Music
and
SOLIDARITY

Questions of Universality,
Consciousness, and Connection

Peace & Policy, Volume 15

Felicity Laurence and
Olivier Urbain, editors

Transaction Publishers
New Brunswick (U.S.A.) and London (U.K.)

Library of Congress Catalog Number: 2010051407
ISBN: 978-1-4128-4230-3
Printed in the United States of America

Library of Congress Cataloging-in-Publication Data

Music and solidarity / edited by Felicity Laurence and Olivier Urbain.
        p. cm. -- (Peace and policy ; v. 15)
    Includes bibliographical references.
    ISBN 978-1-4128-4230-3
    1. Music--Social aspects. 2. Solidarity. I. Laurence, Felicity.
    II. Urbain, Olivier, 1961-
ML3916.M872 2011
781'.1--dc22

2010051407

Contents

**Section 3: Reflections: Two Musical Concerts in Which
"Ideal Relationships" of Solidarity Are Explored**

Prologue
Misunderstanding and Reunderstanding

Christopher Small

On May 12, 2005, in Washington DC, a group of ultra-right-wing United States Republicans calling themselves the American Conservative Union gave a testimonial banquet, admission $250 a plate, in support of Tom DeLay, the besieged majority leader of the House of Representatives. Mr. DeLay was at the time fighting accusations of corruption, gerrymandering, influence peddling, and a whole heap of other congressional crimes, and had been described in the media as "one of the most reviled thugs to hold public office in American history" and "the most corrupt and vindictive politician in Washington." He enjoyed on Capitol Hill the nickname of "The Hammer," in tribute to his successful bullying tactics.

They hired for the occasion a bluegrass band, and it is reported that among the numbers the band played and sang was the 1949 song "If I Had a Hammer" by Pete Seeger and Lee Hays. The song is a defiant affirmation of democratic values, sanctified by nearly sixty years of singing at antiwar and civil rights rallies. The most famous performance must have been that by Peter, Paul and Mary at the 1963 civil rights march on Washington, where Martin Luther King gave his great "I Have a Dream" speech. The song is described in the *Encyclopedia of the American Left* as "one of the most optimistic paeans to the possibilities of constructive social change" (Taskin 1992). It goes like this:

> If I had a hammer,
> I'd hammer in the morning,
> I'd hammer in the evening
> All over this land.
> I'd hammer out danger,

> I'd hammer out a warning,
> I'd hammer out the love between my brothers and my sisters,
> All over this land.

In the second stanza the singer sings "If I had a bell," the third "If I had a song," while in the last the hammer, the bell and the song are brought together:

> Well, I've got a hammer,
> And I've got a bell,
> And I've got a song to sing
> All over this land.
> It's the hammer of justice,
> It's the bell of freedom
> It's the song about the love between my brothers and my sisters,
> All over this land.

A timely song, we might feel, to be sung in the United States today, where a warning of the danger to the Republic is in great need of being hammered out and rung out and sung out as loudly as can be. Maybe we could use a new verse, beginning "If I had a blog."

One might wonder what a song composed by one of the great folk-hero musicians of the political left is doing in this kind of extreme right-wing company? We may ask of it, what's a nice song like you doing in a place like this? There is, of course, the coincidence of the word "hammer," and the choice of the song might even have been the musicians' own, made for that reason. But, knowing the care with which events of this sort are orchestrated in American politics, this seems to me unlikely. In addition, the fact that the press thought the choice of song was worth reporting suggests that even the reporters sensed that something significant had occurred.

The image of the hammer is ripe for appropriation, seeing that it has long functioned as a metaphor for the crushing of disruptive people, as in the nickname "Hammer of the Scots" given to Edward I of England, or in the fifteenth century witch hunters' handbook "The Hammer of Evildoers"—a fact that in our libertarian innocence we—and possibly Seeger and his collaborator—overlooked. So that it's not difficult to see how easily an optimistic paean to the possibilities of constructive social change can be turned into an anthem for this most extreme section of the political right wing.

So I don't think it was just for the coincident appearance of the word "hammer" that the song was chosen for this occasion. I think that those who chose it understood, what generations of musicologists have failed to understand, that the meaning of a song, or indeed of any piece of music, is not just that of the text on the page. That's just the beginning of it. Only when a song is performed will its multiple layers of meaning reveal themselves, and in this case the satisfaction of having appropriated one of the American left's most sacred anthems must have been a major element in the enjoyment of taking part in this performance. Musical meanings are not permanent and stable, and are certainly not built into any musical text, but are labile and changeable, with each new context in which performance takes place.

This is true even with the classical repertory. The stability of scores is inclined to blind us to the labiality of the meanings of performing from them. To perform and to listen to, say, Beethoven's Fifth Symphony in our own time is a very different affair from doing it in the composer's own time, so that what was then an in-your-face affirmation of the values of a rising European bourgeoisie, with the French Revolution under its belt and looking for new worlds to conquer, has today become a source of comfort and a vision of security to the middle classes, with their—perhaps I should say "our"—values and status under attack. Even my father, who was not a sentimental man, used to call it "the dear old Fifth Symphony," which I don't think would have pleased Beethoven. We understand the piece quite differently now from how they did then. That is not to say we *mis*understand the piece. We just understand it differently. A work of art "means" whatever the beholders, in whatever "here" or "now" they might find themselves, think it means. There is no final arbiter of meanings. Everybody brings their own mindset and their own history to bear on the performance, whether it be of a symphony by Beethoven or of a song by Pete Seeger. Scholars may try to reconstruct the original meaning intended by the creator, but audiences, and performers, will make up their own minds about that.

In the case of the DeLay banquet the choice of a bluegrass band is also significant. Bluegrass is a style that is associated with the conservative blue-collar working class, who may have been devastated by the Bush administration's policies, but who for reasons of their own still contributed to his electoral success in 2004. The style is characterized first and foremost by a driving beat and a general high level of tension, which is enhanced by a high vocal tessitura unlike that of other country music. I can't know for sure, of course, since I wasn't invited to that particular bash, but I would surmise that the performance would have stood in great contrast to the laid-back style of the song's most celebrated performers,

Peter, Paul and Mary, not to mention the exuberant Latin manner of Trini Lopez, who also had a big hit with it in the sixties. I would go so far as to speculate that that night's performance would have celebrated, not love or brotherhood and sisterhood but the striving and the tensions of those who believe in their mission to make money and to rule.

In taking the song and giving new meanings to the act of performing it, those Republicans were exploring, affirming and celebrating what they saw then as their victory in the American culture wars. That this should be possible is due to something in the nature of music that I'd like to explore here. The most important aspect of this I have already been suggesting. It's this. Music is not a thing at all, or a collection of things. It is essentially action, something that people do. It is primarily two kinds of action, namely performing and listening. In many musical cultures, most notably on the African continent, dancing is also an essential musical activity, so that if no one is dancing then no music is happening, but generally it is performing and listening. Other musical activities are secondary, such as composing, rehearsing, organizing and researching. The performers, of course, are the primary listeners, in both senses of the word "primary," since they are both the first listeners, in the temporal sense, and the most intense and committed listeners. There need not, in fact, be any listeners apart from the performers themselves.

There may not be any composer apart from the performers, or any fixed and stable musical text. Many highly sophisticated musical cultures get along perfectly well without them. But—and I must emphasize this—even if there is a fixed and stable text, that text is not the whole of what music is about. It is only when a text is performed that the totality of its meanings emerge.

I came to the conclusion many years ago that if music is action and not thing, then the word that designates it should be not a noun but a verb. Accordingly, I coined a verb, the verb "to music," with its present participle or gerund, "musicking," for this purpose. I define it quite simply: to music is to take part, in any capacity, in a musical performance.

For the reader interested in following up the implications of this verb, they're in my book *Musicking* (1998). Broadly, using the verb emphasizes that not only is music an activity, but also it's a form of human encounter in which everyone who is present is taking part, and for whose success or failure as an event everybody who is present has some responsibility. It is not just a matter of active performers doing something for, or to, the passive listeners. Whatever it is that is being done, we are all doing it together. So that in discussing the nature of music I really should have been talking about the nature of the music act, or musicking.

So, what is it that is being done when people come together to music, which is to say, to take part in a musical performance? What meanings are being created? I believe the answer lies in the relationships that are created when the performance takes place. Relations not only between the sounds that are made—that's an important part, but only a part—but also between the participants, that is, among the performers, between the performers and the listeners, and among the listeners. These relationships, in turn, model, or act out, ideal or desired relationships as they are imagined to be by those taking part. And since who we are is how we relate, then to take part in an act of musicking is to take part in an act of self definition, an exploration, an affirmation and a celebration of one's identity, of who one is. In an act of musicking those taking part are exploring, affirming and celebrating their sense of who they are—or who they think they are, or who they would like to be, or even what they would like to be thought of as being.

The relationships brought into existence in a musical performance are enormously complex, too complex in fact to be articulated in words. But that does not mean they are too complex for our minds to encompass. The act of musicking, in its entirety, provides us with a language by means of which we can come to understand and articulate, precisely and clearly, those relationships and through them the relationships of our lives.

Exploring, affirming, celebrating. I use those three words a lot, so I'd better explain what I mean by them.

A musical performance brings into existence relationships that are thought desirable by those taking part, and in doing so it not only reflects those ideal relationships but also shapes them. It teaches and inculcates those ideal relationships—we might call them values—and empowers those taking part to try them on, to see how they fit, to experience them without necessarily having to commit themselves to them, at least for more than the duration of the performance. It is thus an instrument of exploration.

In articulating those values it empowers those taking part to say, to themselves, to one another, and to anyone else that may be paying attention: these are our values, our concepts of how the relationships of the world ought to be, and, consequently, since how we relate is who we are, to say, this is who we are. It is thus an instrument of affirmation.

And, thirdly, in empowering those taking part to explore and affirm their values, it leaves them with a feeling of being more completely themselves, more in tune with the world and with their fellows. After taking part in a successful performance one is able to feel that this is how the world *really* is, and this is how I *really* relate to it. In short, it leaves the participants feeling good about themselves and about their values. It is thus an instrument of celebration.

Of course, we don't all view the world and its relationships in the same way. Tom DeLay and Pete Seeger will surely have different ideas on the relationships of their lives and on how they should be. On the other hand, to the extent that both are white men who were born and grew up in the United States, there will probably be more overlap between those ideas than one would expect, more indeed than either of them might like. They would both, for example, have absorbed from childhood similar ideas about their country's place in the world and about matters such as the uniqueness of the American style of freedom and justice. I believe that "If I Had a Hammer" could only have been written by an American, not only in its ways of articulating those ideas in words but also in its Anglo-Celtic pentatonic melody and its blues-inflected flattened seventh.

Now we cannot question the propriety of taking a song—or indeed any piece of music—that is intended for one social context and performing it in another. It happens all the time, and in fact if it were not possible concert halls and symphony orchestras would lose a great part of their repertoire. As I suggested earlier, this is not a distortion of meanings but the creation of new meanings, new understandings. We may not like those new meanings—that's definitely so for me in the case I am discussing—but we cannot deny their existence. In the struggle for possession of the song and its meanings there is a veiled, or often not so veiled, struggle for political power and for what we might call legitimacy. Only time will tell whose meanings will prevail, and the struggle for control of meanings is never-ending.

There are sites where the struggle for control of musical meanings has been settled, it seems permanently, for instance the concert hall and the opera house. As I suggested when talking of the Fifth Symphony of Beethoven, the message of performing the so-called classics today is one of comfort. However disturbing the performance of those great works may once have been, they can no longer disturb anyone; such performances today belong to the status quo. You can perform a liberation opera like Verdi's *Masked Ball,* which was banned by the Bourbon censors in Naples in 1859, or Beethoven's *Fidelio,* or Chopin's *Revolutionary Study,* in the most oppressed country in the world without provoking any anxiety in the authorities. The work of these musicians resembles those fascinating and often beautiful shapes in the cooled lava from volcanoes, giving testimony to the violence of past eruptions but no longer capable of reshaping the landscape. Even such avowedly revolutionary musicians as John Cage, Mauricio Kagel, and Frederic Rzewski found sponsorship in university music departments, which apparently did not consider them to be any challenge to the landscape of their values.

The image of the volcano may be an apt one, in that volcanoes long thought to be extinct have been known to burst into life and once more reshape the landscape. As we have been learning only too recently, the earth has many surprises in store for us yet, and it could be that ancient volcano we have got used to calling classical music might still burst forth and change our mental landscape. But I doubt it. So many other volcanoes have erupted, especially in African America, since the great Beethovenian explosion that it is no longer easy to detect the fracture lines within the culture of European music.

We can contrast the experiences of Cage and the others with those of many so-called popular musicians, like Fela Kuti, Milton Nascimiento, Sid Vicious, Jim Morrison, Charlie Parker, the Catalan singer-songwriter who calls himself Raimon, who suffered under the Franco regime's censorship, and Seeger himself, whose brush with Senator Joe McCarthy's Un-American Activities Committee earned him a year in prison in 1961. All of those musicians, and countless others, lived in the mouth of the volcano, and their work is still capable of reshaping our landscape of human relationships. All suffered in various ways from brushes with the guardians of social and musical propriety—and it's amazing how often those two roles coincide. It seems that their, and their audiences', musical definitions of who they were did not accord with those of the guardians.

Musical meanings, then, are concerned with relationships, the relationships of our world as we believe they are and as we believe they ought to be. And since how we relate is who we are, we can say that in musicking we are exploring, affirming and celebrating who we are, or at least who we think we are, in relation to fellow humans, to the world and even perhaps the supernatural world—if the supernatural is part of our conceptual world. So it is that in the appropriation of "If I Had a Hammer" at the DeLay banquet we hear a triumphalist affirmation and celebration of Republican Party values, at least as held by those who participated in the event. We could call it the right-wing Republicans' "*Gotcha!*" moment.

I come back to the idea that musicking functions as a means of exploration, affirmation, and celebration of who we are or think we are.

If members of different social groups have different values, or different concepts of ideal relationships, then the kinds of performances that enact those relationships will differ from one another also. But we mustn't be too categorical about this. We have already seen that the degree of overlap between the values of Pete Seeger on the one hand, and Tom DeLay on the other, was enough to allow the appropriation of the former's song by the latter.

It doesn't only work that way, with members of social groups that are, or believe themselves to be, in control of things celebrating that control by appropriating the musical rituals of those they believe they have overcome. For more generations than we can count, underdog groups have been making through musicking their own exploration, affirmation, and celebration of who they think they are, often in the face of those who would say, that is who you are, or even, that is *what* you are, which is to say, less than fully human. Because that is what the slave masters in the American and Caribbean colonies tried to insist to the Africans who were under their control, and their descendents.

It is in fact this serial appropriation of musical meanings that has fuelled what must surely be one of the greatest outbursts of creative musical energy in human history—the African American musical culture. By that term, I mean the musicking that took place not only within the United States but also right across the two Americas and the Caribbean, throughout the cultural region that Paul Gilroy (1999) has called The Black Atlantic, and eventually across the whole human race. I call it *serial* appropriation, because it didn't happen only once and for all or in one direction only, but again and again over the nearly five centuries since the first Africans were landed on the shores of the Americas. Sidney Mintz and Richard Price (1976) date the beginning of a new African American culture to "the moment when one person in need received ritual assistance from another who belonged to a different cultural group." Such ritual assistance must have included musicking and dancing. Over and over again, and back and forth between blacks and mainly poor whites, from African drummers, singers and dancers, from Christian hymn-singers of the two waves of religious fervor that are called the Great Awakening, from fiddlers and singers not only white but black too—since a slave who was adept on an instrument could find his or her condition greatly alleviated on the plantations—from traveling guitar-playing blues men and women, from gospel quartets and choirs to Elvis Presley, from such an unlikely source as Guy Lombardo to Louis Armstrong, from Chuck Berry to the Beatles and Muddy Waters to the Stones. And so on and so on. Who benefited from these crossovers in terms of fame and fortune is of course another matter.

In my book, *Music of the Common Tongue* (1987) I suggested that for members of one social group to take to themselves elements from the musicking of another social group requires a certain empathy or respect between the members of the two groups, a certain recognition of a common humanity, even possibly envy, and even in the teeth of denial in the formal social processes of the dominant group. I doubt if the DeLay Republicans would have bothered with "If I Had a Hammer" if they hadn't valued the song in the first place. You don't appropriate to yourself things that you don't value.

Neither a song nor a style of musicking crosses unchanged from one social or cultural group to another. Every musician, every listener, brings their own style of performing and listening, their own experience and understanding of how a performance should go, their own ideas for making it better, making it new, making it more powerful and more interesting. This is not to be called *mis*understanding. Rather, it is creating a new understanding, a *re*understanding that keeps the work of creation on the move, adapting songs and styles to our own purposes, resisting those who would impose a single mode of understanding on us.

So it is that the African American way of musicking, far from being a juggernaut that flattens out all local styles into one global gray-out, in fact has accommodated itself over and over to local styles. Coming out of poverty and oppression, it makes an immediate appeal to poor and oppressed people throughout the world, giving them a medium through which they can explore, affirm and celebrate who they are. In New Zealand a few years ago I heard a superb band called Te Vata from the Pacific Islands playing its own brand of blues and jazz. I also heard a fine Maori reggae group and a gospel choir—all with pronounced Polynesian accents. Then there is Mandarin rock, Chinese-American rap, South Korean hip-hop and Korean-American pop, as well as Japanese reggae, complete with permanent-waved dreadlocks. We hear bhangra, rai, and reggae, and a host of other syncretic styles whose characteristics cross and recross those arbitrarily imposed limits that we call stylistic boundaries.

These interactions do not occur at random but are always a sign that members of one cultural group can find something useful to them in the musical practices—I'd like to say ritual practices—of another group, something they can empathize with and which calls to them. It is not a question of conscious multiculturalism, which to be honest is a word I don't much like to use, but rather a question of what we might call cultural permeability. Members of one cultural group don't take on board in their entirety the musical ritual practices of another, they don't *learn* the culture, as we hear said frequently in educational circles these days, but rather take bits and pieces that appeal, and incorporate them into the larger body of their own practices.

It is taking bits and pieces from whatever comes to hand, a process that goes under the fancy name of syncretism, not so-called authenticity or purity, that keeps the work of creation on the move. A pure musical culture, if such a thing could exist—and I can't imagine what such a monstrosity would be like—would be one that was without life. And we needn't imagine that the great European tradition that we call classical music is any exception to this. We are all hybrids, every one of us, all creoles, and we all speak our music with some accent or other. We should strongly resist those who tell us that we speak our music with an accent while they possess the pure language. There is no pure language. If I say that even the queen of England speaks with an accent, and if I say that I find the accent a pretty unattractive one, that says as much about my social attitudes as it does about the royal voice.

As for authenticity, there is only one authenticity, and that is in fidelity to our own experience and to our pleasure in musicking. All musicking is authentic when we are doing the best we can with what we have.

We know that today musical permeation is taking place on a global scale, with everybody listening to everybody else and all musical traditions up for grabs by whoever wants to make their musicking more interesting—or more profitable. This process of musical globalization, which is part of a process that has been going on for some five hundred years, if not more, *ought* to be a cause for celebration, but we all know that the process isn't as politically innocent as that. The much warmed-over dispute about Paul Simon's *Graceland* album shows us how right we are to be suspicious of the ways in which in practice it is being carried on, and how the perfectly natural desire in Western industrial culture for what others have to offer becomes too often a cover for greed and exploitation.

The process of globalization, which is to say, the linking together of the members of the human race by increasingly rapid and sophisticated means of transport and communication, has been going on for hundreds if not thousands of years, almost certainly represents the destiny of the human race, barring accidents. What is new in the last thirty years or so has been the way in which those who would enrich themselves at our expense have hijacked the process, along with the word, and have succeeded in convincing the world that the obscene enrichment of a few and the appalling impoverishment of millions, the uprooting of entire populations, the desolation of communities, the exclusion from work and society of tens of millions, and the increasing devastation of the environment, are all unavoidable and even beneficent consequences of this globalization and of the single global free market that they present to us as inseparably linked to it.

In itself, globalization does not have to mean the destruction of diversity and the graying-out of the world's cultures. On the contrary, it presents ever greater and richer opportunities for us to learn from one another and enjoy one another's company on this planet. What *is* destructive of human diversity is the insidious linking of globalization with those other processes while those who oppose those processes are dismissed contemptuously as mindless enemies of progress.

It is not cultures that we respect, or deprecate, or try to preserve, or destroy, it is people. Culture is an attribute of a person or of a group of people, and the word itself is an abstraction of those attitudes and dispositions that underlie human beings' ways of perceiving, feeling, thinking and acting. The only way we can show respect for a person's culture is to show respect for that person for what he or she is. As all people are by definition authentic in their lives, so the words "authentic" and "inauthentic" don't seem to have much meaning in this context. If enslaved Africans, and their descendants down to the present day, had given any thought to authenticity, or to preserving a culture, we wouldn't have the way of musicking today that we call African American. What they must have had in mind was personal and communal survival, and the preservation of that precious sense of who they were without which survival was not worthwhile, and for that purpose they were prepared to take whatever lay to hand from their musical environment.

When we music we have no responsibility to any culture, not even to our own. Our only responsibility is to the pleasure we and our fellow-musickers derive from our musicking. Because ultimately that's what we do it for—for the pleasure it gives us and the reciprocal pleasure of others which unites us for the duration of the performance in a community of like-feeling people. The rich and complex web of relationships that we create every time we music reaches far into the past and across the whole pattern of the living world. Even the most seemingly trivial and frivolous acts of musicking can be an exploration, an affirmation and a celebration of the way in which we relate to one another and to that pattern.

We need not be afraid of misunderstanding others' ways of musicking. As I have suggested, what some call misunderstanding is more truthfully to be called *re*understanding, and it has always been a powerful force for keeping the work of creation on the move. We need not worry too much, either, about preservation, whether it be of the treasured works from the past or even of whole musical cultures. The true treasure is the human act of musicking, in the taking part in the act of music itself. The ability to do so, indeed the *need* to do so, is part of the evolutionary inheritance of every member of the human race. To be able to say, to ourselves and to anyone else who may be listening, *This is who we are*, is central to human life and dignity, and this is surely the ultimate function of musicking in all our lives.

I cannot help adding a postscript, inspired by an agreeable couple of hours I spent a few weeks ago with a group of German couples, middle-aged to elderly, and their children and grandchildren at a beach-side bar in Sitges. As Germans often like to do, they interspersed their conversation with singing, softly and unselfconsciously, almost as if they were singing to themselves, folksongs mostly and popular songs including the 1930s song "Lili Marlene." During the Second World War Lale Andersson's recording of this song was played constantly over German-occupied Radio Belgrade broadcasting to the Afrika Korps and became a favorite of troops on both sides. Given a new set of English words, the song was quickly taken over by the British and Americans and was bellowed out in hundreds of messroom bars and broadcast across the world, in what must have been one of the most successful acts of appropriation ever.

That afternoon a few weeks ago, listening to my German friends singing so sweetly and inwardly, and joining with them with my English words, I had the thought, *Lili girl, you've come home.*

Sitges, July 2010

References

Gilroy, Paul. 1999. *The Black Atlantic: Modernity and Double Consciousness.* London: Verso.

Mintz, Sidney W. and Price, Richard. 1976. *An Anthropological Approach to the Caribbean Past: A Caribbean Perspective.* ISHI Occasional Papers in Social Change, No 2, Philadelphia, Institute for the Study of Human Issues, 10.

Small, Christopher. 1987. *Music of the Common Tongue: Survival and Celebration in African American Music:* 75). Middletown, CT: Wesleyan University Press.

Small, Christopher. 1998. *Musicking: The Meanings of Performing and Listening (Prelude).* Middletown, CT: Wesleyan University Press.

Taskin, Richard in Buhle, Buhle and Georgakis. 1992. *Encyclopedia of the American Left.* Urbana and Chicago: University of Illinois Press.

Introduction

Felicity Laurence

Preface

Using music to express benevolent intentions is not, in general, one of its most notable functions—the human condition not being intrinsically a peaceful one. Indeed, music has been used throughout time and place for the very destruction of any kind of cross-cultural communion, with music in war very effectively getting soldiers marching, livened up and ready to slaughter, and later—used to calm them down ready to sleep. Music is always a powerful and ubiquitous tool in propaganda, and in facilitating the various political projects in all kinds of inventive ways which have nothing much to do with the pursuit of peaceful and cooperative intercultural understanding, or with helping people to address issues of injustice.

But our topics here are ultimately those of peace, and of the policies needed in its pursuit and building. In this issue of *Peace & Policy*, we move beyond the knowledge of music's power upon humans, however this may be conceived and explained, and to a field of enquiry which is yet—in comparison with all other academic and other effort in the world—a tiny endeavor. The sparseness of serious theoretical engagement with our topic is echoed by the insufficiency of its practice—that of the direct use of music for building a more humane consciousness in the "real world." This is evident, for example, in Elizabeth Bowen's account below of recent musically-based collaborative efforts towards honoring a hitherto despised and cruelly treated group of people, where she makes the point that such projects are still rare, for all the profound effects which she shows us that they are having.

In this Introduction, I hope to "set the scene" for our topic with an initial overview, and to sketch some underpinning terms and tenets, delineate its accompanying contexts and the intricate complexities therein, indicate our specific themes, and having thus portrayed our field of enquiry, to introduce the chapters which will explore it.

Overview

In these pages, we are taking one step at a time in what is still a very new field, that of trying to explore what is actually happening in events, programs and activities where music is being used in the context of a teleological project of discovering and building a more humane universal consciousness than is evidently now the case. To this end, we are here, collectively, looking at notions of what a universal consciousness might in fact "look like," and how music might become a part, even a basis, of such a linking-together of human minds and souls. For this, we need ideas and ways of describing and conceptualizing what are in fact universal qualities within musical sounds, patterns, and practices among peoples throughout our planet. The disciplines of musicology and ethnomusicology, linguistics, and philosophies of music, ethics, morality, and many others, all have their part to play in taking our collective theoretical probing forwards; and further, we need to have *sight* of work in the field which exemplifies the ideas we are putting forward.

To these ends, in the following pages, the reader will encounter analytical discussions and explorations alongside and interwoven with vivid stories from the field. In a global and somewhat kaleidoscopic picture, theories are described, stories are told, and conundrums are presented, with insights and knowledge newly available through translation of a number of chapters from their original French. In all these ways, the concepts within our underpinning topic are scrutinized, argued about, turned this way and that, sometimes in tension with each other and other times in harmony. We question the validity of music as a "universal language," but we acknowledge collectively the universality of musical response.

Christopher Small, in characteristic fashion, has thrown down the gauntlet right at the start, with his unequivocal pointing out of the stark reality that—no matter how lovely the music, how nobly conceived, how peaceful or persuasive it is intended to be—the music "object" can be, and frequently is, appropriated for *other* purposes than those originally intended, and can arouse emotions and move people in ways never intended or imagined by its original makers (be they performers or composers). Whatever we may find of music's potential to help us as a species to try to move along a less self-destructive path, and whatever we find in terms of universally accessible elements within musical structures and sounds, and the universal neurobiological patterning which predisposes us to certain kinds of musical reactions and responses, in the end the music can be sabotaged, manipulated, and appropriated; music *itself* is not a universal "good." But perhaps it can be a *tool* for good, and for us to understand how best to use make this tool "work," we need to delve into its essence, and look very closely at how it has been and can be used in specific contexts where such use is both explicit and evident.

Within this collection, a valuable North African perspective holds a mirror up to a discourse permeated by assumptions into which those of us coming from the Western heritage have been inculcated, and of which we need to become aware, to interrogate, and to be prepared to relinquish. Among these, and quite likely to be shared by our reader, is the narrative of music as subject to a linear progression, from the "simple" to the "complex," wherein Western classical music is understood as the pinnacle of the complex, and where "other" music is judged against this (whether these are other genres within Western society, or the music of another culture). Those further "behind"—in this model—are considered to be unable to have real access to aesthetic judgment or experience. You don't have to dig deeply at all to discover this thought—it hardly lies buried, and it's there right in the term "serious music," which has an instant connotation; "serious music" means Western classical music. World music is something else.

This, written, seems extreme and irrelevant today, in times where so many of us listen to music from everywhere, and where the possibility of gaining enjoyment from doing so is manifest. But we need to be very clear that this narrative remains firmly in place. How many university music departments concern themselves with the topic we pursue in this publication? What are they in fact foregrounding and preserving over and over again? How often do we hear stated as a legitimate goal that we must try to increase our (specifically) classical music audience, and educate children accordingly—and what has this to do with music as a way and a tool of developing those empathic and humane attitudes which might help us move towards a less violent and cruel world?

Accordingly, as we search here for ways both of arguing for and understanding universal values, structures and meanings in music, we are inevitably moving against a long discourse where this idea is not necessarily a welcome one; John Sloboda has noted in uncompromising terms that "The notion that music could be engaged in purely for [...] the building up of community and friendship [...] is a strange, almost reprehensible, concept in many people's minds" (Sloboda 1999, 455), and his words, though written more than a decade ago, resonate still. If there are indeed universal values in music, then it is not too long before someone will argue that the music of one culture or genre not only might be understood by people from another, but that there may be values and sophistications in the "Other's" music not evident in our own. This is exactly what some of our contributors, with both firmness and grace, help us to understand, as exemplified by Soufiane Feki as he highlights the early ethnomusicological prejudices that tended to obstruct any real understanding of music's potential to *unite* across cultures. There is thus a heritage of thought that we must recognize if we are to move towards the concept of a benevolent universal musical consciousness.

These dilemmas are reflected in compelling ways in Vanessa Agnew's recent investigation into cross-cultural musical encounters between European and Polynesian populations in the Enlightenment period (late eighteenth to early nineteenth century) in which she sought, as she explains, to "examine the utopian possibilities and dystopian warnings about music's capacity for either constituting or dissolving society" (Agnew 2008, 7). Universal powers of affect were by implication attributed to music in its use by European travelers in Polynesia to make friendly relationships with the indigenous people, this being possible only with an underlying assumption of shared elements within the music of each group and shared responses. But, paradoxically, there was also a deep assumption by the Europeans of the musical naivety of those whose shores they were visiting, and the impossibility of their having access to the assumed higher level of European music. Even when evidence of musical complexity and sophistication was *heard,* it was—by many but not all—refuted. Agnew writes of the understanding then that music "could indeed be used to militarize, pacify, subordinate, and make friends or enemies" (ibid., 116); what she recounts however, is that its use in this last purpose—our topic in these pages—was in the end defeated:

> The lovely dream of hospitality and shared music making had been replaced by a self-imposed injunction to resist the other's song (ibid., 119).

Yet, the expressions we are using in designating our topics, "solidarity," "universality," and "connection" in relation to music, reveal an opposing kind of narrative, a narrative which is perhaps at this point one of hope and optimism, served often by rhetoric rather than the meticulous and painstaking efforts needed to construct a strong framework resilient enough to defy what is still extant and pervasive. It is such efforts which are recounted here, as we investigate the ways in which music might be utilized to construct spaces in which people feel drawn together in that solidarity which we seem so readily to engender, often through music, in situations of war. Instead, we seek to explain how we can use those same attributes and affordances of music, and the bonds and connections which can be made in the activity of musicking, to reduce tensions *before* violence can occur, and to contribute to a transformed sense of the "Other" as human and worthy of respect and care. Music is not enough in itself of course; we also need intention, will and consensus even to get as far as the metaphorical table, and then "tools" to get people to sit down at it and to hear each other. Music, we suggest, has potential as one such tool.

Finally in this overview, we have taken up questions of the universal, both within and beyond music, and here is also the concern to find ways of developing a sense of solidarity not only with those we might meet "at the table," but with people whom we may never meet at all. Philosophical reflection and direct empirical evidence both suggest that being able to feel connection with an invisible "Other," and certainly to the extent of this feeling stirring us to actions of solidarity, constitutes a hurdle of imagination not easily achieved. Again, there has to be an underlying will, intention, and what the philosopher Edith Stein described as the "striving" to "grasp" the other's consciousness (Stein [1917] 1989). But of course, it happens, as Olivier Urbain describes below, famously in the case of those millions attending Bob Geldof's *Live Aid* concert, those people who came to express their solidarity with the suffering and the starving.

I move now to a brief scrutiny of this "solidarity," to offer some ideas about what we intend to convey throughout this collection in our constant use of this term.

Solidarity

At the center of our collective discourse, and rippling ubiquitously through the chapters below, is the concept of "solidarity." Defined as the "harmony of interests and responsibilities among individuals in a group, especially as manifested in unanimous support and collective action for something" by the Encarta Dictionary, this term thus connotes not only the awareness of the other's needs, but the desire to *support* those needs. In many languages, the adjective which allows us to describe actions and events of solidarity is in common use and working hard; in English, not yet—but it is there, a nice word, nestling in the Oxford English Diction-ary—*solidaric*: defined as "*characterized by solidarity or community of interests*" (Oxford English Dictionary). This word can allow us to move away from some reified "thing" called "solidarity," and instead, towards learning to "*be with*" in a certain way, to "do" "solidarity"—and to *be* "solidaric."

What I would suggest is that being solidaric is more to do with the sense of the other as "*an*other" rather than as the "Other"—where "Other" can take us eventually to "less than human." We can be solidaric towards and with "another" (person) who is *allowed to be different*, but who still has the right to *be*, and to flourish. This asks us to work against some of our evolutionary inheritance, that which impels us to compete for resources, but it calls on other innate human characteristics, those which urge us to cooperate. For this, we need an *empathic* stance, as a core element of peaceful and harmonious relationships in which we have both to build and to maintain the solidaric consciousness which will in turn sustain and characterize our relationships with each other.

Being solidaric is to show care for and commitment to another, or to many others, and to be inclined and able to listen to them, to allow their voice, and to act humanely in response.

Contextual Complexities

As we take up those questions of solidarity and universality, consciousness and connection that exercise us in this volume, we find something of a mesh of conundrums and paradoxes. For example, we speak of music helping processes of reconciliation; we must then acknowledge the wider implications of reconciliation and forgiveness, and be clear about what is really happening in practices that aim to "bring people together." We can ask whose agenda is being served, and whether there is, as may often be the case, some underlying repositioning of power which still may leave some people with more (power) over others. In a musically based project of reconciliation between those who have murdered and massacred and those who have survived these actions—how can we speak of mutual forgiveness? What is there—in fact—for the former victim to forgive? Inasmuch as musical means are being employed, we would need to question the legitimacy of such a project.

Where we seek to use those feelings of empathic connection and of bonding that may arise in our musicking to help people engage in cross-cultural dialogue between groups who are historically mistrustful of each other—what are we really doing? Is it "real" to create bonds via a music which may have its own specific cultural connotations for some participants in such a project, or is it more of a "synthetic" encounter, which will dissipate pretty much as soon as the music stops, and prove as ephemeral? In applying music, with whatever "power" it possesses, without a very deep understanding of these issues and of the particular relationship between music and the people involved, might we be doing more harm than good in this musical application of our good intentions?

Music can get us dancing and singing together—but what then? In some of the musicking for a common global consciousness exemplified by those massed concerts for peace which proliferate in the current landscape, perhaps what we are doing is providing little more than a refuge from the painful realities; perhaps such events are even contributing to a stasis, where music's expressiveness and the emotional response it evokes is really being used (by us, and by those musicking with and for us) to cope with things as they are, rather than to change them.

It is my contention that without specific *intentionality* to go forth and *act*, we seldom do so; we emerge from our musically-produced emotional "bath," refreshed perhaps, inspired perhaps, but only rarely do we then march off to make peace. Most commonly, if there is any movement, it is to fight, even where the fight is for justice, as with the civil rights movement; we can certainly argue this as the *precursor* to peaceful relationships. But sometimes though, we do act; having been moved, we then move to action.

A further dilemma is the question of how much change at the individual level can eventually translate into change at the collective level. Again, we have a narrative that seems to articulate this as an axiom; how often are we assured that change begins with each one of us? Reinhold Niebuhr would challenge such a position in his view that what might "work" at a moral level for us as a person does not work when we are in groups. He argues that while as individuals we might be capable of sympathy and taking another's needs into account, even at our own expense, in groups we are not so, and that a radically different sense of morality must be applied to the group, to which indeed he ascribes an "inferiority" of morality (Niebuhr 1960). So we might ask then—should we look at music as a social phenomenon? Or should we find out about music and consciousness at the individual level? Michael Golden suggests below that this is indeed where we must look in order to have a chance of linking individual consciousnesses into a universal consciousness.

Ours is a complex field, in which these and countless other questions frame those upon which we are focusing. My final point here concerns the issue of sustainability, that criterion now increasingly argued as a core prerequisite for the kinds of work described in the following. In some of the "stories from the field" presented in this collection, a case for the fundamental necessity of sustained work might well be made, for example in the accounts of solidaric work in Australia mentioned above, and in Colombia as described in María Elisa Pinto García's following chapter about musically-based reconciliation projects. There is a growing interest with issues of sustainability in this area, and an argument that without plans for a long-term project, such work may not be beneficial, and may even be damaging.

But others look for the "magic moment," when a musical experience seems suddenly to allow a "shift of the light," as in Olivier Urbain's account of the transformation during a single concert of the feelings of one person towards a hitherto hated culture, and perhaps also in Barbara Dunn's stories of such moments in her music therapy work. Perhaps the most dramatic such "shift" can be witnessed as we read of June Boyce-Tillman's *Space for Peace*, where many accounts testify to a profound and transcendental experience through a night of interfaith musicking.

"Magic Moments," and Interculturality, Intermusicality and Identity

One such producer of "magic moments" is the Tunisian singer Sonia M'barek. For her audiences, this is what she hopes her performances will be; but for herself, there is certainly sustainability in that her ultimate goal is to contribute to what she describes as "interculturality," and as she carries out this work she is constantly reflecting upon its effects, and its meaning. There are musicians across the world, some of whom we encounter in the following pages, who are deeply concerned to make their music matter beyond its immediate beauty and sound. Here is her own account of this; we can thus hear in her own words what one such musician is attempting, and how this feels to her:[1]

> With my plural musical identity anchored in the Berber heritage, in the Arab-Islamic and Arabo-Andalusian traditions, and in Turkish, Eastern, Western influences, if I had to talk about my experience, I would say that music expresses all of my humanity. From an education anchored in the Arab imagination, I travel across the musics of the Mediterranean, a place of encounters, of continuities and of break-ups in search of a better understanding of my music, of my history, of its evolution and of the role that I can play to communicate this passion. Music allows me to put up bridges between peoples which are imaginary, but also deeply emotive. My song allows me to communicate, or even to commune with other humans, to find my humanity in its most noble sense, with a sense of sharing understanding and respect, but also of creativity. I feel that I am "rocketing" across all the different kinds of music whose richness I can feel, and to which I can bring all my feelings and my identity.

When I sing my Arab-Andalusian songs in Tunisia, France, or Egypt, Berlin, Washington, these moments are precious, for they engage the feelings of human beings in all these places, and it seems that music holds the power to unite all the peoples of the world, regardless of their differences. It seems to me that the impact of an encounter between musicians belonging to different cultures can go beyond the politics and the speeches, for it encourages sharing, transmission, exchange for a better understanding of one another, in respecting the unique, special features of each one, ultimately going to the deepest part of their soul (M'barek 2010).

In this voice direct from the field, we have the truth of one person's experience and of how this musician thinks and feels in using her art to try to move people towards a shared and mutually attentive consciousness. She is clear that her task is the building of interculturality, which she describes thus:

Interculturality implies the will to live together, to talk to one another, to understand one another, to listen to each other and to see each other, to welcome the music of the other. Interculturality also implies the consciousness of the other as both identical and different, and it differs from the very fashionable notion of multiculturalism, which sets up the diversity of cultures and of identities, without considering a dynamic, positive give-and-take between them. One of the fundamental questions which arises from this debate on interculturality is based on the role of artists and, here, of the musician in particular, in promoting interculturality; and this can be seen as placing the musician at the center of an argument about the universal and the specific, the global and the local. The musician, perhaps thanks to the dazzling technological progress initiated at the end of the twentieth century, seems to be able to be increasingly communicative and interconnected with others (ibid.).

This provides an interesting counterpoint to the concept of "intermusicality," which is conceptually distinct, but related. The fairly recent concept of intermusicality emanates from the ethnomusicological field, and is already being taken up as a useful conceptual tool within the field of music education in discussions that surely relate to our own, of educating our young people in the music of others. In his discussion of this, and drawing on Ingrid Monson's original use of the term, John O'Flynn explains intermusicality in terms of musical conventions and practices being taken from one performance context into another (O'Flynn 2005, 199);[2] while Michael Webb, in turn drawing on O'Flynn's 2005 article, speaks of Western musicians "reconceptualising aspects of their musical practice through a kind of reflective intermusicality"(Webb 2008, 16). This concept is explored in more depth by Fakher Hakima in this volume, and also exemplified in Itır Toksöz's chapter on the case of Turkish music.

A further theme, which can already be glimpsed in Sonia M'barek's account above, is that of identity. Thomas Turino has pointed out the

ethnomusicological consensus that: "Music is a key resource for real-
izing personal and collective identities [...] identities [which] are at once
individual and social" (Turino 1999, 221). He adds: "The crucial link
between identity formation and arts like music lies in the specific semiotic
character of these activities which make them particularly affective and
direct ways of knowing" (ibid.). The Tunisian musician and musicologist Mohamed Zinelabidine also raises questions of identity in music in
his essay "The Human Being as Musician; identity and context,"[3] and
wonders if the pressure to determine identity, in this case in a country
such as Tunisia, in fact "calls into question the creative freedom of the
artist." He asks: "Is musical identity a matter of regulation by political
powers, or is it rather a matter of conscience, or even moral judgment?"
(Zinelabidine 2010, 1) and indeed he questions the whole concept of
a musical identity tied to time, place or tradition, suggesting that the
"aesthetic mutations and transformations of Tunisian music during the
twentieth century prefigure its vulnerability as a firm and clear notion
of identity" (ibid., 4). While Zinelabidine's concern here is with the
tension between artistic freedom and the adherence to a supposed "duty
of identification," his underpinning theme of identity recurs in various
chapters here, within our specific context of the possibility and even
desirability of intercultural musical communication, and is the central
topic of Itır Toksöz's discussion of multiple identities expressed within
Turkish music.

I turn now to the chapters themselves, with a brief "overture" followed
by an introduction to each one.

The Chapters

I have arranged the chapters in a constellation which I hope will help
the reader build reference points and insights, and as she or he moves
through the volume, to perceive interconnections between them, seeing
the themes in the various different lights. Many other groupings of the
chapters would of course have been possible; but our attentive reader
may be able to find resonances that appear only serendipitously from
holding one piece up to another. Many themes recur, for example those
of dialogue, of identity, of the sacred in relation to music, of diversity,
and others.

There are accounts from Tunisia and Morocco with a strong and
even salutary perspective that turns a Eurocentric view on its head and
admonishes the hegemony of a "universal" set of values, and from Colombia, USA, Japan, Africa, Europe, Australia—which together give a

representation of contemporary global scholarship and practice in the field. There are stories from those already exploring the use of music in fields of helping connection and dialogue where there may be none, and possible ways of transferring understandings and techniques from one musical discipline to another, as in the cases of Vanessa Contopulos, Barbara Dunn, and June Boyce-Tillman who each, respectively, "word-paint" for us a clear picture of themselves at solidaric work through music. Accounts such as those from María Elisa Pinto García, Ahmed Aydoun, Elizabeth Bowen, and Itır Toksöz, witness and analyze what they are witnessing, while others give us stories which inspire them, as in the accounts of Soufiane Feki and Olivier Urbain. In several investigations of where music's universal elements and its resonances with a global consciousness might lie, we are taken into realms of neurobiology, philosophy, history, ethnomusicology... (Michael Golden, Soufiane Feki, Ahmed Aydoun, Fériel Bouhadiba, Fakher Hakima); and we hear directly from musicians and composers—for example in June Boyce-Tillman's chapter and my own.

Prelude: Inspiring Global Solidarity

Olivier Urbain's opening chapter takes us to a broad view of some examples of work in the field which illustrate the topics of this volume in practice across the globe; and he gives also, in a personal account of his own response simply to *knowing about* these projects, a sense of how one person can be moved indirectly by music's evident power in these compassionate and solidaric endeavors. This seems to affirm the seriousness of sharing such experiences so that other people might be inspired to join this work. Crucial also to this is the exploration of its conceptual underpinnings, where, as described, we are at a very early point. Thus, in the next section are grouped a number of chapters which tackle this task.

Section 1: Exploring the Conceptual Base: Music and Universality, Consciousness, Intermusicality, Diversity, Dialogue, and Identity

This section begins with Michael Golden's examination of universal consciousness, and what this might "look like," accompanied by a wide-ranging but careful scrutiny of the "relationships between music, its connective functions and consciousness" which takes us on an intellectual journey, from a view of music in the sacred, into the intricacies of recent discoveries in neurobiology, and beyond.

Moving "out" from the individual response to music, Soufiane Feki picks up the thread with his exploration of the universal within music;

bringing an ethnomusicogical perspective, and indeed a critique of earlier failings of ethnomusicological enquiry that tended to conceal what musics might have in common, he investigates what we can find within music itself which recurs in all of its forms, everywhere and always.

With these insights in mind, we then consider Fakher Hakima's discussion of the notion of intermusicality, which also looks at underlying universal structures in music but this time taking inspiration from literary theories of intertextuality, considering this question in the specifically Tunisian context.

Fériel Bouhadiba's account of dialogue and diversity in music offers a particular focus upon the current homogenizing pressure threatening that diversity which in fact, she argues, must constitute the basis of the dialogue necessary to intercultural meeting points, and to any solidarity between peoples resulting from such (musical) meetings. Her themes of diversity, specificity, dialogue and solidarity are echoed in various ways in others' chapters, perhaps with a particular relationship to the concluding chapter by June Boyce-Tillman, where we can see diversity celebrated within that dialogue of which Bouhadiba writes.

This section ends with Itır Toksöz's investigation of identity in music, here with a focus upon the illuminating example of plural identity expressed in music in her native Turkey, where there is an ongoing and probably unique meeting of East and West. She uses the case of Turkish music to challenge the pessimism of Samuel Huntington's apocalyptic "clash of civilization" thesis; if one of our main predicaments is indeed this apparently irreconcilable tension between East and West, as can be gleaned in the particularly North African perspective influencing this collection as a whole, then the question of our identity and of music's place in strengthening and allowing multiple identities, is fundamental.

Section 2: Case Studies: Music at Work in Interpersonal, Intra- and Intercultural Connection and Building a Solidaric Consciousness

The following section addresses the musical expression of our initial concepts, in the stories told here of musicking for healing and for reducing conflict, in contexts of reconciliation, community well-being, and within the field of music therapy. Once again, we see the value of *knowing about* what can be possible, in the first two accounts in which their authors describe and reflect upon projects in their respective countries of Australia and Colombia. In the next two "stories," the authors take us right into their own experience, so that what they are describing is indeed "first hand" and, as with the portrayal above of Sonia M'barek's vision, there is an immediacy that adds a further dimension to our collective study. Concluding this section is a closely described account of a dance from a community of people living in Morocco, wherein community values are shaped and expressed, with music (in its forms as sound and dance) and the associated poetry enabling very specific and beneficial changes in attitude and in behavior.

Elizabeth Bowen's *Voices from the Living Heart* chronicles exchanges between Indigenous and white musicians in Australia that have given "voice to the voiceless"; such exchanges are coming both to symbolize and to engender the processes now begun, but with a very long way to go, and thus constituting the seeds of reconciliation.

María Elisa Pinto García offers a powerful story of human rights abuses, and attempts to come to terms with the past and prevent such occurrences in the future, using musical means. Music may be argued to be saving lives here, in the long run. She brings to bear the particular analytical tool of John Paul Lederach's "paradoxes" in peacemaking, specifically invoking the paradox of outcome and process.

Barbara Dunn writes of her own work and the communicative power of music on which it depends. She introduces tools of music therapy and discusses the crucial importance to this work of total concentration and awareness, again, offering specific aspects on which we might reflect in considering how it might be possible to extrapolate from the music therapeutic setting to that of building intercultural connection.

In the following chapter by Vanessa Contopulos, we find a direct link into this possibility of application of music therapy beyond the clinical setting. She describes and reflects upon her own work, where she has sought to employ tools and practices from music therapy to the process of facilitated dialogue, where dialogue is seen as integral to rebuilding relationships between communities.

Ahmed Aydoun is the author of the final chapter in this section. He gives a description of a musical process and event which, going beyond entertainment, has a specific function of reducing conflict that might otherwise escalate, even into violence. This story from Morocco has much to teach us, because it makes clear what might seem to be a remarkable level of care and also of precision within this musical process. Its elements have evolved over a long period of time, and the responses to the music (including dance and poetry) are deeply and precisely understood. This example stands in quite dramatic contrast to the pervasive idea within other milieu that merely to stand and sing together can "make friends," or that simply going off somewhere and "doing music" with people is going to help them better understand each other. In this story we can begin to glimpse the layers upon layers of complexity of such a project.

Section 3: Reflections: Two Musical Concerts in which "Ideal Relationships" of Solidarity Are Explored

These layers of complexity are also evident in the final two chapters, which each tell the story of its author's own musical strivings, as composer and musician, to use their music in the making of solidaric relationships, where people hitherto divided might experience a way of that "being together"—and *for* each other—which underpins our notion of solidarity. Here are two composers *at* work putting their music *to* work; both are exploring the ways in which this musicking might be serving the intention, jointly held with the participants, of moving towards the sense of a shared consciousness which can also celebrate diversity.

In the first story, I revisit my musical piece *African Madonna*, using Christopher Small's concept of musicking and the idea of empathy, an implicit notion up to this point in the various accounts, to look closely at what might have been going on in two early performances of this piece. These two concepts form the basis of my developing theory, which posits the possibility of conceptual and experiential links between them, and I introduce these ideas in a framework of "real" stories of "real" events.

June Boyce-Tillman then brings us a vivid account of a performance of the musical event *Space for Peace*, in which she addresses themes of diversity, liminality, space and dialogue, with what we might see as a parallel text running along within, which documents the intensity and often transformative nature of the experience of those who took part, or who witnessed it. This account concludes this collection with, perhaps, an intimate vision of what we are talking about when we try to conceptualize solidarity and to *make it happen*.

The chapters which follow document what may in the future be seen as being among the earliest vanguard of the attempts to understand what is "going on" when participation in certain kinds of "musicking" (to put immediately to work Christopher Small's term, explained by himself in the Prologue above) seems to facilitate progress towards a sense of solidarity beyond cultural and national boundaries, and ultimately towards a sense of universal and connected consciousness. In this volume, we take up again Agnew's "lovely dream" depicted above—of that shared music-making which might lead to a solidaric consciousness, where, accepting the other's song for what it is, we might move together with our different songs towards a collective "imaginary" of where our musicking *could* take us.

Notes

1. For a fuller account of Sonia M'Barek's explanation, see her article at: www.toda.org.
2. Ingrid Monson introduced the term "intermusicality" in 1996 in her book: *Saying Something: Jazz Improvisation and Interaction.* Chicago and London: Chicago University Press; this will be further explained in Fakher Hakima's chapter.
3. For a fuller account of Mohamed Zinelabidine's article, see: www.toda.org.

References

Agnew, Vanessa. 2008. *Enlightenment Orpheus: The Power of Music in Other Worlds.* Oxford: Oxford University Press.

Niebuhr, Reinhold. 1960. *Moral Man and Immoral Society.* London: Continuum.

O'Flynn, John. 2005. "Re-appraising ideas of musicality in intercultural contexts of music education" *International Journal of Music Education* 23, 3: 191-203.

Sloboda, John. 1999. "Music-where cognition and emotion meet" *The Psychologist*, 12, 9: 450-455.

Stein, E. [1917] 1989. *On the Problem of Empathy.* Washington, D.C.: ICS Publications.

Turino, Thomas. 1999. "Signs of Imagination, Identity, and Experience: A Peircian Semiotic Theory for Music" *Ethnomusicology* 43, 2: 221-255.

Webb, Michael. 2008. "Gilles Apap's Mozart cadenza and expanding musical competences of twenty-first-century musician and music educators" *Music Education Research* 10, 1: 15-39.

Inspiring Musical Movements and Global Solidarity: *Playing for Change, Min-On* and *El Sistema*

Olivier Urbain

Introduction

In 1992, the essay *Music Beyond Apartheid?* was published. The author, Denis-Constant Martin, suggested that the musical situation in South Africa in the 1980s reflected the political tensions and confusion. After years of oppression by the apartheid regime, during which both musical and political creativity were suffocated, South Africans started to express their longing for liberty for all, both politically and musically. This resulted in an explosion of musical expressions, which was an integral part of the profound transformation the country was going through. I find this point very important because even though musicking did not bring down apartheid (boycotts and sanctions did), it surely played a crucial role, as Martin intimates in the following excerpt:

> Contemporary South African Music is fundamentally mixed [...]. If a fear of the Other is inextricably linked to desire for the Other, a passage may be more readily initiated by music, in that music ignores the language censor, to let the body speak [...]. The acceptance of the community of the Other may well be discreetly announced by a widening of musical tastes (Martin, cited in Garofalo 1992, 204).

Martin's essay can serve as a reference point and a source of inspiration for those who believe that music has a role to play in the enhancement of a universal consciousness of solidarity in today's world. Indeed, in recent years, certain individuals have clearly been inspired by such a belief to establish whole movements that, through the use of music, they hope might promote understanding and mutual respect across social, national and even transcontinental borders.

One of the most famous examples of an individual launching a movement that can be argued to have raised consciousness, in its transforming of the way millions of people viewed the relatively marginalized issues of poverty, hunger and third world debt, is that of Bob Geldof, who organized the *Live Aid* concert in 1985 and its follow-up *Live 8* in 2005, both of these events attracting global audiences. It is clear that if society is to change for the better, it is firstly the people within them who have to change. It is therefore especially encouraging to see what one individual can do. For this opening chapter, I have chosen three case studies of such musical movements which all started with the decision of one single person to do something for the world through music. These are: *Playing for Change* in the USA, *Min-On* in Japan, and *El Sistema* in Venezuela.

I will be looking at these three case studies as inspirational examples of current practice across the globe in people's attempts to foster solidarity, as this term has been defined in the Introduction to this volume, through the human activity of musicking. These three examples have spurred me to write this chapter and as Director of the Toda Institute to strive towards the publication of this volume, and also to organize an ongoing series of conferences exploring the power of music for peace. What, then, is it about them that has such potential to inspire that sense of solidarity with our fellow human beings … at least for me?

The founders of these three movements, respectively Mark Johnson (*Playing for Change*), Daisaku Ikeda (*Min-On*) and José Antonio Abreu (*El Sistema*), were inspired by musical experiences to start activities which all reached spectacular proportions within a few years, eventually reaching across the globe. The first two soon developed into organizations with the explicit purpose of promoting solidarity in various ways, whereas *El Sistema*'s goal was (and remains) to offer a better future to children through the discipline and skills which musical practice can provide them. Much has already been written about *El Sistema*, but in this chapter the achievements of this organization will be given a new "twist": for I find it a source of revelation in terms of my own feelings of identification with and care for the children whose lives are transformed within the project. However, through discussions with others who are perhaps equally concerned about issues of universal justice and peace, it is clear that such a response to this particular "story" is neither inevitable nor obvious. What is it about *El Sistema* that touches me in such a way? Does it depend on my own conception of solidarity, or perhaps the extent to which I am "ready" to be moved by what I know of this project?

In the section entitled "*El Sistema* Revisited," I will suggest that this huge organization can be seen as testament to the possibility that people, all people, no matter how poor or hopeless, can be inspired by music and change their lives in radical ways for the better. The most spectacular example of this is that of Gustavo Dudamel, who started in the children's orchestra in his hometown in Venezuela, learned the violin and today conducts some of the world's greatest orchestras. The fact that Dudamel's life was transformed by music, as were those of thousands of children, enhances this author's feelings of solidarity with the rest of humanity.

For me, it is crucial to feel that "this person is inherently precious." This feeling comes easily with our loved ones, but what about people we have never met in person? In order to build a culture of peace in a world ridden by violence and struggles for power, it is crucial to enhance the conviction that "this person, that person, any person is *inherently* precious." In this context the example of *El Sistema* is crucial. The fact that one or two children were able to change their lives for the better through music would already be remarkable, but in the case of *El Sistema*, the current number is no less than 300,000. If that many people can leave the anonymity of a life of misery in the barrios, and show the world that they are "inherently precious," then there is no reason why the numbers could not be enhanced to 3 million, or 300 million, 3 billion, or 6.8 billion.

Too many decision-makers think that power, control, resources and strategic advantages are more important than people. Too many of us complacently watch them wreak havoc on the planet. The more people are convinced that *other* people—those beyond their kin, or their "tribe"—are precious and irreplaceable, the more we will be able to move towards a culture of peace.

In the musical projects *Playing for Change* and *Min-On*, the intrinsic rationale was the direct pursuit of this culture of peace and the nurturing of intercultural understanding necessary to this. I tell the story now of the first of these, *Playing for Change*.

Playing for Change

In March 2005, while walking down the 3ʳᵈ Street promenade in Santa Monica, California, USA, Mark Johnson heard a street musician singing "Stand by Me." He was deeply touched by the quality of this performance and decided to find ways to share this experience with the entire world. The singer was Roger Ridley (who passed away on November 16, 2005), one of the thousands of anonymous people who play music in our neighborhoods. Johnson decided to film and record his street performance and to distribute it widely on the Internet. Then he added more musicians from other places and mixed the recordings in a single video of "Stand by Me" (Stand by Me 2010).

This was the beginning of the *Playing for Change* (PFC) movement. Based on his expertise as a technician with some of the most renowned musicians and producers in the film, television and music industries, Johnson created a mobile recording and filming technique to capture the work of musicians throughout the world. He and a small group of filmmakers then combined the recordings together to create the CD and DVD *Songs Around the World*. The result is a series of short videos with a single song as soundtrack for each, but in which viewers can see and hear people performing that song in different countries and continents. The website of PFC states:

> The idea for this project arose from a common belief that music has the power to break down boundaries and overcome distances between people. No matter whether people come from different geographic, political, economic, spiritual or ideological backgrounds, music has the universal power to transcend and unite us as one human race (*Playing for Change* 2010a).

The PFC crew became closely involved with the people of the communities they visited, and developed a culture of mutual respect and participatory democracy while filming and recording musicians all over the world. After traveling around the globe recording *Songs Around the World* and sharing them with an ever-growing audience through virtually every means available (concerts, Internet, CDs, DVDs and more), they created the Playing for Change Foundation (PFCF) in 2007, a separate nonprofit corporation. In early 2008, they established Timeless Media, a for-profit entity that funds and extends the work of *Playing for Change*.

Their goal is to bring PFC's music, videos and message to the widest possible audience, and they describe the production of the album *Songs Around the World* as an attempt to enhance a universal sense of connection:

> We traveled from streets and subways to Native American reservations, through African towns and villages, up to the Himalayan Mountains, and beyond. Throughout this journey we have created a movement connecting the world through music. This album is a collective statement from over 100 musicians spanning five continents. Many of them have never met in person, but through their different cultures, these songs demonstrate a profound human connection and willingness to unite. Through music we can understand our differences and create a better world (*Playing for Change* 2010b).

In this way, the clip based on Roger Ridley's original singing of "Stand by Me," now digitally "accompanied" by numerous musicians playing in their locations throughout the world, is symbolic of a spirit of universal solidarity on different levels. By promoting Ridley's music worldwide, as well as that of many other street musicians, PFC has brought the music of common people to audiences of millions through the Internet.[1] The lyrics of the song itself are about the friendship and loyalty of people who care about each other—the most basic elements of solidarity, while the performers, although they are from different civilizations and cultures, blend happily in the video. It is also notable that this format for performance and the deliberate attempt to build a unified consciousness has occurred in at least one other video, which follows the same technique in a different context. For example, the Turkish group Doğa İçin Çal (Play for Nature) acknowledge this debt to PFC on their website and at the end of their video (Doğa İçin Çal 2010). It shows musicians and singers from different cities in Turkey playing the same song, following the example of "Stand by Me" and other "Songs Around the World." In this way, it can be seen that PFC has the potential of instigating a global movement.

On a more concrete level, the PFC movement staff members have started founding music and art schools using the proceeds of benefit concerts and other financing sources coming from the PFC Foundation. As of April 2010, three schools are already running and two are under construction. One of these is the Ntonga PFC Music School.

Established in a community that is plagued with drugs, crime, and poverty, the Ntonga PFC Music School in Gugulethu, South Africa offers a place for the children where they can go after school and learn music, without having to pay any tuition fees. In addition, the whole community is supporting this project, and this in turn gives them hope and a sense of dignity. The school offers eight-week class sessions and weekend workshops as well as a holiday workshops series. Classes are provided in the afternoon after normal school is finished for the day. Well aware of the dangers of cultural imperialism, the PFC staffs are sensitive to the needs of the local people and respectful of their ancestral cultures. At the same time, while grounding their efforts in the historical and cultural richness of the local community, they also provide opportunities to learn about other types of music, as described in their brochure:

  • In an effort to preserve history and cultural traditions, each school's curriculum is focused on regional music and instruments. The global role of music is also explored via interaction with other schools, students, teachers and musical cultures.

- These are not *our* schools; each school belongs to the people in the community. The community is invested in the school and its success. The people create the energy that the schools—and the community—need to succeed (PFCF Brochure 2010, 3).

This is also exhibited in the work of the Bizung School of Music and Dance in Tamale, Ghana, where youngsters can learn dance, and various musical instruments including voice. Elders can teach traditional music, and students can also get acquainted with the musics of other cultures. The PFC music Program at the Tintale Village Teaching Center in Nepal offers humanitarian aid along with support for music education. More such programs are being planned in other countries; and these together contribute towards a picture of an organization that exemplifies a worldwide movement that started with one person's vision. Other groups have started to emulate their example in different countries, showing that the power of music to enhance solidarity through complex techniques can be reproduced and has the potential of becoming universal.

Min-On

Amongst the ruins of post-war Tokyo, Daisaku Ikeda, having lost his elder brother who was killed towards the end of the war in Burma, having seen his family house destroyed, and being forced to work in an ammunition factory, was confused and in poor health. It was during this period in his life that he listened to music to encourage himself, especially Beethoven's Fifth Symphony. Beethoven's music gave him hope, and this was the starting point for his conviction that music could inspire people to rise above their circumstances.

During a trip to South-East Asia in the early 1960s, while flying over Burma, Ikeda had vivid memories of his elder brother who was killed there. He wondered again what could be done to avoid a repetition of the tragedy of war and to promote peace, and the thought came to him that if only Japanese people could have more chances to appreciate music and the arts, and thereby learned to feel the depth of the human heart, they might be less tempted to take up the path of war again (Kobayashi 2010). Two years later, in 1963, he established the *Min-On* concert association.

The name Min-On is an abbreviation of *Minshu Ongaku*, which means "Music for the People." At the time of its inception, the vast majority of Japanese people had no opportunity to enjoy live music performances of top quality since they were too expensive and reserved for the elite. By founding *Min-On*, Daisaku Ikeda decided to change this. His first motivation was to make live musical performances accessible to "ordinary" people in all parts of Japan (Kobayashi 2010). Today it can be said that this goal has been reached: since its birth in 1963, *Min-On* has organized more than 70,000 concerts attended by more than 100 million people, inviting musicians from more than 100 different countries to perform in Japan. It is supported by one million volunteers who promote *Min-On*'s programs and encourage their neighbors to attend its concerts. Accordingly, *Min-On* may be argued now to be contributing to the enhancement of a spirit of commonality, in Japan and even beyond.

This evolution is reflected in the structure of their mission statement, which states first its concern to locate the movement "among the people," followed by the wish to enhance artistic progress, and finally announcing the ultimate goal of addressing inter-country relationships:

1. We shall aim to develop a multifaceted music and cultural movement that is firmly rooted among the people so as to share with still more people the pleasure and inspiration that come from enjoying music and the performing arts.
2. We shall endeavor to contribute to a flourishing of music and art in the new age by enhancing musical and cultural activities and developing musical programs designed to cultivate the artistic sentiments of children and youth.
3. We shall seek to deepen mutual understanding and friendship among all countries by promoting global music and cultural exchange that transcends differences of nationality, race and language (*Min-On* 2010).

In Japan, *Min-On* organizes international competitions for young conductors, and also for composers, through which original ballets, operas, and other pieces have been created. People from around the world come to Japan to participate. *Min-On* also organizes lectures and conferences about music, and brings young musicians from abroad to perform in Japanese schools. Thus two goals are fulfilled, those of allowing ordinary Japanese people to enjoy top level performances, and also of introducing cultures from abroad to Japanese audiences. Along these lines, one of their most spectacular achievements is to have brought the whole La Scala opera company to Japan in September 1981.

This was the very first time that Japanese audiences had a chance to see and hear La Scala performing Verdi, Puccini and Rossini. Here "the whole company" means all the singers, the musicians, the dancers, a total of 500 artists and staff members together with 80 truckloads of stage sets. As one person put it at the time, *Min-On* brought "Everything except the theatre itself" (Roderick 1981).

The current president of *Min-On*, Hiroyasu Kobayashi recently described in an interview[2] what for him stands as the fundamental spirit of the association, invoking Daisaku Ikeda's acceptance speech given in response to receiving an honorary doctorate from Moscow State University in 1975.[3] This "spirit" can be discerned in the following passages from the speech, where, firstly, Ikeda talks about the rich exchanges that took place along the ancient Silk Road, which used to link such distant places as the Mediterranean and Japan:

> What was the reason for the wide cultural diffusion that took place along the Silk Road? Certainly, trade and conquest are two causes of dissemination of cultural traits, but I believe a more important one lies in the very nature of culture as an instrument of exchange. Culture is essentially universal; it is the breath that enlivens the activities of human life. Joy strikes a sympathetic chord in the hearts of all people and causes harmonious reverberations. Similarly, culture is a fundamental human undertaking that conquers distance and stirs the hearts of peoples everywhere. I believe that this sympathy among human hearts is the point of departure for cultural exchange and the basis of culture itself (Ikeda 1996, 66).

A second excerpt from the same speech addresses the gap between what are considered rich and poor countries, the North and the South:

> It is desirable to use standards other than economics in evaluating the achievements of a people. For example, what would we find if we examined the nations of the world in terms of musical achievements? (70)

I believe that by putting these two quotes together, especially Ikeda's conviction that "sympathy among human hearts is the point of departure for cultural exchange and the basis of culture itself" with his suggestion that we examine "the nations of the world in terms of musical achievements," we obtain a powerful formula for the mission of Min-On in terms of a fresh look on international relations. Instead of promoting military, political or economic power, Min-On aims at promoting musical power in order to enhance humanity's capacity for harmony and peaceful, humanistic exchanges. One example of how this can be achieved, one heart at a time, follows.

In his interview, Kobayashi shared a letter from a 60-year-old Japanese man whose feelings towards the "other" were transformed by one performance. He was born in the far north of Japan, in an area that was taken over by Russia at the end of the Second World War, and he and his family had to escape to the south of the new border, into what had become a slightly smaller Japan. For him the Russians were enemies. He had reluctantly attended a *Min-On* concert featuring music and dance from Russia, and what follows is a shortened translation of his letter:[4]

I really didn't want to come. I had bad feelings towards Russia because of the Northern Territories Dispute. I used to live in Kushiro and Nemuro, which were occupied by Russia. However I came here today, and when I heard the music and the singing, I could not hold my tears, which flowed freely throughout the performance. I realized then that I should not judge people based on stereotypes. The people of Russia are now my friends for all eternity (Kobayashi 2010).

Kobayashi commented that it was very hard to change 60 years of prejudice. Even though this man had been exposed to books, photos, CDs and videos about Russia, he could not open his heart. However, a single performance of two hours had such a profound impact on him that he was able radically to change his attitude. Such can be the power of live music (Kobayashi 2010). Gomart and Hennion suggest that "active work must be done in order to be moved" (cited in Tia DeNora 2001, 168); this notion might also be useful here. If this man had absolutely no intention of "being moved," he would probably not have attended the concert at all…

Besides inviting musicians from abroad, *Min-On* also sends Japanese artists to all corners of the world. Audiences in many different countries learn something of Japanese music and dance, while the Japanese artists can be influenced and enriched by their experiences abroad, which may subsequently, in turn, have an impact on their compatriots once they return home. Thus, by promoting live music in Japan and throughout the world with the mission of establishing what we might call a "spiritual silk road," *Min-On* allows countless people opportunities to make connections and learn about each other.

Just as *Playing for Change* started with one individual inspired by a street performance, *Min-On* started with the encouragement that one ordinary Japanese man felt while listening to Beethoven after the war. The third organization also started from the motivation of one person.

El Sistema Revisited

As described above, El Sistema is a music education program in Venezuela which gives free lessons to 300,000 people, mostly youngsters, so that they may learn and perform Western classical music. It was established in 1975 by amateur musician **José** Antonio Abreu, who would later become minister of culture in that country. This is how Abreu explains its humble beginnings:

Since I was a boy, in my early childhood, I always wanted to be a musician, and, thank God, I made it. From my teachers, my family and my community, I had all the necessary support to become a musician. All my life I've dreamed that all Venezuelan children have the same opportunity that I had. From that desire and from my heart stemmed the idea to make music a deep and global reality for my country (Abreu 2009).

Whereas Mark Johnson was inspired by a single performance of "Stand by Me," and Daisaku Ikeda by the rejuvenating melodies, rhythm and chords of "Beethoven's Fifth," José Abreu found a source of energy in the joy provided by his early musical education.

Most of the members of *El Sistema* come from the most vulnerable sectors of society, many of them from the slums surrounding Caracas, known as the barrios, where millions of people live without roads, a functioning sewage system, reliable access to water or electricity, and with so much violence that the barrios have one of the highest levels of criminality in the world. In contrast, this is the way an article in *The Guardian* of 27 July 2007 describes what happens when children join *El Sistema*:

> Across Venezuela, young barrio-dwellers now spend their afternoons practicing Beethoven and Brahms. They learn the "Trauermarsch" from Mahler's fifth symphony while their peers learn to steal and shoot. They are teenagers like Renee Arias, practicing Bizet's Carmen Suite at a home for abandoned and abused children, who when asked what he would be doing if he had not taken up the French horn, replies straightforwardly: "I'd be where I was, only further down the line—either dead or still living on the streets smoking crack, like when I was eight" (Vulliamy 2007).

The very first rehearsal in a Caracas garage was such a challenge that Abreu felt he could have given up right there and then. He was expecting 100 boys, but only 11 came. Abreu was able to surmount this initial obstacle: "I decided to face the challenge, and on that same night, I promised those 11 children I'd turn our orchestra into one of the leading orchestras in the world." He did keep his promise and this orchestra, called the Simon Bolivar Youth Orchestra, hugely impressed the audience at the BBC proms in 2007 and later that year, also performed in the Carnegie Hall in New York. To quote Abreu again:

> In [their] essence, the orchestra and the choir are much more than artistic structures. They are examples and schools of social life, because to sing and to play together means to intimately coexist toward perfection and excellence, following a strict discipline of organization and coordination in order to seek the harmonic interdependence of voices and instruments. That's how they build a spirit of solidarity and fraternity among them, develop their self-esteem and foster the ethical and aesthetical values related to the music in all its senses. This is why music is immensely important in the awakening of sensibility, in the forging of values and in the training of youngsters to teach other kids (Abreu 2009).

The Venezuelan government began fully financing Abreu's orchestra after it succeeded brilliantly at an international competition in 1977 in

Aberdeen, Scotland, and it has been funded by each successive government ever since. Moreover, in 2007, the Inter-American Development Bank carried out extensive research about the beneficial effects of its musical programs, and found so much evidence of social improvement and drop in criminality rates that they granted a loan of US$150 million (Lubow 2007).

Thus, based on his positive experience as a child learning music, Abreu was able to create a huge movement allowing Venezuelan youth to improve their daily circumstances. But I would suggest that it accomplishes much more than this, arguably strengthening feelings of solidarity around the world on several different levels.

As Gustavo Dudamel and the Simon Bolivar Youth Orchestra became famous, it has made many people throughout the world aware of the existence of the barrios of Caracas, and of the fact that many more potential "Dudamels" are living in appalling conditions. In the minds of the people who have been deeply moved by their music, the "poor" of Venezuela are not nameless masses anymore, but *real* people, with talents and value like everyone else. This awareness is reinforced by the fact that most news about *El Sistema* mentions the origins of Dudamel and of the whole enterprise, describing the situation of the poor in Caracas (Carroll 2007; Higgins 2006; Lubow 2007; Vulliamy 2007; Wakin 2006). In addition, *El Sistema* has exerted a profound influence on different countries; for instance this is the description of El Sistema USA:

> El Sistema USA is a support and advocacy network for people and organizations inspired by Venezuela's monumental music education program. It will grow to provide comprehensive information on the El Sistema philosophy and methodology, and host a variety of resources that will aid those building, expanding and supporting El Sistema programs in the US and beyond (El Sistema USA).

People in other countries and regions, such as Scotland and many South American nations have started to implement similar systems.

Conclusion

It is often said that it is difficult to create unity towards peace. It is much easier for people to organize themselves effectively in order to commit crimes or wage wars. How can we make peace and solidarity as attractive and exciting as violence and war, or even more so? One answer is: through music. The three case studies presented here have shown that, based on a positive musical experience, individuals can be inspired to establish worldwide movements, themselves based upon musical activity. These organizations can then in turn touch millions of people. These kinds of musical activities can thus be powerful tools towards the construction of a better world at the dawn of this second decade of the twenty-first century.

Notes

1.   At the end of a promotional video for the Playing for Change Foundation entitled *Playing For Change Sizzle Reel*, we find the following information: "Over 30 million views on You Tube." See Concord Music Group. 2010. *Playing For Change Sizzle Reel*, Accessed: April 28, 2010 from http://www.concordmusicgroup. com/video/pfc_sizzle_reel_20100129.html.
2.   The interview took place in Tokyo, at the Min-On Culture Center, on January 6, 2010.
3.   Min-On was established in 1963, but today it is the content of the 1975 speech which constitutes the fundamental spirit of the association, according to its president, Hiroyasu Kobayashi.
4.   The letter was provided in Japanese by Hiroyasu Kobayashi, and translated into English and summarized by this author.

References

Abreu, José Antonio. 2009. Acceptance speech for the TED prize, delivered on 5 February 2009. Accessed: January 18, 2010 from http://www.ted.com/talks/jose_abreu_on_ kids_transformed_by_music.html.

Carroll, Rory. 2007. "Chávez pours millions more into pioneering music scheme." *The Guardian,* 4 September 2007. Accessed: April 27, 2010 from http://www.guardian. co.uk/world/2007/sep/04/musicnews.venezuela.

Concord Music Group. 2010. *Playing For Change Sizzle Reel*. Video introducing the work of the Playing for Change Foundation. Accessed: April 28, 2010 from http://www. concordmusicgroup.com/video/pfc_sizzle_reel_20100129.html.

DeNora, Tia. 2001. "Aesthetic agency and musical practice: new directions in the sociology of music and emotion" in Patrik N. Juslin and John A. Sloboda (eds.) *Music and Emotion.* Oxford: Oxford University Press.

Doğa İçin Çal (Play for Nature). Accessed: April 26, 2010 from http://www.dogaicincal. com/index.asp?sayfa=aboutpfn.

El Sistema USA. Accessed: April 26, 2010 from http://elsistemausa.org.

Garofalo, Reebee (ed.). 1992. *Rocking the Boat: Mass Music and Mass Movements.* Cambridge, MA: South End Press.

Higgins, Charlotte. 2006. "Land of hope and glory." *The Guardian,* 24 November 2006. Accessed: April 27, 2010 from http://www.guardian.co.uk/music/2006/nov/24/Classicalmusicandopera.

Ikeda, Daisaku. 1996. "A New Road to East-West Cultural Exchange." Speech delivered at Moscow State University on 27 May 1975. In *A New Humanism: The University Addresses of Daisaku Ikeda.* New York and Tokyo: Weatherhill.

Kobayashi, Hiroyasu. 2010. Interview by the author on 6 January 2010 at the Min-On Culture Center in Tokyo.

Lubow, Arthur. 2007. "Conductor of the People." *New York Times.* 28 October 2007. Accessed: April 27, 2010 from http://www.nytimes.com/2007/10/28/magazine/ 28dudamel-t.html?_r=1.

Martin, Denis-Constant. 1992. "Music Beyond Apartheid?" In Reebee Garofalo (ed.). *Rocking the Boat: Mass Music and Mass Movements.* Cambridge, MA: South End Press.

Min-On. (2010). Mission Statement. Accessed: April 26, 2010 from http://www.min-on.org/about/index.html.

PFCF Brochure. 2010. Playing for Change Foundation brochure. Provided as attachment in a personal email to this author dated April 24, 2010 by Alowie Ahmad, staff member of Playing for Change.

Playing for Change. 2010a. Official website. Accessed: April 21, 2010 from http://www.playingforchange.com/journey/introduction.

Playing for Change. 2010b. Official website. Accessed: April 21, 2010 from http://www.playingforchange.com/journey/locations.

Roderick, John. 1981. "La Scala to Visit Japan." *The Spokesman-Review*, 24 August 1981. Accessed: January 18, 2010 from http://news.google.com/newspapers?nid=1314&dat=19810824&id=cNMRAAAAIBAJ&sjid=du4DAAAAIBAJ&pg=4982,4064930.

Stand by Me. 2010. Video featuring Roger Ridley. Accessed: April 26, 2010 from http://www.playingforchange.com/episodes/2/Stand_by_Me.

Vulliamy, Ed. 2007. "Orchestral manoeuvres." *The Guardian*, 29 July 2007. Accessed: April 27, 2010 from http://www.guardian.co.uk/music/2007/jul/29/classicalmusi-candopera1.

Wakin, Daniel J. 2006. "A Youth Movement at the Berlin Philharmonic." *New York Times*, 8 May 2006. Accessed: April 27, 2010 from http://www.nytimes.com/2006/05/08/arts/music/08yout.html.

On Music, Interconnection, and Consciousness

Michael Golden

Introduction

Broadly viewed as a phenomenon (rather than as a "fine art"), music exists in every human culture on earth. With other diverse but universal human phenomena (e.g., our use of language), we recognize and seek to explain their value to humanity, to our development. It is common, however, in our contemporary civilization, to view music either as a commodity, frivolous or extraneous to the essential activities of human beings ("auditory cheesecake" is Stephen Pinker's term), or as a tool for divisiveness along one or more of the fracture lines—religious, cultural, political, ethnic, gender, class—that plague our species. In this chapter I will be considering the relationships between music, its connective functions and consciousness, and proposing some alternative views of the significant contribution music makes (or might make) to the positive development of humanity.

To begin, we need to consider the complex and somewhat elusive meaning of "music." As we learn more about the extraordinary diversity of human activities that might be encompassed by the word "music," we realize the need to adjust our understanding if we are credibly to assert anything universal about it. Therefore, I propose the following working definition:

> Music is an activity of human beings involving sound, the purpose of which is to facilitate and enhance our connection to our environment. "Environment" here is intended to be inclusive of both the natural/physical and social realms.

By focusing on human music I do not mean permanently to exclude from consideration the sounds of other living things or even the earth itself or the cosmos. I also assert here and hope to show that the connection we experience through music is both broader in scope and more powerful than that which we achieve through speech.

After a brief survey of examples from around the world which illustrate the function of music as defined above, I will examine some ideas about the origins of and evolutionary "reasons" for human musical activity, and then look at the particular strengths of sound and our sense of hearing in enabling connection with our environment. Among the specific beneficial impacts of music on individuals are an expanded sense of self, and an enriched awareness of time, and I will explore both of these in subsequent sections of this chapter, along with discussion of studies in neurobiology as they relate to these issues. Finally, I will return to some general questions about music, consciousness and universality.

The "Music-as-Connection" World Tour

It seems that music is everywhere closely affiliated with the sacred, with connecting to the sacred, however that may be defined by a people, and in this "tour" I am going to focus on illustrating this aspect, as it seems closely related to our theme. However, having defined "connection to the environment" as including both the cosmic and social realms, let me quickly note that the notion of connectivity as the central purpose of music is not limited to religious practices or even expressions of spiritual ideas; examples of music from around the world used for social bonding of all kinds (mother and child, female and male, even soldiers or athletes) would be equally easy to present and would not invalidate my working definition.

Pythagoras is known for the discovery of the relationship between number and sound. This led him and his followers to the idea that since our organisms, the music we create, and the celestial elements of the cosmos (the "spheres") all move and vibrate, "proper" music has the power to harmonize our lives with the sublime order of the universe. Thus, the power to "soothe the savage breast" meant for the Pythagoreans music's power to realize the underlying mathematical resonance between the cosmos and ourselves (James 1995, 28-40).

The Bayaka of the central African rainforest (sometimes referred to as "pygmies") understand their music-making, which is almost continuous, as communication with the forest that sustains their lives. Their singing[1] contributes a human voice to the natural "orchestra" of sounds in their environment, and is used, Louis Sarno writes, to create "a reestablishing of the natural and harmonious relationship between community and cosmos." (Sarno 1995, 79)

The Shona people of Zimbabwe are known (musically speaking) for playing *mbira*, a metal-keyed lamellaphone. Paul Berliner writes,

> In the past, as today, the *mbira* has been used in traditional Shona religious ceremonies to create the essential link between the world of the living and the world of the spirits. The *mbira* is believed to have the power of projecting its sound into the heavens, and attracting the attention of the ancestors, who are the spiritual owners and keepers of the land and the benefactors of the people's welfare (Berliner 1993, 43).

The classical music of India, another tradition going back over four thousand years[2] is based on a concept remarkably similar to that of Pythagoras. There are said to be two kinds of sound: unstruck sound ("the sound of the universe, ever present and unchanging" writes Ravi Shankar, but like the "music of the spheres" unheard by human ears), and struck sound. In the Hindu tradition, sound is God, and so, in Shankar's words, "The highest aim of our music is to reveal the essence of the universe it reflects... [T]hus, through music, one can reach God" (Shankar 1968, 17).

In ancient China, the two major influences of Confucianism and Daoism also point to the role of music as a powerful means of connection to the environment, Confucianism focusing on the harmony among humans in society (through music's capacity to increase the virtue of the individual), and Daoism focusing on bringing the individual into harmony with nature (DeWoskin 1998, 7:97).

David Harnish, discussing the gamelan music of Bali, writes that "gamelan and music cannot be separated from the balance of Balinese life" and that music and the gamelan instruments "harmonize humans with God, nature, and all humankind... Music... is developed upon structural elements shared with cosmology, and has an efficacy to transform reality (time and space) and to create balance and harmony" (Harnish 2006, 125).

Among the traditional peoples of the Bolivian Andes, the natural landscape, indeed the cosmos, and humans and other living beings are understood as part of a single entity, and *animu*, the living energy in all things, is manifested in sound, movement, or light. Henry Stobart writes, "From this perspective, sound is equivalent to life and its shaping in music may be seen as the shaping of life" (Stobart 2000, 31). The Andean peoples make the specialized sounds we might call music in order to strengthen the *animu* in themselves (as in overcoming illness), to support the function of the natural forces around them, and to express their respect and appreciation for those forces.

Among the Aborigines of Australia, David Turner writes, "music is the principal means of accessing the 'eternally uncreated' domain we have translated as the 'Dreamtime'" (Turner 2000, 35). The didgeridoo player and singer, through their music, cross to the "other side" of existence and return.

Expressing a common understanding of the role of music in the Christian West, here are the words of American pastor John Mellen from a 1773 sermon, "But such poetic compositions set to music, increase the pleasure, and by still further fanning the fire of devotion, serve to waft and elevate the soul to God."

Ideas on Origins and Evolution

Let us now consider why such a universal (and universally diverse) practice may have evolved and proven beneficial to humanity. Ellen Dissanayake argues that the arts in general offer significant evolutionary advantages to humans because of the value of what she calls "making special." The nature of our awareness of ourselves and the world calls forth the need to transcend the ordinary in our expression (poetry and music extending or enhancing speech, dance extending basic movement, and so on) and this serves several beneficial aims for us: more powerfully influencing our environments (or at least providing the therapeutic notion that we can), uniting and strengthening bonds among groups of people, and transmitting important information to future generations more effectively than mere speech, among others (Dissanayake 1999, 27-38). Concerning music specifically, she writes, quoting Viktor Zuckerkandl, "music provides 'the shortest, least arduous, perhaps even the most natural solvent of artificial boundaries between the self and others'" (Dissanayake 1995, 119).

Composer and musicologist François-Bernard Mâche, discussing the universality of sound models and the link between music and myth, writes, "Obstinately to imitate the cry of the prey one is chasing is not only to pressurize it by appropriating its "spirit," it is also to be already certain of possessing it by allowing oneself to be possessed by its voice." And further "The accuracy of these imitations fulfils both the practical function of attracting the quarry and the magical function of identification" (Mâche 1992, 36-39). Significantly, he argues that the practical success of such behavior may have led to the expansion and extension of the practice of using musical sound to both communicate and identify with our environments, sometimes through increasingly abstract or symbolic associations.

Steven Mithen believes that rather than music extending or deriving from language, music and language both emerged from a "proto-language"—a holistic sound-based mode of communication—that developed among early humans. He calls this mode "Hmmmmm" (Holistic, manipulative, multi-modal, musical and mimetic) and argues that the ability to communicate and influence each other through the qualities of sounds we make was essential to the cooperative behavior necessary for survival (Mithen 2006, 172). Language, he believes, emerged later from the segmentation of these sounds and the assigning of symbolic meaning to the segments.

These three authors have different focal points, of course, but I believe their ideas all resonate with the notion that there seems to have been, from earliest times, some innate drive in human beings (and perhaps our primate ancestors as well) to establish powerful and holistic communication amongst ourselves and with our environment. Let us next consider why music might provide a particularly powerful channel for such efforts.

A "Connectivity Survey" of the Senses

Our five senses are the links between our consciousness, our bodies, and the environment and all five serve important functions in our survival. Clearly, the ideal channel for connecting with the environment, in the sense discussed here of holistic identification, would enable two-way communication with the greatest possible range of interaction. Furthermore, the communication will be all the more powerful if we ourselves are directly engaged in it, rather than communicating through the medium of artifacts, however cleverly fashioned. With these criteria in mind, consider our sensory channels. Taste can give us important information about the state of something from our environment, and can produce a profound impact on our physical and emotional states, but as a rule, it's not practical to feed ourselves to other tasting beings as a means of communicating with them. Smell may also be a powerful communicator of health and emotional state. Although not as well developed in humans as in some other animals, smell enables us to gather important information about our environment; however, although we do often exert effort to communicate (especially to other humans) through altering our scent, the physical range of effectiveness in this "outward" direction is somewhat limited. Touch powerfully conveys two-way information; heightened experience or our sense of connection can be profound through touch, but again, it has a very limited range.

Our sense of sight of course has the greatest physical range of reception (we gather light from the stars), and we also exert effort to communicate to others through our appearance. However, since we do not emit light ourselves (setting aside the possibility of electromagnetic auras for the moment), the most we can do in the "outward" direction is to attempt to control how we *reflect* light. Since light doesn't penetrate or impact our bodies except in the nerve-endings in our eyes, it doesn't touch our physical organisms as powerfully as the other senses. We cannot see behind, above, or below our heads without moving (smell and hearing are omnidirectional) and, of course, if we consider the early development of our species, we must have been very limited in visual communication of any kind after dark. The level of connection to the environment through vision is necessarily one step removed or abstracted from our physical experience, and functions within a narrower range of circumstances than other senses.[3]

And so we come to our sense of hearing. We can generate sound, and feel it, deep within our bodies. We hear the sounds of our bodies all the time. We hear the environment in all directions day and night (our ears are never closed) and we begin hearing in the womb, well before we see. We can hear sounds from a great distance, and send sounds out a greater distance than touches, tastes, or smells. Stephen Handel, concluding his book on the physics, biology and psychology of listening, writes of:

> the experience of listening, the experience of being in the auditory world, listening to one's self and to the world. Although there are equivalent expressions—looking at and listening to—listening, more than looking, puts us in the world. Looking makes each of us a focused observer, listening makes each of us a surrounded participant (Handel 1989, 546).

The physical characteristics of sound and hearing, then, make this an ideal path or channel for our endeavors to connect with each other and the universe around us.

I would note here that while speech is also a sound-based mode of communication, to the extent that it relies on what Susanne Langer calls "conventional or assigned meaning" (Langer 1953, 82) in order to be effective, it is limited in its capacity to satisfy by itself our needs to connect. In speech, the most powerful communicative factors are often tone, rhythm, intensity, and "body language" or gesture, all elements of sound production associated with music, or "Hmmmmm," to use Mithen's term. Clearly language, the assigned meaning of the words, can be and often is contradicted or "overruled" (or, on the other side, enhanced) by the musical and gestural qualities of speech, and thus these qualities become for us, even if subconsciously, the more reliable and powerful tools for connection with others. Writing about the possibility of a universal mode of communication (which he argues cannot be called "music" as thought of in the West), Kenneth Gourlay notes, "This [possibly universal] form of expression[4] is used on occasions of heightened feeling, when speech is inadequate, and it is necessary for communication to attain a new level of intensity." (Gourlay 1984, 36) In other words, when we *really* want to connect with our fellow humans, nature, gods or others, we sing it more than say it.

Music and Expanding the Self

I turn now to the aspect of music as contributing to an expanded sense of self, as suggested by the above-cited words of Viktor Zuckerkandl. Composer David Dunn writes:

> For me, the aesthetic response is what Gregory Bateson referred to when he said, "beauty is the pattern that connects." I interpret that to mean that the aesthetic response, the perception and apprehension of beauty, becomes a sort of resonance: we see and feel our own individual mind expand to include something that we previously didn't assume to be part of us (Dunn 1989, 94-105).

Another composer, Claude Schryer, writes about sublime aesthetic experience. Describing one of his own experiences, similar perhaps to one that most of us may have had at some point, Schryer notes that the music:

> literally "lifted" my spirit into another level of perception. The work carried me *into* listening. I don't recall what this particular piece was about, but I clearly remember and cherish the sensation it has left me (Schryer 2001, 123).

Mithen applies the idea of "expanded self" to examination of the social benefits of music-making, citing William McNeill's "notion of 'boundary loss,' the manner in which group music-making leads to 'a blurring of self-awareness and a heightening of fellow feeling...'" (Mithen 2006, 209).

Daisaku Ikeda, in a lecture at the Académie des Beaux-Arts, notes that "art worthy of the name consists in seeking this fundamental reality that creates the link between man and man, man and nature, and man and the universe" (Ikeda 1989).

The expanded sense of self we experience when engaged with music, then, seems to be a primary benefit of this activity, and is applicable to our need to connect with each other, our immediate environs, and the cosmos.

Music and Temporality

One further distinction among the senses which perhaps explains the importance of hearing and sound, and hence music, to humans is the inherent temporality of the experience. With our other four senses, while of course there is always some minimal time involved in perceiving the sensory input, perception can generally be reduced to a "snapshot," a momentary totality. In contrast, Handel writes that "it is almost impossible" to do this with an auditory event.

Sound perceiving must always be anticipating, hearing forward as well as retrospecting, hearing backward. The 'present' gets its meaning from both preceding and succeeding sounds (Handel 1989, 163).

The inherent temporality of auditory experience makes it an ideal medium for embodying (if in ephemeral form) the temporal experiences of living. Langer describes what makes art in general most effective as, "Living form—such form is 'living' in the same way that a border or a spiral is intrinsically 'growing': that is, it expresses life—feeling, growth, movement, emotion, and everything that characterizes vital existence" (Langer 1953, 82). She also writes, "But, although a work of art may abstract from the temporal character of experience, what it renders in its own logical projection must be true in design to the structure of experience" (Langer 1953, 373). Here again, the particular power of music may lie in the fact that it does not need to "abstract from" our experience of change over time; its existence itself is, at a level we directly perceive, parallel to our own.

Igor Stravinsky, among many others[5] of course, discusses music in terms of its capacity to create a kind of temporal experience independent of "ontological" or real time; like the "variations in psychological time," which we experience "only as they are related to the primary sensation—whether conscious or unconscious—of real time," music because of its temporal nature has the power to create its own time, or rather, to allow us to simultaneously inhabit ordinary "ontological" time and "musical" time (Stravinsky 1942, 30-1).

Understandably then, music from cultures around the world reflects those cultures' ideas about the nature of time, but more directly and significantly, music enables the people who engage with it to *experience* time in specially constructed and especially impactful ways. Stravinsky and Mâche (again, among many others) write about the spectrum of temporal structuring from repetition/sameness to continuous change/variety and the different effects and purposes of each. From around the world, we find approaches quite different on the surface, but related at the deeper level of being common human practice.[6] Shaping and experiencing meaningful temporal processes is a means of connecting with the life that goes on within and around us.

Furthermore, it seems that at a practical level, the mental processes involved in musical activity may be closely connected with the qualities of mind that make us human, that are particular to our form of intelligence and consciousness. Stravinsky writes, contrasting the processes of perception involved in the plastic arts, "music is based on temporal succession, and requires alertness of memory" (Stravinsky 1942, 28). To return to Stephen Handel's point, listening is never just a single or simple act of perception, but always involves both memory and anticipation, thus expanding the meaning of the "present moment." These processes (memory and prediction) clearly are essential to our survival, and music may therefore be closely linked with optimal functioning of our intelligence.

Another aspect of temporality, related of course to prediction, is expectation. David Huron describes a theory of expectation that includes five component response systems: imagination, tension, prediction, reaction, and appraisal. Each of these component processes has potential emotional or feeling states attached to it, which emerge during the time before and after the "expected" event. He writes:

> I propose that these five response systems arise from five functionally distinct neurophysiological systems. Each response system solves an important problem in tailoring behavior so that it is optimally adapted to a given environment (Huron 2007, 17).

The evolutionary purpose or survival benefit of expectation is to prepare an organism for the future, and the emotional states connected with this process are "motivational amplifiers" (Huron 2007, 4). Huron's research into the process of expectation in music uncovers a complex web of biological and cultural factors, which suggests the possibility that because, in its temporal aspect at least, music is primarily *about* expectation and its consequences, it may play an important role in our development. The assertion that musical activity, among its other important functions, may enable us to enhance our capabilities in these crucial temporal skills has not yet been proven, but it would certainly make a plausible argument, of a different sort from those presented earlier, for the evolutionary value of music to our species, an additional reason why our early ancestors may have found this activity worth the effort and not merely "cheesecake."

There is also a growing and highly diverse body of empirical evidence (from research in psychology, medicine, cognition, and education) that suggests that there may be quite measurable benefits to human development from engaging in musical activity.[7] I will focus next on some recent work by neurobiologists which, while not directly addressing music, may connect with the other ideas under discussion from a different direction.

Neurobiology and the Foundations of Consciousness

Rodolfo Llinás discusses the relationship of time to consciousness in terms of neural activity. While a complete technical summary of his findings is beyond our scope here, the essential point is that scientists have been able to measure a consistent and coherent 40-Hz electrical oscillation produced by the coordinated interlocking activity of our neurons, and that Llinás and others believe that this temporal coherence is "the neurological mechanism that underlies perceptual unity, the binding together or conjunction of independently derived sensory components, called 'cognitive binding'" (Llinás 2001, 121). He continues:

> This temporally coherent event that binds, in the time domain, the fractured components of external and internal reality into a single construct is what we call the *"self."* It is a convenient and exceedingly useful invention on the part of the brain. It binds, therefore I am![8] (Llinás 2001, 126).

The essential capability for prediction, the need for which, Llinás argues, is the "cause" of the evolutionary development of nerves and brains in living organisms in the first place, is centralized in what we call the self, but it is neither tangible nor fixed. Rather it "is generated by the dialogue between the thalamus and the cortex," a continual process of communication and temporal coordination between different parts of the brain associated with different functions (Llinás 2001, 126-8).

This raises a potentially interesting connection to the idea that musical activity fosters an expanded sense of self. Perhaps our ever-active neurons, engaging in intensive predictive dialogue "about" sound when it is *not* immediately linked to our individual survival, both improve their capacity to do so when it may become necessary for survival in the future, and are able to expand the self beyond the narrow, to, in Dunn's words, "include something that we previously didn't assume to be part of us."

Neurobiologist (and Nobel Prize winner) Gerald Edelman, discussing temporal processes in the brain, notes that while we may think we experience past and future, "in a strict physical sense, only the present exists" (Edelman 2006, 93). This present[9] itself lasts somewhere between 200 and 500 milliseconds at the conscious level, because of the time necessary for the integration of the various brain states that make it up. But, writing about the function of future planning, he notes that:

unconscious neural activity leading to action can lead to much faster responses. Many such responses... require conscious training. After deliberate practice, habitual responses are then mediated nonconsciously and rapidly by subcortical structures interacting with the cortex (Edelman 2006, 93).

Edelman, an avid musician, developed the theory called Neural Darwinism, and argues that experience of interaction with the environment coupled with "deliberate practice" leads to the development of our human capabilities through selectively improving the coordinated functioning of our neurons. Again, this suggests the possibility that engaging in musical activity, by "consciously training" our temporal responses and "deliberately practicing" our temporal functions, may serve to enhance our ability at the neural level to imagine and plan for the future.

Recapitulation: Social Benefits of Musical Activity

To this point, I have looked at potentially beneficial effects of musical activity in terms of sound and time, the two essential aspects of music, mostly from the perspective of the impact on the individual. I would argue that the social value of musical activity is, in part, inherently derived from this; since we are social organisms and dependent on each other, the growth of an individual will ultimately benefit the group. There are also some specific social benefits, described in a substantial body of literature (some referenced earlier), which I wish to emphasize here.

Mithen writes extensively of the value of the cooperative and interdependent behaviors in group music making as strengthening bonds of trust (think here of "practicing" in Edelman's sense or training our social network to function together as we "train" our neurons), while Dissanayake stresses the value of the arts specifically in the transmission of important information to future generations, one of the hallmarks of human culture. And John Blacking reverses the common expression "humanly organized sound" and writes of "soundly organized humanity" in developing his thesis that we use music to modify our own behavior, and to impart important values through the musical sounds we make. He notes, "Musical behavior may reflect varying degrees of consciousness of social forces, and the structure and function of music may be related to basic human drives and to the biological need to maintain balance among them" (Blacking 1973, 100).

To recapitulate, music, as defined above, may have developed out of the social calls of our primate ancestors and become our way of "practicing" the temporal coordination needed for our self-awareness, intelligence, and predictive capabilities, enabling us to experience a flexible and expansive sense of self, and promoting the social cooperation essential for our survival.

I turn now to the question of how music might contribute to the betterment of the world from today onward.

Looking Ahead: Music and Expanded Human Consciousness

As stated in my introduction, music can be and has been used by people as a tool for promoting egoism, hatred, and divisiveness, and rampant violence. The capacity of music or musical activity to promote social cohesiveness can be applied to promoting (unified) destructive behavior, behavior quite antithetical to what I have argued to be its original and beneficial function as part of human existence. Plato and Confucius, among others, recognized and feared this potentially degrading or disruptive function.[10] Since the potential power of music to affect us is great in either direction, we have to recognize that the *intent* of the humans involved, which at first seems to be an extra-musical issue, is an important factor. This raises the question of how (with what intent) those of us who are committed to promoting a greater consciousness for humanity might inspire and assist its development through music.

First, a (true) story from my experience as an educator. Some years ago, I was teaching an introductory course in world music at a university in the midwestern United States. At the conclusion of our unit on music from sub-Saharan Africa, a very bright and talented graduate student presented a report to the class on Shona *mbira* music. At the conclusion of her report, she explained to us that she had been taught from childhood that what the Shona were doing in making this music (practicing ancestor worship and spirit possession) was evil. Then she said, "But when I listen to this music, there's no evil in it. And when I read what the musicians say about their music, there's no evil in that either." I was inspired by and caused to reflect on the meaning of her comments. Of course, it's hazardous to read too much into a single piece of anecdotal evidence (although I have observed similar phenomena on many occasions), but I think that here was an intelligent human being who was able to experience something remarkable through listening to the sounds themselves, in spite of the fact that her cultural conditioning would have closed her off to what these other intelligent humans were doing; even the musicians' words would have provoked a negative response in her without the music. Her experience suggests that while it seems extremely unlikely that any of us can truly experience music from a very different human culture in the ways in which members of that culture do (and indeed she did not do so in this case), the music of the Shona enabled her to transcend differences of culture and religion—perhaps finding some common human aspiration to expand their lives, to connect to the sacred in their environment—and to expand her own humanity as a result.

As many others have pointed out, including various of my co-authors in this journal, unless we were to dissolve all differences of culture and all make music in the same way, music will never be a "universal language." What I suggest, if we want to promote appreciation of our common humanity, is that rather than prescribing a certain way of making music, we focus on education aimed at appreciating and promoting the common human *practice* of music-making, the common aspects of human existence itself and the ways in which music serves our most fundamental needs. Evolutionary biologists use the term "convergence" to describe the phenomenon that occurs when species with no obvious genetic link develop distinctive but related solutions to common challenges or needs, and I believe the term applies to music as well.

In his concluding chapter, Llinás raises the question of whether universal consciousness is possible, and what it might "look like." He notes that the temporal coordination among cells that enables consciousness and is essential to our ability to function evolved over a *very* long time. The temporal coordination among humans that might enable us to function as part of a universal consciousness certainly would also require a long evolution. He considers (and largely dismisses) the possibility that the World Wide Web is the beginning of such a consciousness (Llinás 2001, 250-256). I would submit, and have argued here, that musical activity is *already* a human universal (and does not require computers) and, because it is "about" temporal coordination and interconnection through sound, seems a natural direction to pursue in the development of some form of universal consciousness.

We need to go further. To carry through the analogy, as the harmonizing behavior of our neurons enables a larger consciousness whose behavior in turn benefits the individual cells, expanded human consciousness, it is to be hoped, would bring with it a mode of behavior more beneficial not just to the rest of human life, but to all life on our planet. It is not a hard argument to make that most if not all of the troubles we inflict on ourselves as humans stem from the fact that the dismissive stance we have taken towards the rest of life on earth—attempting to disconnect ourselves from the balancing forces inherent in life as a system—carries over to our relationships with each other as well. In other words, to establish a universal consciousness we must aim beyond the human realm in order to bring the activity of that realm into a contributive role in the system of life on earth.

Consider again the role of music from the viewpoint of "systems thinking" or the idea that we are an inseparable part of a complex interconnected system called life on earth. Music, as we noted, is ultimately about connectivity, a holistic means of resonating with our environment, as the neurons in our brains do with each other. Music might be thought of as the kind of signaling, or, to use Fritjof Capra's term, "structural coupling" (Capra 1997, 287-9), that enables the elements in a system to function together as part of a higher order. As such, it may well have a unique potential to contribute to the ongoing dynamic balance and development of life itself.

If we are to realize this potential, it seems to me that the following suggestions, some of which have been touched on earlier in this chapter, become significant. First, learning from the system of life on earth, we should actively seek to preserve the diverse traditions of music-making from around the globe; diversity is essential for music as it is for life itself. Second, we should, through education, raise the awareness of the importance of music to humanity and foster appreciation for our deeper commonalities and the level of universality of function that I have discussed here. And third, we should work to ensure that music-making is not restricted to experts or professionals, and instead promote active music-making among all people (but especially youth), so that as many individuals as possible contribute to this human endeavor.

And so, I conclude with Socrates' statement from *Phaedo* (Rouse 1999, 463), "In my past life, the same dream often used to come to me, in different shapes at different times, but saying the same thing, 'Socrates, get to work and compose music!'"

Acknowledgments

I wish to express profound appreciation to two of my colleagues: John Kehlen, whose extraordinary range of reading and knowledge led me to many of the discoveries herein, and to Jim Merod, whose support and adventurous spirit encouraged me to pursue them.

Notes

1.   This music was apparently known and valued by the Egyptians from at least 2300 BCE, as there is a written request from a pharaoh to an Egyptian noble who traveled up the Nile to the rainforest to bring back the "dwarf" musician who "gladdened the heart of the king" (Locke 2009, 135).

2.   The systematic theory of *ragas*, the melodic bases for this music, makes explicit the relationship between the sounds of music and times of day, seasons, and emotional

states, and traditional performances are synchronized with these temporal factors so as to produce the most desirable outcome—the appropriate and harmonious state of mind or emotion—for musicians and audience. This is a clear example of an articulated link between humans, time, and the environment (Shankar 1968, 24).

3. None of this is meant to depreciate the visual arts; the focusing of attention on appearance and creation of virtual space, as Susanne Langer points out, can certainly function to expand the awareness of both artist and observer (Langer 1953, Chapters 4 and 5).

4. Gourlay, as can be seen from his title, insisted on just calling this form of expression "non-music."

5. Stravinsky chiefly credits Pierre Souvtchinsky for his ideas on the subject of time.

6. To mention a few examples: the "forms" of classical Western art music (and the eschewal of such forms by musicians from the same tradition in much of the twentieth century), the interlocking cycles common in sub-Saharan Africa, the coinciding end-accented cycles in Indonesian gamelan music, the large-scale three-part acceleration or building of intensity in music of Japan (*jo-ho-kyu*) and India (*alap-tanam-pallavi* in the Carnatic style), the irregular phrase lengths built into complex multi-part structures in songs common among the Indians of the Americas, and so on.

7. For two very different and useful approaches, see Oliver Sacks' *Musicophilia* and Eric Jensen's *Music with the Brain in Mind*. Sacks, a physician and psychologist, relays a remarkable collection of case studies involving patients he has worked with over the years. Jensen has collected and surveys a wide range of experimental evidence related to the value of music in supporting childhood development and education.

8. The italics here are in the original text.

9. Edelman describes the shortest unitary experience of consciousness as "the remembered present" (Edelman 2006, 15, 38, 93).

10. See Bowman (1998, 19-47) and DeWoskin (1998) for detailed discussion of these issues.

References

Berliner, Paul. 1993. *The Soul of Mbira*. Chicago: University of Chicago Press.

Blacking, John. 1973. *How Musical is Man?* Seattle: University of Washington Press.

Bowman, Wayne. 1998. *Philosophical Perspectives on Music*. New York: Oxford University Press.

Capra, Fritjof. 1997. *The Web of Life*. New York: Random House.

DeWoskin, Kenneth. 1998. Chinese philosophy and aesthetics. In *Garland Encyclopedia of World Music*, ed. Bruno Nettl, Ruth Stone, James Porter and Timothy Rice, 97-101. New York and London: Garland Publishing Inc.

Dissanayake, Ellen. 1995. *Homo Aestheticus: Where Art Comes From and Why*. Seattle: University of Washington Press.

Dissanayake, Ellen. 1999. "Making special": An undescribed human universal and the core of a behavior of art. In *Biopoetics: Evolutionary explorations in the Arts*, ed. Bret Cooke and Frederick Turner, 27-38. Lexington, KY: International Conference on the Unity of the Sciences.

Dunn, David and Lambert, Michael. 1989. Environment, consciousness, and magic: An interview with David Dunn. *Perspectives of New Music*, 27, no. 1:94-105.

Edelman, Gerald. 2006. *Second Nature: Brain Science and Human Knowledge*. New Haven and London: Yale University Press.

Gourlay, Kenneth. 1984. The non-universality of music and the universality of non-music. *The World of Music*. 26, no. 2:25-36.

Handel, Stephen. 1989. *Listening: An Introduction to the Perception of Auditory Events*. Cambridge, MA: The MIT Press.

Harnish, David. 2006. *Bridges to the Ancestors: Music, Myth, and Cultural Politics at an Indonesian Festival*. Honolulu: University of Hawaii Press.

Huron, David. 2007. *Sweet Anticipation: Music and the Psychology of Expectation*. Cambridge, MA: The MIT Press.

Ikeda, Daisaku. 1989. Art and Spirituality in the East and the West. *The Seikyo Times*. 7:53-56.

James, Jamie. 1995. *The Music of the Spheres: Music, Science and the Natural Order of the Universe*. New York: Springer-Verlag.

Jensen, Eric. 2000. *Music with the Brain in Mind*. Thousand Oaks, CA: Corwin Press.

Langer, Susanne. 1953. *Feeling and Form*. New York: Charles Scribner's Sons.

Llinás, Rodolfo. 2001. *I of the Vortex: From Neurons to Self*. Cambridge, MA: The MIT Press.

Locke, David. 2009. In *Worlds of Music: An Introduction to the Music of the World's Peoples*, 5th edition, ed. Jeff Titon, 134-143. Belmont, CA: Schirmer Cengage Learning.

Mâche, François-Bernard. 1992. *Music, Myth and Nature, or The Dolphins of Orion*. Trans. Susan Delaney. Chur, Switzerland and Philadelphia, USA: Harwood Academic Publishers.

Mellen, John. 1773. Religion productive of music. Early American Imprints, Digital Edition, Series I: Evans, 1639-1800. http://infoweb.newsbank.com/.

Mithen, Steven. 2006. *The Singing Neanderthals: The Origins of Music, Language, Mind and Body*. London: Orion Books, Ltd.

Rouse, W.H.D., trans., Eric Warmington and Philip Rouse, eds. 1999. *Great Dialogues of Plato*. New York and London: Penguin Books.

Sacks, Oliver. 2008. *Musicophilia: Tales of Music and the Brain*. New York: Random House.

Sarno, Louis. 1995. *Bayaka: The Extraordinary Music of the Babenzélé Pygmies*. Roslyn, N.Y.: Ellipsis Arts.

Schryer, Claude. 2001. The Sharawadji Effect. In *The Book of Music and Nature: An Anthology of Sounds, Words, and Thoughts*, ed. David Rothenberg and Marta Ulvaeus. Middletown, CT: Wesleyan University Press.

Shankar, Ravi. 1968. *My Music, My Life*. New York: Simon and Schuster.

Stobart, Henry. 2000. Bodies of sound and landscapes of music: A view from the Bolivian Andes. In *Musical Healing in Cultural Contexts*, ed. Penelope Gouk. Aldershot, England and Brookfield, USA: Ashgate.

Stravinsky, Igor. 1942. *Poetics of Music in the Form of Six Lessons*. Cambridge, MA: Harvard University Press, 14th printing, 2000.

Turner, David. 2000. From here into eternity: Power and transcendence in Australian Aboriginal music. In *Indigenous Religious Musics*, ed. Karen Ralls-Macleod and Graham Harvey. Aldershot, England and Burlington, USA: Ashgate.

Universals in Music: Music as a Communicational Space

Soufiane Feki

Introduction

The power of music to establish peace in our societies, to break down divisions in our communities, and to promote the harmony of living together in multiethnic and multifaith societies is, as my co-authors illustrate in various ways, evident in many contexts, both historical and contemporary. Even partisans of war understand this. To begin my account, I would like to recount a story which might seem to be far away from the main topic of this chapter (that is to say, universal elements in music) but which in fact is profoundly illustrative of its main purpose. There was an Algerian city perched at the top of two steep rocks and hidden there, called Constantine. Muslims, Christians, and Jews used to live there together in quiet harmony. In mutual respect of their religions, they would share with each other moments of joy or of sadness, until 1934 when a sad and unexpected incident and a series of misunderstandings and mistakes triggered clashes between Jews and Muslims. Cohabitation and trust took a hard blow (Ageron 1973; Stora 2007).

Raymond Leyris was born on July 27, 1912 in this society of Constantine. He was Jewish, his father was Jewish, but his mother was, as would be said then in Algeria, "European" (Christian). He represented the sometimes harrowing meeting place of the three dimensions representing Algeria: the Jewish, the Christian, and the Arabic (Draï and Etienne 2000, 107). Raymond was a musician of the secular Andalusian musical tradition. His mastery of Andalusian song and the Arabic musical genre "muwashshahāt,"[1] as well as of the *oud* (lute) earned him the honorary title of "Sheikh" and this is why he is known as "Sheikh Raymond."

This extraordinary musician was the symbol of "living together" in the society of Constantine. In his band, musicians from the Muslim and Jewish faiths played music and sang together. Besides the fact that they were all Algerians, they shared the same love for their ancient traditional musical heritage, around which they felt a kind of communion, namely, the Malouf, a musical genre found in the Andalusian classical music tradition of Algeria, Tunisia and Libya. Sheikh Raymond animated celebrations such as weddings or circumcisions of all Algerian families without distinction of ethnicity or religion whatsoever. In a tense geopolitical environment where colonial forces and also discrimination and social tensions prevailed, Sheikh Raymond and his followers were involved in healing and reconciliation among citizens. In this regard Martin Stokes wrote: "Raymond's world was an Edenic musical paradise, reconciling Christians, Jews and Muslims in North Africa. What French colonialism and the current turmoil have divided, the Sheikh's music joins together" (Stokes 1997, 676). This man who became a symbol of love and brotherhood among the different communities has shown that despite religious and racial differences, it is possible to share many things, including love of a specific music, and belong to the same culture and to the same country.

Thanks to him the music of the funduks[2] was fully revealed to the city that had served as its casing. Those who knew him saw in him the living synthesis of the Western world, the culture of which he wanted to be well known and understood, and the orient, made up of its different facets, Jewish and Arab Muslim. When he sang on the radio or the television the streets of the Jewish and Arab city were empty (Draï 1994, 12).

Since those unexpected clashes of August 1934 between the Jewish and Muslim communities who had lived previously in mutual understanding, a degree of fear had permeated people's minds, but social peace was not fully endangered, and for a long time, through the power of his music, his voice and his oud, this musician amalgamated, so to speak, the two communities. This is why Sheikh Raymond was probably the ideal target for those who did not want this peace between Muslims, Jews, and Christians, those who were disturbed by their harmonious coexistence; for in the camp of hatred, all means were acceptable to undermine social peace and to sow division within Algerian society. One of those ways was to silence the music.

On June 22, 1961, while shopping in the market with his daughter, Sheikh Raymond was shot with a bullet in the neck. The assassination was not merely that of a Jew (which, surely, would be a fairly simplistic and reductive interpretation), but that of a whole symbol. Raphaël Draï states:

> Raymond Leyris was killed by a gunshot, probably because he had become the living symbol of a human and cultural conciliation which history did not want (Draï 1994, 9).

Benjamin Stora, historian and specialist of the colonial period in Algeria, establishes a link between the events of August 1934, the demise of Sheikh Raymond, and the beginning of the mass exodus of Algerian Jews to France, which ensued soon after this assassination.

> This fear has been revived June 22, 1961, with the assassination of Raymond. In the Jewish community of Constantine, everyone was shocked. The great Malouf singer [...] known as "Sheikh Raymond Leyris" had been murdered in the market. [...] That was the turning point, the moment when what remained of the Jewish community of Constantine in 1961 chose to go to France (Stora 2007).

The question haunts my mind still: who killed Sheik Raymond, who wanted his death? We have the right to think that his assassination was sponsored by people who were enemies of the civil tranquility that prevailed between the two communities at that time. It seems that these people had realized the apparently magical power of music in reconciling these communities, and so they stopped the music.

There were other similar places, for example in Tunisia, where Jews and Muslims shared the same musical heritage and because of that even shared the joy of celebrating different non-religious festivals respective to the two communities. This is unfortunately unimaginable these days as the rift deepens day by day between the two communities; everything seems to separate them. Music has its role to play in calming these tensions, and it may help people to smooth out racial and religious differences, but it is still necessary for people to have a real will to live together.

Today, in our globalized world, all cultures are opening up to each other, in particular thanks to methods of dissemination that are ever more elaborate and sophisticated. Music benefits from this social and technological evolution and contact between minds can grow, through musical activity, while barriers of all kinds, linguistic, cultural, and religious, can be crossed in many new ways.

My intention here is to bring a musicologist's perspective on the sources of music's potential and even remarkable ability to allow dialogue, certainly between musicians of diverse cultural horizons, but equally and indirectly (through the intermediary of musicians) between different social groups which nothing else seems to unite or bring together *a priori*.

The Interconnections between Musical Cultures

The perception of cultural and religious otherness is no longer as it was at the time of the first European expeditions to distant lands, where the musical practices of the *Other* were called by all sorts of names: "barbaric," "savage," "primitive." Some ethnomusicological references from the early twentieth century show a disparaging, even racist, attitude toward non-Western musical practices; one has only to thumb through Jules Rouanet's article on "Arabian music" in the *Encyclopedia Lavignac* to realize the extent of such prejudgment and disapproval (Rouanet 1922, 2937-2939). However, this was the case with only a very few Western ethnomusicologists or musicians, whose ethnocentric judgments from then on form a part of history and can be relegated thereto.

Today, we are all in search of new sounds, new rhythms and new musical colors. Artistic productions involving music spring up every day inside an extraordinary operation of intermingling and musical-cultural hybridization never seen before. But so that musicology and the anthropology of music acknowledge the thousands of existing non-Western musical practices as having the right to be studied just like their counterparts in the West, it has been necessary to spill a lot of ink.

To explain this mosaic of musical practices we have seen the comparative theory upheld by European musicologists from the beginning of the twentieth century (Von Hornbostel, Sachs, Schaeffner); subsequently, and in reaction to this stance, there was the culturalist doctrine proposed in turn by North American ethnomusicologists and anthropologists, for example Merriam, Blacking, and Nettl. Comparative musicology suffers in two crucial aspects: firstly, from the linguistic, cultural, and historical incompetence of its protagonists in relation to the music they study, and secondly because these protagonists have tried to analyze and explain different types of musical systems through the sieve of Western tonal theory, making these analyses on the basis of only a few records and some not-very-reliable written transcriptions (Picard 2007, 37-38).

Anthropologists of music have rigorously objected to the comparative thesis, notably at the beginning of the second half of the twentieth century, pointing to the necessity of reviewing the sociocultural context that produced the musical practices in order to successfully define them, thus favoring the relativist doctrine. And it is only during the last three or four decades that we have witnessed a somewhat coherent discourse on universals in music, far from the ethnocentric or relativist theories of the beginning of the last century. In what follows, I will offer a summary of the evolution of the regard toward the Other and their music, and also discuss the underlying mechanisms of the communicational space embodied by music.

My thoughts begin with the following questions, also shared by many others: how can I be deeply moved and affected by music that I hear but which comes from a musical system and culture different from mine? Is it a question of a simple infatuation for a musical exoticism, or must it be admitted that despite the extreme variety visible on the surface of musical productions, there are shared universal characteristics emanating from a type of structural precedence? In other words, what is there in common between different musics of all eras and all cultures?

Since the work of the seventeenth-century French composer Jean-Baptiste Lully, we have witnessed many tangible borrowings from non-European traditions in Western art music, for example as in his music for the final ballet of Moliere's *The Bourgeois Gentleman (Le Bourgeois Gentilhomme)*: "Court ballets in France in the baroque and classic periods always highlighted exoticism" (Bartoll 2007, 159). This was also evident in the use of melodic and rhythmic motifs from Ottoman military music called "turquerie" in the works of some composers such as Haydn, Mozart, and many others. Composers of the romantic period, such as Schumann, did not hide their admiration for melodies and rhythms from elsewhere. In view of the mysteries suggested by unknown musical civilizations, it can, however, be argued that the reaction of European musicians has been, for a long time, to "tame" the apparently unconstrained musical sounds and patterns of the world beyond their frontiers by reducing these to a series of aural clichés, themselves translated into musical idioms which are in turn integrated into the syntactic system of tonal music (Pasticci 2007, 186 and *passim*).

With the development of methods of recording sound, and the emergence of comparative musicology, we begin to become aware of the extreme variety of musical practices and languages which pour in from the four corners of the planet. The first reaction of European comparative musicologists was to compare them to Western tonal music. Considering this to be the purest and the most elaborate of all, they adopted the evolutionary theory which led them to consider Western tonal music to be the culmination of an evolution of several stages, whose origins are presumed to be the very first, "simple" musical expressions.

In a logic of cultural domination, tonal music and its panoply of equal tempered scale, harmonic bipolarity, dominant and tonic, quickly invaded the world, as remains evident today. Everywhere—in India, in China, as in the Arab world, in soundtracks of movies, pop songs, military music—music is made uniform under the tonal system. The hegemony of European culture in this domain also relies on a theoretical legitimization that, in an approximate logical analogy, links the natural harmonics of a sound and the notes making up the harmony, hence the claim of conformity in the tonal system with the laws of natural resonance. Some Arab musicologists have even bowed to the assertion that tonality systematizes the laws of nature and that Arabic modal music is on the other hand artificial (Hage 2005). Yet there have been challenges to this belief in the superiority of Western tonality; "the knowledge of ethnic music along with the new music of the twentieth century exploded the framework of tonal music: one realizes that what one had until then taken for universals was nothing more than one system among others" (Molino and Nattiez 2007, 345). The revelation of a musical *elsewhere*, thanks to recording and broadcasting, opened new musical perspectives to Western composers at the beginning of the last century, such as Debussy, Bartók, Stravinsky, and Varese, who wanted to bring an element of universality to their music by letting themselves be inspired and influenced by traditional musics of all kinds. They were able ingeniously to integrate rhythmic or melodic motifs into the ultra-coded, well-marked universe of erudite Western music, thus creating the clash, not of civilizations, but of alien melodies, and timbres, and doing this while respecting all traditions.

In his analysis of the *Requiem* by Florentz, Appolinaire Anakesa makes it clear that "traditional music has allowed alternate solutions to aesthetic problems to the debate posed by the crisis of functional harmony in the Western music of this century [twentieth]" (Anakesa 1998, 282). Debussy himself was said to have found in Javanese music: "all the nuances, even those that one can no longer name, where the keynote and the dominant were nothing more than empty illusions used by naughty little children" (Debussy 1980, 70).

The use of sounds and forms originating from other cultures, par-ticularly by French composers and researchers during the second half of the twentieth century, was a sign of a new compositional approach different from the "sole worship of writing on which an entire musical avant-garde ended up foundering" (Mache 2001, 19). But despite all these enlightening initiatives, musicologists show a rather surprising delay in researching universals or foundations common to all music, a delay also in the formulation of hypotheses in this sphere of enquiry. One must acknowledge that to speak of the universal or universality is often to risk incurring sharp criticism. At a certain point in the history of musicology, musicologists interested in the universal saw their initiative accused of colonialism for, say their detractors, the temptation to impose the European or Western model as universal is always compelling.

Cultural relativism came about in reaction to the evolutionary theories born of the comparative approach mentioned above. Its doctrine is to consider as ethnocentric every enterprise not first founded on the categories of the "native" culture. The position of a large number of ethnomusicologists, especially those swimming in the culturalist current of American anthropology, is the following: each culture has its own music, which cannot be reduced to a comparison with other music, and it should be studied in its uniqueness. Because of this every musical culture is denied the right to influence or to be influenced by another, to mix with another, or to experience hybridization.

However, musical hybridization is undeniable today, and this jeopardizes the thesis of radical relativism. Let us take, for example, the case of some musicians in the Arab world: the works of the Rahbani[3] brothers in Lebanon in which they created an alliance between Lebanese popular arts and symphonic-style orchestration; the case of Omar Kheriat[4] in Egypt where Arabic modality and its sweet melodies mix with techniques of contrapuntal musical notation; or the works of Zian Rahbani[5] which demonstrate a musical osmosis between the Maqam melodic system and the harmonic components of jazz. In Tunisia one can also observe several attempts to make Tunisian music speak in the language of jazz, for example in the music of Fawzi Chekili,[6] and Dhafer Youssef.[7] Here, the case of the Swiss musician Stephan Athanas[8] is enlightening; with the cooperation of the Tunisian musician, Samiha Ben Saïd, he "dared" try the Tunisian *nûba*,[9] and each of these two musicians were able to discover relevance in this collaboration.

I suggest that supporters of the premise that musical cultures are irreconcilable err in their ignorance of what is really happening in a world where each of us can know about—without having to travel—the diverse musical systems of humanity, and can even adapt some of them to be used as we wish in our own compositions. As noted by Molino and Nattiez; "Music in all its forms appears today as a human universal in action" (Molino and Nattiez 2007, 352).

The Question of Universals in Music

In the light of the above discussion, and in the wake of what composers have done and are doing as described, it is high time for musicology to take the full measure of musical transculturality as it has been operating for several decades. Is comparative musicology in the process of rising from its ashes? It is very likely so. But it must learn the lessons from the history of comparative musicology (originating in what we call the "School of Berlin") as well as those of ethnomusicology (from the mid-twentieth century). How? By integrating universal elements into the study of its objective without limiting the comparisons to include only the standards of European systemic norms, and without fearing to go beyond cultural frontiers.

Several works of musicology are already following this view. As an example we can mention the works of Harold Powers[10] on modality and modes—who argues these as a transcultural musical phenomenon which is probably universal. We can also refer to the works of Bernard Lortat-Jacob[11] on improvisation in traditional oral music. The question here is of a universal musical phenomenon shared by all the cultures of the world; its principal mechanisms should be studied without having to be limited to one repertoire or another, for it is always in the invariant that the universal resides, and to achieve understanding of this musical invariant it is necessary greatly to increase the number of examples and above all to vary the sources and origins. Following this same tradition is also the work of Annie Labussiere[12] on traditional songs sung *a capella*, which attempts to find the constants functioning in monodies from cultures which historically have had no contact with each other (for example, within children's songs from Madagascar, China, New Caledonia, and other places).

This non-exhaustive list of works reflects a new orientation in musicology which tries to overcome divisions in opinion on the theories of classical musicology and ethnomusicology, and to deal directly with the musical phenomenon as defined by Jean Molino, which "is sound constructed and organized by a culture" (Molino 1975, 41).

At this stage of my discussion, I would draw attention to the contribution of linguistics, which cannot be ignored in this context, and which counts and studies thousands of languages throughout the world. Researchers in this field are indeed searching to locate the invariants, or those factors that are universal, in the languages studied, so that rules can then be established that are shared by them all. These rules are argued to meet the fundamental and pre-cultural needs of human thought, and it is suggested that they can form a type of universal grammar. On the other hand there are rules specific to each language, which modify this universal grammar on a surface level. In this respect we must learn lessons, once again, from the extraordinary quality of the work done by linguists, where the advanced technical and scientific nature of linguistics has eventually silenced its critics who claimed to represent positivism and who constantly disparaged human and social sciences, particularly during the post-war era.

Just as in the case of ethnologists and sociologists, musicologists have indeed, turned to linguistics and become interested in its methods of analysis. In the case of existing musical practices we can discern that certain intervals such as the octave and the fifth are ubiquitous in practically all musical systems. Is this by chance? This seems improbable; it is far more likely that the simplicity of these ratios makes them more easily perceived by our auditory apparatus. There may be a common bio-physical factor that predisposes us to choose from a limited number of compatible elements within the infinite number of possible sounds and intervals, namely the ability and structures of the human mind which condition our systems of sound perception, whatever the era or the culture from which this system comes (Meyer 1998, 26-28). We may thus hypothesize that there are universal as well as culture-specific operations making up a grammar according to which we analyze musical sequences. Examples of such operations include: the segmentation of musical discourse; the grouping of segments by category; and reduction, among others.

Thanks to these operations of segmentation, it has been possible to infer that in a musical *construction* (the term "construction" preferred here to that of the musical "work") there are "periods," and inside these periods there are themes which in turn contain phrases which are themselves composed of motifs, etc. And it is significant that the difference in length of these motifs or these themes does not vary on a scale from zero to infinity, but remains variable within a relatively limited range of duration. Whether it be a symphony by Mozart or by Bruckner, or a Turkish instrumental piece or even a type of improvisation using the *taqsîm*[13] which occurs in the cultured Arab/Middle-Eastern musical repertoire, one can find themes and motifs in all these forms, as disparate as they may be. Our ability to memorize and to process musical information is certainly conditioned by universal biological and psychological imperatives, in the first place, and at a secondary level, by cultural influences. As Molino and Nattiez again make clear, it is this "common anthropological base that explains the frequency of exchanges between music belonging to different traditions. It very much seems that one has always appreciated forms of art other than one's own" (Molino and Nattiez 2007, 385).

The phenomenon of repetition, which gives rise to other terms such as duplication or redundancy, is equally universal. In all the music of the world, "repetition" is an essential component. "The relationship that duplication has with human psychology reminds us that music is anchored in human origins as well as in the subconscious" (Gorge 2008, 170). Repetition allows the marking of the boundaries of each unit and the defining of its role within the global structure. Efforts to abolish this phenomenon within certain genres, especially in serial music, remain marginal. In music, the experience of repetition is basic, not only in creation and in listening, but also in learning. Through repetition the musician tries to do away with time, which seems irreversible. Through his or her work, he or she "aims to symbolically transform the evanescence of time into fullness and stability" (Mache 2001, 240). It is in this way that the link in identity appears among the repeated fragments.

Physically speaking, no repetition is identical; there is always a shift between the statement and its repetition, more, or less, important. This shift often leads to the variation that occupies an immense space between two limits: absolute innovation and absolute repetition. Variation is another of the categorical universals shared by practically all music on the planet. It intervenes at every level: melodic, rhythmic, harmonic, but also at the level of orchestration and modality. Contrast, repetition and transformation are the three fundamental processes for all formal construction in music.[14]

In systematic terms, the notion of a scale is also equally shared by all. A little of everything is found here, from simple two-degree scales to octave scales, including pentatonic scales which exist in different forms in Africa and Asia. It is these pentatonic scales which allow Alia Sellami,[15] for example, to combine Afro-American gospel and Moroccan Gnawa songs. It is always the same principle: each culture makes a selection from an infinite number of possible sounds, and this results in a scale which is set up as a system managing every act of composition. Next to the question of the formation of the scale, are the problems of organization of the notes delineated by it, which leads us unavoidably to the question of modality and mode.

Therefore, in music one can speak of universals of substance, embodied by the concept of theme or of motif, and of categorical universals such as: the notion of repetition and variation; scale and organization.

It is equally appropriate to talk about the musical instruments, and for over a century, within the discipline of organology there has been an endeavor to examine, compare, and classify different types of instruments in order to reveal human genius in the conceiving of all these instruments. We can perceive here further common denominators in the differences or specificities by classifying instruments according to the procedures of production of sound (among others); for example, flutes, struck instruments, and skin drums are found practically everywhere and in all possible and imaginable forms, in Asia, Africa, and Europe.

There are many more examples, to the point where it is not possible to list them all, which, moreover, is not the goal of this chapter. I conclude my discussion thus:

- Universals exist in practice at the level of all the essential parameters of music: at the categorical, structural, and systemic levels. This does not indicate that we should assume a "perfect" and complete conception of the universal in music; as our colleague Ahmed Aydoun[16] succinctly puts it: "the 'pure' universal does not exist, nor does the 'pure' specific."
- Music is a kind of organization of audible material in time. It is simultaneously unique and plural and it varies according to era, place, language, and culture. From this come the differences and even the oppositions between musical styles and the study and use of symbols that follow from it, peculiar to each people and each civilization. But, as Anakesa states:

the initial organization of this same audible material remains the same: tension-relaxation, ascent-descent, with such values as: melody, polyphony, rhythm (Anakesa 1998, 281).

Epilogue

This being said, music must never claim to be as specific a vehicle of communication as spoken language, which is the only one capable of faithfully transmitting a message, but it can be, as Jean Molino has said, a "process of symbolic exchange" (Molino 1975, 58). As illustrated in several of the accounts accompanying my own, during a concert or a show, music can embody a space of communication where political, religious, ethnic, and communitarian prejudices fall and are stamped out in favor of a dialogue involving the most human of qualities: the capacity to feel emotion.

Nowadays, few people believe at this moment in the possibility of the peaceful coexistence of the Jewish and Arab peoples, and it seems that the chances of reconciliation are dwindling. Yet the Israeli Sephardic Jews from North African countries, just like North Africans from the Maghreb, cannot contain their emotion and sometimes even their tears when listening to Malouf. As we speak, such communion is unthinkable, even utopian, but this underestimates the power of Malouf. In reviving the memory of Sheikh Raymond, we need to hold music's universal elements in mind, as did he in his work, through the practice of music, in building that dialogue so fundamental to relationships of peace.

Notes

1. *Muwashshah,* is an Arabic poetic form, as well as a secular musical genre in the western part of the Arab world using *muwashshah* texts as lyrics. The poetic form is also used in Andalusi *nuba* which similarly originates in Al-Andalus.
2. Funduk is a "place of the mystical, in which "silent dreamers" are to be found spread out along the balcony, on the verge of falling, on the brink of the cliff, in the pockets of the rock, the refuge where they would find each other night and day, with the smell of basil and mint, the taste of mouldy tea, cedar, storks, the chirping of cicadas..." (Stokes 1997, 676).
3. Fairuz, *Jerusalem in my Heart,* Compact Disc, 2005, Production of the Rahbani Brothers.
4. Omar Khariat and Elies Rahbani, *Arabian Moods Instrumental,* CD Album, EMI Arabia, coll. Arabian Masters, 2002.
5. Ziad Rahbani, *Live at Damascus Citadel,* CD, Artemisia Music, 2009.
6. Fawzi Chekili, *Echihem,* CD, Blue Jasmin, 2004.
7. Dhafer Youssef, *Abu Nawas Rhapsody,* CD, Universal Music Division Jazz, 2010.
8. Stephan Athanas, *Jazz Suite in Nine Mouvements-Nuba Hsin,* CD, Musi, Switzerland, 2000.
9. Secular repertoire of vocal and instrumental music that mixes the Andalusian musical heritage with a portion of local Tunisian music.
10. Powers, Harold. 2001. "Mode," *The New Grove Dictionary of Music and Musicians, (éd.).* Stanley Sadie, London, vol. XVI; 775-860.
11. Lortat-Jacob, Bernard (dir.). 1987. *"Improvisation in music of oral tradition" ("Improvisation dans les musiques de traditions orales"),* Paris, Selaf.
12. Labussiere, Annie. 2007. "Gesture and modal structure in *a capella* traditional song," ("Geste et structure modale dans le chant traditionnel à voix nue"), *Music. An encyclopedia for the twenty-first century (Musique. Une encyclopédie pour le 21ème siècle),* Jean-Jacques Nattiez (dir.), vol. 5, *The Unity of Music (L'unité de la musique),* Paris, Actes Sud; 980-1024.
13. An instrumental form that is improvised but very heavily codified and marked thanks to a secular musical tradition. The *taqsîn* is limited to so-called erudite repertoires in Turkey and in the *mashreq* (Arab Middle-East).
14. I can put it thus: the contrast A-B, the repetition A-A, and the transformation A-A' are the three fundamental processes for all formal construction in music.
15. Musicologist, French-Tunisian musician specializing in lyric and scenic art (opera). She is included here for an article that treats the questions of musical correspondence among several styles and body language.
16. Remarks collected during the International Colloquium on Music for the Universality of a United Consciousness (colloque international sur La musique pour l'universalité d'une conscience solidaire) Tunis, February 6-8, 2010. Cf. as here the chapter of Ahmed Aydoun.

References

Anakesa Kululuka, Apollinaire. 1998. "The Space of Traditional Music and its Interaction with Contemporary Creation" ("L'espace des musiques traditionnelles et son interaction avec la création contemporaine"), *Space: Music/Philosophy (L'espace: Musique/philosophie)*, Jean-MarcChouvel and Makis Solomos (dir.), Paris, ed. L'Harmattan, 279-288.

Ageron, Charles-Robert. 1973. "Une émeute anti-juive à Constantine (août 1934)," *Revue de l'Occident musulman et de la Méditerranée*, vol. 13, no. 13-14, pp. 23-40.

Bartoli, Jean-Pierre. 2007. "Orientalism and Exoticism of the Debussy Renaissance" ("Orientalisme et exotisme de la renaissance à Debussy"), *Music: An Encyclopedia for the Twenty-first Century (Musique: Une encyclopédie pour le 21ème siècle)*, Jean-Jacques Nattiez (ed.), vol. 5, *The Unity of Music (L'unité de la musique)*, Paris, ed. Actes Sud; 155-181.

Debussy, Claude. 1980. *Correspondence (Correspondance)*, edited by François Lesure, Paris, ed. Hermann.

Draï, Raphaël. 1994. "Cheikh Raymond Leyris. Music From Eden," *Anthology of Algerian urban music, Sheikh Raymond*, compact disc vol. 2, Al Sur.

Draï Raphaël and Bruno Étienne. 2000. "Le non-voyage d'Enrico Macias en Algérie," *La pensée de midi*, no. 2; 106-111.

Gorge, Emmanuel. 2008. "Music and Otherness" *(La musique et l'altérité), Mirrors of a style (Miroirs d'un style)*, Paris, ed. L'Harmattan.

Hage, Louis. 2005. *Modes of the Syro-Maronite song (Les modes du chant syro-maronite)*, Kaslik, Lebanon, ed. USEK.

Mache, François Bernard 2001. *Music in the singular (Musique au singulier)*, Paris, ed. Odile Jacob.

Meyer, Leonard. 1998. "A universe of universals" ("Un univers d'universaux"), *Philosophy (Philosophie)*, No. 59, Paris; 26-28.

Molino, Jean. 1975. "Musical fact and semiology of music" ("Fait musical et sémiologie de la musique"), *Music in play (Musique en jeu)*, No. 17, Paris, ed. Seuil.

Molino, Jean., and Nattiez, Jean-Jacques. 2007. "Typologies and universals" ("Typologies et universaux"), *Music. An Encyclopedia for the Twenty-first Century (Musique: Une encyclopédie pour le 21ème siècle)*, Jean-Jacques Nattiez (ed.), vol. 5, *The Unity of Music (L'unité de la musique)*, Paris, ed. Actes Sud; 182-203.

Pasticci, Susanna. 2007. "Influences of Non-European Music on the Western Music of the Twentieth Century" ("Influences des musiques non européennes sur la musique occidentale du 20ème siècles"), *Music. An Encyclopedia for the Twenty-first Century (Musique: Une encyclopédie pour le 21ème siècle)*, Jean-Jacques Nattiez (ed.), vol. 5, *The Unity of Music (L'unité de la musique)*, Paris, ed. Actes Sud; 182-203.

Picard, François. 2007. "For a General Musicology of Traditions" ("Pour une musicologiegénérale des traditions"), *Review of Musical Traditions of the Arab and Mediterranean Worlds (Revue des Traditions Musicales des Mondes Arabes et Méditerranéen) (RTMMAM)*, No. 1, Lebanon, Antonine University, ed. UPA, 37-56.

Rouanet, Jules. 1922. "Arabic Music—Arabic Music in the Maghreb" ("La musique Arabe—La musique arabe dans le Maghreb"), Albert Lavignac (ed.), *Encyclopedia of Music and Dictionary of the Conservatory (Encyclopédie de la musique et dictionnaire du conservatoire)*, tome V, Paris, 2813-2942.

Stokes, Martin. 1997. "Voices and Places: History, Repetition and the Musical Imagination," *Journal of the Royal Anthropological Institute*, Vol. 3, No. 4); 673-691.

Stora, Benjamin. 2007. *Representations of the Algerian War in French Cinema*, Conference given on April 8, 2003, Georgetown University, French version published in: *Études Coloniales*, Online Revue, http://etudescoloniales.canalblog.com.

Examples of Tunisian Intermusicality: Particularism and Universalism

Fakher Hakima

"Music seemed to me to be more than an identity, it was a truth! A truth that goes beyond the moment, tradition, customs, forms and convenient arrangements. It is itself an emerging form, escaping from materiality, longing for what Hegel described as being a contemplation sensitive to the existence of the idea."[1]

Introduction

Instances of interaction between different languages and musical styles seem in recent decades to be more and more frequent, and new genres and experiences continue to appear throughout the world. Musical, literary, and artistic fusion in general has experienced a renewal of interest within contemporary societies, and has been gradually increasing. Indeed, perhaps we could argue that the new generation of artists and musicians needs a dose of multiculturalism daily to learn to coexist in a world that, many argue, is transforming into a village. And highlighting this sense of transformation are the many artists who are attempting—through their art—to build bridges between the cultures of the world, with stated intentions of promoting a sense of solidarity and universal responsibility (as indeed documented in other chapters in this volume).

Tunisian artists might be seen as being among the pioneers of the integration of this new universal cultural landscape, seeking to establish a position from which they might play a real role later in an honest representation of Tunisian culture with its diverse characteristics.

The concept of intermusicality was introduced to the field of musicology by Ingrid Monson in 1996.[2] Monson, an ethnomusicologist, was inspired by the literary movement of intertextuality, which was developed in the seventies by the literary critic Julia Kristeva. The latter showed that "all future texts cannot exist without a dialogue with preexisting texts" and she explained that "all text is intertext, because other texts are inserted into a fundamental text with more or less recognizable forms."[3] Applying this definition to music, we get "music on top of music," that is to say, one or more pre-existing musical themes which have been restructured in order to give new meaning and a new direction towards universality in music, this being termed the intermusical trend. Some musicologists relate the notion of intermusicality to the time of the seventeenth century, and consider Bach's *Goldberg Variations* an exemplar, since some influences from contemporary popular music can be found in them. We can also cite the example of the Hungarian composer Béla Bartók, who was inspired by popular Algerian songs to compose his *"Suite for Piano Opus 14,"* as well as his *"Concerto #1 for Piano and Orchestra."* In addition, we can detect some Chinese melodies in the compositions of Puccini, especially in the opera *"Turandot,"* with a further example in the work of Tomás Marco, who in 1942 composed *Oculto Carmen* with melodic, orchestral, and interpretative inspiration from Isaac Albéniz's *Granada.*

I would also offer the evolution of jazz music as an example that illustrates this trend of intermusicality, using existing musical elements to create new styles of interpretation and improvisation. How could we speak of the era of *bebop* if there had not been any intermusicality between *classic blues, ragtime, and Dixieland*? Likewise for the *freefunk* style—which surely owes its form to intermusicality between the styles of *free jazz, soul, funk,* and *hip-hop.*

In the case of Tunisian music, we may speak not only of a multitude of influences from African music, Berber music, Turkish music, and Andalusian music, but also of the influence from music originating beyond the country. This influence has become increasingly noticeable in the Tunisian musical landscape, and at the end of the twentieth and beginning of the twenty-first centuries, the new tendency of *intermusicality* has given rise to new musical creations, and opened new horizons for composition, imagination, and creativity among Tunisian composers. The past decade has seen an *"explosion"* of new musical experiments. These days, the Tunisian "scene" includes music called *Malouf-funk,* universal Tunisian music, Tunisian "ethnojazz," music notated and arranged for Big Bands of Tunisian music, and others; in short, there are innumerable attempts at composition, arrangement, and interpretation which may be classified as experiments in intermusicality.

The emergence of this tendency prompts us to ask numerous questions essentially concerning particularism and universalism in Tunisian musical practice. The question of particularism and universalism is complex, especially when it relates to culture. On this topic Jacques Demorgon explains that: *"too much openness, and it becomes submersion. But no openness is fossilization. Humans must also renew themselves because their environments change. These two vital necessities (closure and openness) cannot disappear."*[2] The study of intermusicality requires an analysis of the combination of original elements constituting the distinctive features of the local musical identity with the invented and novel elements that make up universalism. In other words, each example of intermusicality is inevitably a musical synthesis between elements of a specific identity, and universal elements.

A number of questions arise, among these questions the following:

- How might we conceive intermusicality as proof of the progress of Tunisian music and a reservoir of evolution and advancement?
- Can one adopt universalism with open arms while at the same time keeping one's feet firmly anchored in tradition?
- Can one describe the examples of intermusicality in Tunisia as inspired genius or as a way of thinking that inspires?
- After analyzing some instances of intermusicality, can we demonstrate a logic of intermusicality, and outline a vision of local identity and of universalism?
- In other words, has the new generation of Tunisian composers and performers succeeded at safeguarding their identity, while at the same time taking on a certain amount of creative latitude?

This chapter is, therefore, a conceptual and analytical approach to the tendency called "intermusicality" of Tunisian music. It is structured in two major parts, the first devoted to a brief analysis of the Tunisian sociocultural setting (cultural heritage, political choices, technological resources, system of education). The second part examines several examples of so-called intermusicality; the goal here is to throw light on the rationale of musical universalism, and to describe approaches to intermusicality, and finally to explain the musical reasoning peculiar to this style of creation.

The Sociocultural Approach to Intermusicality in Tunisia

The use of the terms "world music," "music of mixed race," "music of the world," "universal music," is becoming more and more common. To find the "true" sense of these terms, it is necessary to acknowledge that there are no human cultures which have not been intermingled, and that, consequently, all music has always been a result of such cultural intermingling. Thus, musical "universalism" in its most pure and simple form represents absolutely nothing new except for designations and classifications.

From a sociocultural point of view, music is created and developed from the internal dynamics of a society. This characterizes all cultural practices in every human society, and is brought about on the one hand by its social organization, and on the other, by aesthetic concerns which flourish in this system by integrating stimulating forces borrowed from the outside world. As a result, every example of intermusicality must be presented in the light of two aspects: an aspect inspired by preexisting music, and an aspect related to the creativity and influence of music from outside the culture.

It is from this thesis that every example of intermusicality is considered to be a link, a re-permeation, and a re-equilibration, harmoniously arising from what is already present, and from different cultural behaviors emanating from given sociocultural settings and a well-defined musical landscape.

In the Tunisian context, one can readily see that this tendency is favored by several factors, including:

- Tunisia's remarkably diverse cultural heritage.
- What is at risk politically regarding culture and music.
- The role of institutions of musical education in intermusicality.
- New technologies in music that are available to every musician, both professional and amateur.
- The revolution in the field of telecommunications, with broadcasting by satellite and on the Internet.

I take each of these in turn.

A Country with an Age-Old Cultural Heritage

- Tunisia has always been a land of intertwined civilizations and cultures, its history, thousands of years old, showing many ethnic groups, belief systems, languages, and cultures following one another. Its unique geographic location has made Tunisia a part of Africa, and at the same time, a country anchored in the Mediterranean—with all the cultural diversity this brings. A part of the Arab-Muslim world for more than fourteen centuries, it is nevertheless a modern society, and open toward the West and the rest of the world.

Musicological research confirms the multiple influences upon Tunisian music, evident enough in its diverse musical styles (traditional, Sufi, military, ceremonial, and rural and urban pop). These include:

- The influence of African music, clearly present in the repertoires of both traditional Malouf music and popular music.
- The influence of Berber music, observed in the musical traditions of some regions.
- The influence of Ottoman and Turkish music, always present in our musical traditions.
- The influence of Andalusian music, characterizing our repertoire of North African Malouf.
- The influence of Western music, appearing in the use and adoption of certain elements that make up the Western musical language (score, vertical musical notation, Western musical instruments, methods of distribution).

The Political High Stakes of Culture and Music

Throughout the last decade, the Tunisian government has placed culture among its highest priorities. This strategy is plainly clear in the statements of President Ben Ali.

> We have always considered culture as supporting change and development, the way toward evolution and progress, the means of expressing the conscience of the people, translating their uniqueness, and making their creative genius known. Due to this fact, we have given special interest to this area, and have made it a strategic area in our policies.[4]

It is clear that political policies consider culture to be a factor in development. This is based on the national identity taking root and at the same time upon active support of the process of developing a universal culture. Thus, many political decisions have been undertaken to support artists and musicians. Among those decisions we note:

- The establishment of the Superior Council of Culture 2007[5]
- The development of legislation to modernize laws related to the protection of the rights of the composer
- Paid leave for artistic creative work
- The edification of the city of culture project.[6]

Institutions of Music Education Promoting Intermusicality

The last decade has seen an expansion of the number of institutions of musical education, with, currently, six university-level institutions[7] in Tunisia offering an education in music and musicology. The creation of these institutions has led to a clear evolution of musical practices (creation, arrangement, composition, instrumental and vocal interpretation, etc.) and research in musicology, with many graduates from these institutions contributing in a real way to the musical scene as well as to scientific activity. The institutions certify approximately 500 students each year. The education offered within these institutions is not only diversified and multidisciplinary, but is also carried out by teachers of diverse backgrounds and different specialties. The Music Institute of Higher Education of Sousse (L'institut Supérieur de Musique de Sousse), as an example, relies on 30 foreign teachers out of a staff totaling 100 teachers. The foreign teachers, of Romanian, Bulgarian, Russian, Polish, Korean, Italian, Iraqi, and other backgrounds, are intermediaries of their cultures. They involuntarily exert an influence on their students and, as it were, bring about the first attempts of intermusicality.

Thus, I would argue here that pedagogical action leads to a type of intercultural intermusicality. In other words, it is an interaction between two musical identities, a foreign professional teacher[3] and a local student/ future promoter. Although this may occur "unconsciously," this context of transmission is an important element which encourages intermusicality and which influences the local musical identity, contributing indirectly to both the growth and diversification of examples of intermusicality.

The many and increasing numbers of graduates in music and musicology are trainers, practitioners, and researchers, with a growing effect upon the field of music in Tunisia. It seems clear that the multicultural aspect already evident in schools of music offers a fertile ground for experiments in intermusicality, and serves as an advocate of the tendency called universal Tunisian music.[8]

New Technologies in Music and New Methods of Telecommunication

New technologies in music, broadcasting, and communication have been an important factor in accelerating intermusicality and emphasizing its impact on new Arabic musical productions of the last decade. The current generation of artists and musicians has these same tools of creation at their disposal everywhere in the world, with the phenomenon of sampling allowing composition, arrangement, and even performance in home studios. Indirectly, these technological inventions have allowed a global context for these new musical productions.

It is important to emphasize that previously—for example just 20 years ago—in order to have intermusicality, it was necessary to have contact. This contact was demonstrated by the sale of records, by the direct relationship between performers and musicians, by visits to concerts, etc. This contact is now immediately possible with composers and musicians able to access the entire collection of musical output in the world at any time by a simple "click." Furthermore, one can compose, be influenced by, and affect music coming from quite distant horizons without the human bearers of this music ever meeting. The technologies of distribution and communication (satellite and Internet) offer a reservoir of music of every genre and style existing on the planet, generating new fields of knowledge and building a shared cognitive process. In short, a new musical culture is being established.

The use of these new technologies in the areas of music and telecom-munications requires a redefinition of culture and of musical identity. Indeed, a new dimension of culture and of musical taste is emerging. It combines the traditional concept of a musical identity as linked to one sociocultural setting, with that of plural musical identities linked to a global sociocultural setting.

Our inventory of new musical production confirms:

- An important interaction between the musical languages of the world.
- Some resemblance between the musical systems.
- A wide-spread instrumentarium.[9]

To summarize this brief sociocultural approach, we can say that the interaction between these factors (geographical, political, sociocultural, technological, and communicational) has given rise to many examples of fusion between musical styles. In the Tunisian context, Tunisian music can be placed at the center of an interaction with a number of musical styles and languages from the outside. Taking stock of these examples shows us that each one is based on the argument of intermusicality, and on a vision of universal music. Thus, we now turn to a brief exploration of the concept of intermusicality.

Reasonings and Processes of Intermusicality

In this analysis I will try to clarify the identifying elements of some examples of so-called intermusicality and will attempt to unveil the techniques of mixing and exchanging with other musical languages. This will then lead to a concluding focus on an explication deriving from the tenets of intermusicality, which may elucidate each of these examples of so-called universal music.

From viewing the repertoire, and an initial outline of some examples, I have located three levels of intermusicality: that is, three views of local identity and of its advancement toward a universal dimension. An ex-ample is offered to illustrate each view, each of the three examples being recurrences of pre-existing themes. I hope to focus my analysis on the mixing between the local culture and the universal dimension, and at the same time to avoid any possible confusion with those new compositions known as "standard." These are, of course, notional analytical categories; practice and reality are generally much more complex.

The First Aspect: Combination of Themes and of Instruments

This approach to intermusicality depends in essence on the combination of instruments of diverse origins and therefore, gives a view of universal music based on the use of instruments. We know very well that for each language and musical genre, there are appropriate instruments that faithfully interpret its musical characteristics. Some Tunisian artists have made use of this classification to give a universal dimension to their pieces; according to them, the act of combining instruments from different cultures can qualify their music as universal. These kinds of pieces are in constant evolution. For example, we have seen combinations of a saxophone with an *oud*, a clarinet with a *ney* (Arab flute), a *qanoun* (zither) with an accordion, a guitar with a *doudouk*, a piano with an Indian zither, in short, instruments of classical and popular Arab-Tunisian music associated with instruments coming from the entire world. Here, the concept of intermusicality is fundamentally based on the sound of the instrument and on its interpretive uniqueness for contributing to different musical languages.

It should be noted that this type of piece can sometimes call on prototypical instruments or instruments which have been modified to carry out the interaction between two musical languages. We can name as examples the "guitar-oud" of Nabil Khmir, the "Arab trumpet" of Nassim Malouf, the quarter tone Egyptian accordion, the Turkish clarinet, and the modified saxophone.[10] This is an argument of intermusicality based on the association:

- Of elements of local identity: authentic instruments representing the local culture (the instrument *oud* and the *maqam* style of improvisation).
- Of elements making reference to the outside world: foreign instruments in the local culture, themes and improvisations interpreted by these instruments (the electric guitar and the modal style of improvisation).

It is an encounter between two or several musical languages where heterogeneous elements form a whole but remain clearly juxtaposed.

The Second Aspect: The Fusion and Orchestral Arrangements of Songs

Intermusicality at this level is essentially based on the choice of the repertoire and on the orchestral arrangement. On the one hand, there is a local repertoire representing identity and authenticity, and on the other hand an orchestral arrangement with a vertical musical notation symbolic of "universal" music.

This example of intermusicality is based on a bi-dimensional reasoning, where an "authentic" vocal interpretation of a repertoire representative of the identity, is "seasoned" with the sounds of instruments of the symphonic orchestra and of the jazz band, and sometimes "spiced up" by local rhythms. This view of intermusicality resides in this balance between Tunisian identity (choice of songs and themes with an exceptional level of interpretation) and of elements from symphonic music (vertical musical notation).

Intermusicality here is thus defined by:

- The choice of songs and of themes (popular urban, classic traditional) representative of the local identity.
- The style of vocal interpretation, representative of the local identity.
- Retaining a rhythmic section from local music.
- The use of authentic instruments (oud, ney, and *qanûn*).
- The introduction of elements referring to the universal, such as large symphony orchestras and vertical musical notation.

In other words, it is a universal presentation (orchestration) of Tunisian identity embodied by the choice of repertoire and by the style of vocal interpretation.

This universalism can be argued as a result of media coverage of symphonic music and the impact of this musical genre on the world; it is a universalism based on a prejudgment of the superiority of Western classical music and on its complex aspects of harmony and counterpoint.

Intermusicality is characterized by a larger interweaving of the elements which enter into the mix, but where the elements are still discernable.

There are numerous examples, including that of the Tunisian singer Saliha's arrangements of traditional Tunisian songs performed by the Orchestra of the Mediterranean under the direction of the musician Kamel Ferjani.

The Third Aspect: Synthesis and Interaction between Performers of Diverse Backgrounds

This version of intermusicality is based on the meeting of individuals of diverse cultural origins around the same musical theme in order to start a discourse of universal music. The fulfillment of this type of experimentation must be undertaken in specific social conditions, under the impetus and creative will of innovative individuals and artists. This view of musical universalism puts the instrument and the instrumentalist at the center of an interaction between several cultures. In this type of work, instrumentalists with their instruments are representatives of their culture. It is an intermusicality that puts into play the cultural "background" of the instrumentalist and the potential sounds of his or her instrument. In other words, the instrument is transformed into a tool of language and the instrumentalist might play the role of a poet-artist-translator. This is an intermusicality based on the intertextuality of the musical discourse. In this way, artists of diverse cultural backgrounds meet around the same text. In this style, the musical theme representing the identity is transformed into an inter-theme, a new original form.

It is important to add that in order for this type of work to succeed, it is necessary to have at least a minimal knowledge of the music of the Other, and also a predisposition to interaction. Indeed, at this level of musical interaction the identity of each instrumentalist is transformed into a subject of interchange. From then on, each musician must make a great effort to move towards the others; if not that musician will risk remaining cloistered in his or her local musical universe even while being on the universal scene. It is only in these conditions that the musical dialogue can occur, and perhaps a new language.

With this form of intermusicality, the local identity is represented by the recurrence of original elements, the themes and the use of instruments of local music, and the elements of musical universalism by the interaction between musicians of diverse cultural backgrounds.

At this level of intermusicality, I would suggest that the original elements have completely blended in and are no longer identifiable. It is from this point that the overall interpretation acquires a universal aspect. The examples of Tunisian works that can illustrate this level of intermusicality are exceptional. We can name the musical project entitled the "Silence of Passions," under the design, production, and art direction of the musician Mohamed Zinelabidine. This project was carried out on the occasion of the first session of the Ben Ali Chair for the Dialogue of Civilizations and Religions. Twenty-one musicians from 14 continents convened on themes of Tunisian music and on Mohamed Zinelabidine's compositions. The "global" performance of these songs and compositions puts together two principal elements:

- A musical theme representative of the local identity.
- Improvisations of varying styles (from diverse cultures) on this theme.

These elements gave a universal dimension to the work and permitted artists of different cultural backgrounds to cooperate in working on a single theme. In other words, it was a musical dialogue between diverse cultures on a theme of Tunisian music.

Conclusion

Tunisia's music is clearly furnished with examples of intermusicality. This artistic landscape, richly diversified, is aided by a quite specific sociocultural setting, by a special educational system, and by favorable political policies.

Examples of intermusicality are based on the combination of instruments of diverse cultures, on the orchestral arrangement, or on the cultural membership of performers.

Each example of intermusicality rests on a vision of local identity and renovation. This vision is generally thought of as being in two main parts: preexisting music and music outside the local area. It is in this way that ancient elements acquire a new universal dimension. This latter is conditioned by a good mastery of characteristics and specificities of one's own music. To this, we can add respect for the aesthetics and the history of the borrowed material.

Furthermore, we must remember that the three levels of intermusicality that we have outlined are analytical categories. They do not in any way represent a classification by order of merit. Practice and reality always remain much more complex. However, each example of intermusicality outlines an approach and justifies a logic and vision in order to explore, attain and even create universal values in music, which might in the end help us to reframe cultural, religious, national, regional, and other *differences*, and allow us to conceive of the borders now tending to divide us, and which are at the origin of conflicts between people, as nothing but symbols.

Notes

1. Zinelabedine, Mohamed. 2007. "L'Etre musicien: identité, textualité et contextualité," in *Le Dictionnaire Critique des Identités Culturelles et des Stratégies de Développement en Tunisie*, Laboratoire de Recherche en Culture, Nouvelles Technologie et Développement, Ministère de l'Enseignement Supérieur, April 2007.
2. Assistant Professor at the Department of Music, University of Chicago.
3. Margarita Celma, Intermusicalité, Rencontre entre Sens Public et le peintre Braun-Vega, 25 January 2007.
4. Official Website of the Electoral Campaign of President Zine el Abidine Ben Ali. Accessed: August 12, 2010 from www.benali.tn/dmdocuments/prf_electoral/programme-electoral-fr.pdf 93/98.
5. "This council is called to be a new space of dialogue between the Administration, intellectuals, representatives of political parties and organizations of civil society, concerning everything related to our cultural approach."
6. An avant-garde project in the Arab world. Its objectives are: To establish as complete as possible a platform to guarantee training in every cultural domain, to develop artistic and intellectual production, to promote the Tunisian culture in its diverse aspects, to facilitate its diffusion as much within the country as outside it.
7. Tunis 1981; Sfax et Sousse 1999; el-Kef 2005; Gafsa 2005; Gabes 2006.
8. Already as part of end of year projects at the ISM of Sousse (L'institut Supérieur de Musique-Music Institute of Higher Education), several endeavors in composition have been performed. These projects draw from two musical styles: a local style, and a second, from outside; we cite the example of Tunisian jazz compositions, a sonata for piano using the taba' (method) of "mhayer Sikah popular music, the SAXOFAN spectacle, (Big Band which performs excerpts of the repertoire of Tunisian and Arabic music), etc.
9. Collection of instruments.
10. We have put together an Arab saxophone project with keys of ¾ of tone with the help of the Selmer firm.

References

Celma, Margarita. 2007. Intermusicalité, Rencontre entre Sens Public et le peintre Braun-Vega, Espagne, July 2006. Translated by Chantal Gac-Artigas. Accessed: August 12, 2010 from http://www.sens-public.org/spip.php?article374.

Demorgon, Jacques. 2002. *L'histoire interculturelle des sociétés*, Paris, éd. Anthropos, coll. Exploration interculturelle et science sociale, 2002, p. 35.

Fleury, Jean. 2002. La culture, Thèmes et débats, Bréal, September 2002.

Official Website of the Electoral Campaign of President Zine el Abidine Ben Ali. Accessed: August 12, 2010 from www.benali.tn/dmdocuments/prg_electoral/programme-electoral-fr.pdf 93/98.

Zinelabedine, Mohamed. 2007. "L'Etre musicien: identité, textualité et contextualité," in *le Dictionnaire Critique des Identités Culturelles et des Stratégies de Développement en Tunisie*, Laboratoire de Recherche en Culture, Nouvelles Technologie et Développement, Ministère de l'Enseignement Supérieur, April 2007.

Compositional Process and Intercultural Dialogue: The Role of Music in a Collective Harmonious Consciousness

Fériel Bouhadiba

Music carries the seed of diversity within it; consequently, any mention of or argument for diversity in relation to music would come under the heading of pleonasm, that is, within the realm of the self-evident. Laden with diversity as much in its deep structures[1] as in those which are manifest,[2] music is thus a profound source of dialogue and exchange. If it is needless to prove the evident importance of the role of its distinctiveness and unique quality in the process of musical creation, it is nevertheless increasingly necessary today to emphasize the capacity of music to articulate identity within the two poles, those of community as micro-society, and of humanity as macro-society, in an expression of responsibility toward present and future generations and the seeking of a common future for humanity. If diversity is at the heart of the musical, the strengthening of constructive sentiments of solidarity would seem to be a major validation of its successful outcome. Evoking the concept of solidarity also underlines the essential role of dialogue. Three notions will therefore be at the center of the reflections in this chapter: diversity and at the same time, specificity, dialogue, and solidarity.

Humans are social beings, with both linguistic and musical predispositions evident from birth; we are biologically programmed on the one hand to be open toward the rest of humanity, and on the other hand to develop a feeling of belonging on the micro-social level. The capacity for musical perception is a surprising indication of this, for it indicates humans as beings with cultural identities and, simultaneously, beings open to cultural diversity.

As we know, the process of adaptation plays an important role in the development of the cultural markers of human beings; aesthetic markers are an integral part of these, with aesthetic criteria being closely related to the individual's cultural environment. Aesthetics, as such, is not just a question of art, but is related to all human behavior and it is in this sense that I refer to the existence of what I have named an "aesthetic of human behavior," wherein the richness of its variants and characteristics may be argued to constitute a "cultural aesthetic of human behavior." For everything in human behavior can be related to aesthetics: our body language, our way of speaking with accents and intonations peculiar to each culture and each region of the world, our culinary tastes, the artistic movements found in each culture. Thus are displays of behavior, both in daily life and in artistic creation, strongly influenced by the cultural and natural milieu of the individual. Thus, rural farmers often have a different way of speaking from city people, Mediterranean people have a different body language from those from other continents, those residing in the South of France can be distinguished by a characteristic "sing-song" accent; and what is today called the Orientalist school of painting would not have existed without the cultural and natural milieu of the Eastern countries that inspired it.

Musically, this is particularly felt in the perceptive reaction, which appears within the connection between aesthetic and systemic elements of music. There is, in effect, a profound relationship of determination between aesthetic judgment and the musical system related to this, with the concomitant correlation between the systemic and the aesthetic as fundamental elements of musical language. As the individual is progressively immersed in her/his culture, adaptation proceeds in terms of the recognition of *aesthetic deviations* in the context of a given musical system. It will thus be more difficult for an uninitiated person who is discovering a musical genre for the first time to distinguish mistakes made in a performance. However, it has been shown that a newborn baby's musical perception appears to allow him or her to distinguish characteristics of foreign music more readily than in the case of adults. A conclusive experiment carried out in 1990 by Michael Lynch and his team of researchers showed that six-month-old babies were able to detect wrong notes in a native system and in a foreign system far more often than were adults. The results of the experiment suggested an equipotentiality in the abilities of musical perception of the newborn for musical scales of different cultures.[3] We also see here an extraordinary lesson of openness.

Nonetheless, the fact remains that the development of what we would call cultural feelings in terms of the musical begins very early, even before birth. Numerous experiments have shown that the fetus can recognize melodies listened to by mothers during the last three months of pregnancy and will be calmed when listening to that music, while a selective preference has been clearly shown by three-day-old babies for nursery rhymes sung by their mothers during the prenatal period (Satt 1984).[4] Thus the influence of the outside environment as a vehicle of cultural transmission is already implicated in the sense of cultural belonging; a further lesson instructing us (as it is sometimes unfortunately necessary to remind ourselves) that openness does not preclude specificity, and vice versa. These discoveries from the field of human musical perception concerning the equipotentiality of the discrimination of melodic changes and the impact of musical immersion from the fetal period, support the contention that music participates in reinforcing on the one hand a universal conscience of the importance of cultural diversity and thus cultural specificity, and on the other hand, the human's biological predisposition to dialogue. Musical perception expresses the innate human capacity for understanding the culture as a whole and simultaneously reveals a preferential feeling for elements related to fetal experience, and to the subsequently cultural environment, indicating an innate predisposition to *cultural specialization*. It is this double structure that I suggest makes humans creatures of dialogue. Openness and cultural identity are at the heart of cultural dialogue; one cannot converse without being open to others, but neither can one converse without the differences in identity of each social community that cause diversity and thus dialogue, exchange, and contributions to and with one another.

Musical dialogue is certainly a constructive value, permitting knowledge of the other through its intangible culture, and participates in creating new ways of musical expression. However, at this point, it is necessary to define what is meant by "dialogue."

Every dialectic implies an encounter, in the sense of a different entity carrying its own characteristics; by extension, every dialogue necessarily implies diversity as a principal rule of its existence. In the area of music, this principle of existence, which is diversity today, finds itself facing a risk of diminishment due to the spread of what I will designate as a new "aesthetic of standardization of the compositional process." Particularly in the field of modal music, the use of compositional procedures specific to Western music, often inadequate to those relevant to modal musical development, leads to a loss of musical material, and a resulting impoverishment of the richness of the elements of a modally-based music. Musical diversity is thus restricted by the widespread use of foreign procedures, both in compositional terms and in terms of musical interpretation.

This can be seen in the use of the harmonic system to create modal works particular to a monophonic system, without conserving modal characteristics or, especially, melodic coherence. The expression of a given musical language is also closely related to the possibilities offered by the instrumental palette used, the type of instrument used (chordophone, aerophone, etc.) in part determining the opportunities for expression. Limiting the instrumental range leads to less variety in the types of sounds possible and thus fewer ways to express modal musical language. This is seen particularly in the restriction of Oriental modes to only those modes compatible with Western musical instruments, especially in the case of keyboard instruments incorporated without consideration of the opportunities they offer to the expression of modal music. Furthermore, the use of the synthesizer in interpretation and of Virtual Studio Technology (VST) instruments in composition, replacing a number of instruments, especially string instruments, also considerably reduces opportunities for interpretation while distorting the sound (in different ways, depending on the quality) and limits the opportunities for microtonal variations offered by variable pitching. In the same way, the use of drum machines in a musical system of a rich rhythmic complexity tends to diminish the nuancing of rhythmic interpretation.

While some works of music using "exosemic" (originating from an external or foreign source) compositional processes and phrases have been able to preserve coherence with the modal system, there are numerous contemporary works in which we witness the emergence of hybrid musical entities marked by an aesthetic blurriness arising from a lack of cohesiveness. Therefore, from all the inadequacies evident in the tension between those practices which are "exosemic" and those which are "endosemic" (arising from within the culture), and the almost systematic use of the former in current compositional practice (notably in what is labeled "music for young people"), a strange impression sets in of an uncomfortable resemblance between many compositions. The massive distribution of this type of music brings what might be termed as "a new aesthetic of the similar and of the prefabricated."

The need for innovation is not the cause of this; instead, it is the failure of modal awareness, the selective borrowing, and the standardized creative process. In fact, as far as music is concerned, we are witnessing what I would call an "industrialization of the creative act."

This takes me to the connections between the notions of identity and specificity, and of the former as protecting the latter, specificity itself being a guarantor of diversity and therefore of dialogue.

What is identity if not the stratification of a whole unit of acquired knowledge and of fruitful dialogue across the history of a population. Together, these form tradition—a body of customs, learning, and know-how. We have a duty to respect it, on the one hand making sure of its survival and durability, and on the other hand continuing the search for knowledge in an ongoing spirit of discovery and openness. This process, multiplied on a scale of the entire group of identities across the peoples of the world, makes up what I designate as "the cultural structure of humanity." However, the emergence of the single modal system, a product of globalization and mimicry resulting in a reduction in the amount of cultural diversity, its canonization by the mass media, and the replacing of innovation with the denaturing of tangible and intangible cultural heritage, puts this structure at risk by its promise to transform it into a great boulevard of uniformity.

Contrary to some accepted ideas, the preservation of one's legacy of acquired knowledge is in no way contradictory to innovation, for it is necessary to know one's past in order to build one's future in an enlightened way. To forget or distort one's heritage, to confuse the destruction of one's legacy of knowledge with innovation, would mean starting again at zero every time in terms of building a civilization, and thus treading water. We would then be far from the fundamental meaning of the notion of progress. This is valid for music but also for all forms of artistic expression, and more globally, cultural expression.

It is therefore essential to emphasize the difference between innovation and distortion. To innovate is to create new forms and ways of expression, and this is not in any way to consider that one can make one's musical legacy "better" or "more aesthetically correct" by dressing it in a garment which doesn't suit. We can converse with our musical legacy, and even with History with a capital H, by bringing in new compositions and thus adding, with each one, its stone to the cultural structure of humanity, rather than trying to repaint a stone in a different color.

It is important, moreover, in terms of dialogue, to take an interest in the cultural complimentarity between artistic expressions. Beyond the special association that music maintains with poetry, we can find in its connections with architecture, painting, and other arts, as many channels of dialogue enriching the imagination and allowing the emergence of new forms of expression.

In terms of specificity, innovation, and creativity, referring to the "Dasein," -the "being there" and the "being in the world" of Heidegger[3], to Ricoeur's[4] the "having been," and considering Bergson's[5] idea placing duration in its relationship to memory and to the continuity of before and after, I suggest that by maintaining extant characteristics *and* by innovation and creativity, the "being there" integrates the "having been" into a perspective which is fundamentally projectionist.

Identity and cultural contemporaneity thus refer to the positioning of a synchronic time (what is under study at this point in time) in the diachrony (the development over time) of a historical period where collective and individual memory participate in the construction of the civilizational framework of nations and societies. Memory, an awareness of the past, contributes to the awareness of a vision of the future. For if, as Bergson explains, "all awareness is an anticipation of the future,"[6] the cultural act is fundamentally, and at the same time, synthesized of the temporal tridimensionality and a projection into a time yet to come, perhaps, even, a *participation* in a time yet to come. For if humans are creatures of temporal tridimensionality, feeding on the past, living in the present, and projecting themselves into the future and into becoming as a *cultural footprint*, they thus position themselves as stakeholders in a civilizational project. And yet, any projection of the self as part of a civilizational project implies an ethical dimension and a stance of solidarity.

While music is an expression of the self, it is also in some of its manifestations the expression of experience of social life; and using culture and specifically music, people have struggled for a better future. The hardships in the lives of some peoples and social groups have in many cases been expressed through their musical creativity, especially in the many social protests that have been made through music. So it is with the birth of the blues, of free jazz, of Rap... born from a social group's need to express the problems of daily life and to cause society as a whole to become aware of these problems. Experiencing one's humanness, being in the world—is to be inclined to feel the social experience of life, to be a person of empathy and therefore a person of solidarity.

Today, with our awareness of the force of communication presiding over the musical act, it is time to struggle together when confronted by the challenges facing humanity. Despite differences in politics and ethnicities, it is crucial to realize that solidarity is no longer just a noble feeling and a noble behavior but a necessity for survival, particularly in regard to the ecological situation. While humankind continues its killing of one another, the dangers—of global warming, of water shortages—advance with a sure step. Faced with wars, poverty, the environmental challenges, and scourges that touch the earth and humanity, we owe it to ourselves to be, as composers, conscious of the rallying role of music on the right path to tolerance and solidarity, and to integrate this dimension in our creative musical lives.

In conclusion, strong in our diversity, working to build a world of dialogue and tolerance with music, among other forms of expression, we may place the creative, "poietic" act at the heart of a united, constructive consciousness. Much mention has been made, notably by international organizations, of the importance of diversity, of the knowledge of one's heritage, and of encouraging creativity. To that effect, I offer the following examples of publications from UNESCO:

- Convention on the Protection and Promotion of the Diversity of Cultural Expressions (October 20, 2005).
- Convention for the Safeguarding of the Intangible Cultural Heritage (October 17, 2003).
- Unesco Declaration concerning the Intentional Destruction of Cultural Heritage (October 17, 2003).
- Unesco Universal Declaration on Cultural Diversity (November 2, 2001).
- Declaration on the Responsibilities of the Present Generations towards Future Generations (November 12, 1997).
- Recommendation on the Safeguarding of Traditional Culture and Folklore (November 15, 1989).

These initiatives are necessary but remain insufficient as long as they do not pass beyond the stage of individual and social behavior into the framework of a unified consciousness for living in harmony.

Notes

1. Here, I use the terminology used by Greimas in his semiotic model. See Greimas (Algirdas Julien), *Du sens*, Paris, le Seuil, 1970.
2. Ibid.
3. Lynch, Michael P., Eilers, Rebecca E., Oller, D. Kimbrough, Urbano, Richard C., *Innateness, Experience and Music Perception,* Psychological Science, American Psychological Society, Volume I, No. 4, 1990.
4. Cited in Lecanuet, Jean-Pierre, *The Prenatal Auditive Experience (L'expérience auditive prénatale)* in Deliege, Irène, Sloboda, John A. (Dir.), Birth and Development of the Musical Sense (Naissance et développement du sens musical), PUF, Paris, 1995.

5.   Bergson, Henri, *L'énergie spirituelle: essais et conférences*, Presses Universitaires de France, Paris, 1962, p. 16.
6.   Ibid.

References

Books and Articles

Arbo, Alessandro (ed.). 2007. Perspectives de l'esthétique musicale: entre théorie et histoire, L'Harmattan, Paris.

Bergson, Henri. 1962. *L'énergie spirituelle: essais et conferences*. Presses Universitaires de France: Paris.

Bergson, Henri. 1968. *Durée et simultanéité*, Presses Universitaires de France, Paris.

Cresson, André. 1961. *Bergson*, Presses Universitaires de France, collection Philosophies, Paris.

Deliege, Irène, and Sloboda, John (ed.). 1995. *Naissance et développement du sens musical*, Presses Universitaires de France, Paris.

Greimas, Algirdas Julien. 1970. *Du sens*, Paris, Editions du Seuil.

Greimas, Algirdas Julien. 2002. *Sémantique structurale*, Presses Universitaires de France, Paris.

Heidegger, Martin. 1964. *Être et Temps*, Gallimard, Paris.

Leroi-Gourhan, André. 1964. *Le geste et la parole*, Tome I: *Technique et langage*, Albin Michel, Paris.

Leroi-Gourhan, André. 1964. *Le geste et la parole*, Tome II: *La mémoire et les rythmes*, Albin Michel, Paris.

Lynch, Michael P., Eilers, Rebecca E., Oller, D. Kimbrough, Urbano, Richard C., 1990. "Innateness, experience, and music perception," *Psychological Science*, American psychological society, Volume 1, N°4.

McAdams, Stephen, and Bigand, Emmanuel (ed.). 1994. *Penser les sons: psychologie cognitive de l'audition*, Presses Universitaires de France, Paris.

Ricoeur, Paul. 1983. *Temps et récit*, Tome I: *L'intrigue et le récit historique*, Editions du Seuil, Paris.

Ricoeur, Paul. 1984. *Temps et récit*, Tome II: *La configuration dans le récit de fiction*, Editions du Seuil, Paris, 1984.

Ricoeur, Paul. 1985. *Temps et récit*, Tome III: *Le temps raconté*, Editions du Seuil, Paris.

Ricoeur, Paul. 1975. *La métaphore vive*, Editions du Seuil, Paris, 1975.

Wirthner, Martine, and Zulauf, Madeleine (ed.). 2002. *A la recherche du développement musical*, L'Harmattan, Paris.

UNESCO Documents

UNESCO—*Convention sur la protection et la promotion de la diversité des expressions culturelles* (Paris, 20 October 2005).

UNESCO—*Convention on the Protection and Promotion of the Diversity of Cultural Expressions* (Paris, 20 October 2005).

UNESCO—*Convention pour la sauvegarde du patrimoine culturel immatériel* (Paris, 17 October 2003).

UNESCO—*Convention for the Safeguarding of the Intangible Cultural Heritage* (Paris, 17 October 2003).

UNESCO—*Déclaration de l'UNESCO concernant la destruction intentionnelle du patrimoine culturel* (Paris, 17 October 2003).

UNESCO—*Unesco Declaration concerning the Intentional Destruction of Cultural Heritage* (Paris, 17 October 2003).

UNESCO—*Déclaration universelle de l'UNESCO sur la diversité culturelle* (Paris, 2 November 2001).

UNESCO—*Unesco Universal Declaration on Cultural Diversity* (Paris, 2 November 2001).

UNESCO—*Déclaration sur les responsabilités des générations présentes envers les générations futures* (Paris, 12 November 1997).

UNESCO—*Declaration on the Responsibilities of the Present Generations Towards Future Generations* (Paris, 12 November 1997).

UNESCO—*Recommendation sur la sauvegarde de la culture traditionnelle et populaire* (Paris, 15 November 1989).

UNESCO—*Recommendation on the Safeguarding of Traditional Culture and Folklore* (Paris, 15 November 1989).

Orchestrating Multiple Eastern-Western Identities through Music: A Turkish Story

Itır Toksöz

Introduction

In his famous article "The Clash of Civilizations," Samuel P. Huntington (1993) claimed that the next global clashes would be along civilizational lines and that Turkey was one of what he designated as the "torn" countries. However, rapidly increasing coexistence of both Eastern and Western elements in Turkish music can be regarded as a manifestation of how the citizens of Turkey identify themselves with both an Eastern and a Western identity. While politically Turkey may be struggling between its Western orientation and its Eastern roots, culturally people seem to be more at ease with their dual Eastern and Western characteristics: the musicians' preference to express themselves through music that embraces both Eastern and Western melodies, especially in popular music, is a powerful indication of that.

This chapter, against the backdrop of the Turkish case, seeks to highlight the following questions: Can we have multiple identities? How can we express multiple identities through music? Can having multiple identities help societies be more peaceful? And what role might music, as an expresser of multiple identities, have in such a process?

I will argue that we can and we do have multiple identities, and that music is an ideal platform where those identities are both experienced and expressed. Whether or not having multiple identities is conducive to peace is not based on the fact that we have them, but on how we use them. Multiple identities are often accused of creating an identity crisis. But they can be used to build bridges as well. One way of defining identity is to see it as "characteristics that individuals use to group themselves with some people and differentiate themselves from the others" (Morrison 2003, 14). Multiple identities are important as they can mitigate the effects of the opposition between the Self and the Other, create different points of reference for self-identity and thus help enter into dialogues with people coming from different backgrounds more easily, thus, ultimately, facilitating the emergence of a global consciousness of solidarity.

Today, there are many musicians in Turkey who successfully present their music as the "bridge" between the East and the West, the bridge metaphor being commonly used to describe the country. Hüsnü Şenlendirici, a famous and popular Turkish clarinet player, is one of them. His music presents a mixture of Anatolian melodies with those of Western jazz.[1]

His introductory song "Oyun Havası" from his first solo album *Hüsn-ü Klarnet: The Joy of Clarinet* (2005) starts with a Western sound which, in my case at least, invokes for me a feeling of being in any city of the Western world. Some seconds later the clarinet enters, then the "darbuka" (goblet drum) with Turkish rhythms, followed by violins playing Eastern melodies. Thus, there is a slow transition to Eastern melodies as the song progresses, which alternate with unmistakably Western fragments of chill-out lounge music followed by very apparent Eastern fragments. The focus of the sound changes from Western to Eastern and back and forth several times during the course of the four and a half minutes. The piece is a compelling example of how Eastern and Western tunes can coexist in the same song.

If Eastern and Western characteristics can coexist in the same musical piece, can they also coexist in the identity of a person? If, as many have suggested, music is a means of expressing self-identity, a medium through which we express who we are, how we feel, what we think, where we stand, then the popularity of Mr. Şenlendirici's music seems to give an affirmative answer to this question. Not only he himself who creates this music, but also his listeners must find something of themselves in this coexistence, and this is probably one of the reasons why Mr. Şenlendirici is popular in a country where the debate on questions of identity is often positioned on the East-West axis. This is the focus of the first part of my discussion, which now follows.

Multiple Identities, Turkey and the Clash of Civilizations

Marc Gopin (2008) suggests:

> One of the cornerstones of civil society is the capacity to live with more than one identity... Throughout history people have developed the capacity to see themselves as having many identities, and become comfortable with all of them or most of

them... Each one of these identities gives me a slightly different view of the world and a different set of things to think about and feel. The more I can allow all of these identities to coexist inside of me, the broader my perspective will be on coexistence with others, with the diversity of people in my country and on the planet. The more rigid my identity, however, the more singular, the more I tend to suppress all the richness inside me as well as inside others.

He then continues linking his statements with the arguments of the clash of civilizations:

It turns out that this is the same in the political life of civilizations. The more that people and whole civilizations suppress the multiplicity and diversity of our identities, the more they will see themselves in constant struggle with others. A clash of civilizations is something that we human beings choose to create. It does not exist inside civilizations (ibid.).

Another voice, Amartya Sen, a Nobel prize winner, economist and humanitarian, writes:

The main hope of harmony lies not in any imagined uniformity, but in the plurality of our identities, which cut across each other and work against sharp divisions into impenetrable civilizational camps" (Sen 2001).[2]

In the twenty-first century, we increasingly bear witness to an expression by individuals that they indeed do have multiple identities. This situation can be attributed to the effects of migration, communication and information technologies in particular, and of globalization in general. Multiple identities are more common in places where globalization has made the biggest impact, as well as the places where identities have been historically complex. Turkey is a classical example of the latter. A major question, self-posed as well as posed by others, is whether Turkey is a part of the East or the West.

Answering this question has proved to be a futile effort. One could argue both ways successfully and would still fall short of presenting the entire picture. Turkey is not only a country where East geographically meets West, but it is also a country where Western cultures meet with the Eastern ones. It is at the juncture of the Islamic, Jewish, and Christian civilizations. It is the successor of an empire that embraced people with all these identities. At various historical points, it has been at close contact with different nations (French in the West, Russians in the North, Mongolians in the East and Arabs in the South). As a nation-state born in the early 1920s, its modernization project has been solidly based in Westernization. However, its Eastern roots cannot be overlooked either. Today, it pursues EU membership while constantly keeping its connections with the Middle East and Central Asia.

This particular situation creates a cultural richness, perceived both as an asset and as a threat, depending on one's perspective. It is often referred to as an identity crisis, which is not likely to be resolved as long as the categories of the "East" and the "West" continue to exist. This is very problematic for the people of Turkey because it impacts how they perceive themselves and how they are perceived from the outside by others who define themselves either, and only, as Westerners or as Easterners.

A Turkish song from the famous rock band Kargo is a good example of how East and West are seen through the eyes of the Turks. In their song "Boğaziçi" (Bosphorus), entitled after the name of the Istanbul Strait separating Asia and Europe, from their 1998 album *Yalnızlık Mevsimi* (Season of Solitude), the lyrics discuss the positive sides of the West and the negative sides of the East, and then the positive sides of the East and the negative sides of the West, asking the Bosphorus to separate "us," which perhaps sounds less like a true wish and more like a rebellious demand to be understood, hence the line: "Tell them about us without separating us." An excerpt from the song reads:

> To laugh
> in the East means shame, vanity
> in the West,
> it is almost a natural desire
> Knowledge
> in the East means respect, reputation
> in the West
> it is indexed to Money
>
> Separate us, Bosphorus
> tell them about us, without separating us
> Separate us Bosphorus
> save me before I drown[3]

Another song that highlights the existence and expression of multiple identities in Turkish society is by Sezen Aksu, who is known as the Diva of the Turkish pop music. In her song "Oh Oh" from the album *Deliveren* from 2000, and with a somewhat vernacular vocabulary, she talks about how the "wild youth" have adapted their image to the globalized world, hinting again at the sense of this Eastern-Western identity. Some lines in the original Turkish lyrics that were already in English are specified with the use of italics in the translation below:

> Nail it, sugar, come on hop *give me five*
> Global is the world, global is *life*

Cut your swagger, American tune
Mafia in between streets, *fight is fight* [...]

To the bottom, everything is sinking to the bottom
Also there is the analysis, synthesis
Come from the East, come from the West
Do it, do it, just do it, come on![4]

It is the assumption of this chapter, as articulated above in the citation from Gopin, that the possession of multiple identities is a positive thing in that it may give people more flexibility in terms of creating points of convergence with those whom they designate as "outsiders," outsiders here referring to "the culturally other." In Turkey, even those who would see themselves to be completely Western would find Eastern characteristics in themselves and vice versa. As Gopin and Sen imply, a society where individuals have multiple identities might be more open to understanding others. Despite the fact that the above lyrics refer to a tension between the East and the West, both songs indicate an acknowledgment and acceptance of multiple identities and also the tension between them and do not necessarily qualify the tension as a negative thing. Although both songs indicate an ongoing tussle with identity, I argue that this is not necessarily a bad thing and I want to stand with my argument that having multiple identities is of positive value.

Such a perspective on multiple identities would tend to discredit Samuel Huntington's "Clash of Civilizations" thesis mentioned at the start of this chapter. Huntington sees civilizations as cultural entities (Huntington 1993, 23) and defines civilization as "the highest cultural grouping of people and the broadest level of cultural identity people have short of that which distinguishes humans from other species" (ibid., 24). Although he acknowledges that the culture of two villages within the same country may be different, taking as his example a northern and a southern Italian village, he sees them as part of a common Italian culture distinguishing them from the villages of other European countries; and on a higher level he sees them as part of a European community which distinguishes them from others (ibid.). Yet if a civilization is the broadest level of cultural identity, how can one expect that all its members share one single homogeneous identity in such a broad entity as a civilization?

In fact, Huntington acknowledges that "civilizations obviously blend and overlap and may include subcivilizations"; he also sees that they are dynamic and without any sharp lines between them (ibid.). Yet his analysis does not seem to address whether or not these complexities have an effect on how the people of a civilization would act. Huntington argues "the interactions among peoples of different civilizations enhance the civilization-consciousness of people that in turn invigorates differences and animosities stretching or thought to stretch back deep into history" (ibid.). I would argue that on the individual level, people are able to embrace the elements of more than one civilization, which is likely to have spill-over effects on how their societies look at different identities. Different civilizations, different identities are sure to have overlapping elements because they have evolved in interaction with one another.

Huntington's thesis of the Clash of Civilizations can be argued to have become something of a self-fulfilling prophecy, in that during the post 9-11 period, many decision makers and academics have started to see the events of 9-11 within the framework of this term, suggesting that the events of 9-11 "prove" Huntington's thesis; this might be itself argued as having very unfortunate consequences for world peace. Huntington is right in the sense that civilizations clash with one another. What he neglects is that civilizations also borrow from one another. It is not news to anyone in social sciences how paper, compass and gunpowder came from China to the Western world or how Islamic civilization acted as the preserver of the ancient Greek texts during the Middle Ages of Europe. Civilizations and the identities that make up these civilizations can cooperate instead of getting into conflict.

Huntington calls those countries with some degree of cultural homogeneity, yet which cannot decide which civilization their society belongs to, "torn" countries, where the leaders pursue a bandwagoning strategy for becoming a part of the West, despite their non-Western history, culture, and traditions. He sees Turkey as the most prototypical torn country, torn between its secular Westernism and an Islamic revival (ibid., 42).[5] While politically this may be true, in people's daily lives different identities can peacefully exist in Turkey.

Most of the studies on the issue of identity today see identities as social constructions, for example as "complex, hierarchical networks of inter-related constructs," (Hargreaves et al. 2002, 2) drawing attention to the suggestion by social constructivist theorists that people have many identities and that these identities can even be contradictory (ibid., 10). While acknowledging the social constructivist literature, I will be focusing on the expression of these identities through music rather than on how they were constructed.

Turkish Music: Historical Perspective

The Ottoman Empire, the predecessor of modern Turkey, was a multicultural entity. The period of collapse and disintegration of the Empire brought efforts towards Westernization for saving it, and this resulted in questions of identity. One could say that even then music had a role in the Westernization attempts of the Ottoman Empire. For example, Değirmenci (2006, 56) reports that the first Westernization movement in music happened in the Army with the invitation to Guiseppe Donizetti in 1826 to lead the military band of Nizam-ı Cedid. However, the overall Westernization efforts proved to be insufficient to save the Empire and the First World War brought its end. After a war of independence that lasted from 1918 till 1922, the new Turkish Republic was established as a nation-state in 1923.

The transition from a multicultural empire to a nation-state required not only political changes but also cultural ones, including the policy on music. The cultural policies of the Turkish Republic put a Western emphasis on music, with a corresponding neglect of the Eastern musical tradition, as part of the ongoing Westernization project. A new citizenry was to be created to make the transition from a multinational Empire to a nation-state. Tekelioğlu (1996, 194) draws attention to the essential objective of the new republic being "the founding of a nation-state with a new concept of the Citizen or rather a new culture for the people." Within this context, a new (polyphonic) musical taste for the new citizen was to follow the rejection of the monophonic traditional forms of the East. Stokes (1992b, 90) sees this as a "strong central bureaucratic state tradition imposing reform upon a passive (if reactionary) periphery." In general one can say that traditional Turkish music was divided into two categories: (Turkish) classical music, and folk music. The first was the music of the aristocratic circles whereas the latter was restricted to peasantry (Belaiev 1935, 356; 359; 366). The new Republic sought to get rid of the first while promoting the latter.

According to Tekelioğlu (1999, 194) Mustafa Kemal, the founder of modern Turkey, himself spoke and wrote about an East-West or West-East synthesis, which was the result of this cultural process, in which the influence of the Ottoman legacy of the East was reduced and Turkish Classical Music, the music of the Ottoman Palace, was now regarded as an archaic form which could not meet the needs of the new citizen (ibid., 195). Signell (1980, 166) claims that for the first 50 years of the Republic, Turkish classical music "suffered under its Ottoman shame."

Instead, the West-East synthesis promoted Western classical music and Turkish Folk Music (the music of Origin) as part of the nation-building and this was influenced by the ideas of Ziya Gökalp[6] (1978) on music (Değirmenci 2006, 55).

Therefore, during the early years of the Turkish Republic, to eradicate the effects of the Ottoman culture, a series of measures were taken in the area of music, such as: the closing down or transformation of musical institutions like the Palace Symphony Orchestra, Palace Military Band School; the banning of monophonic music education; and the abolishment of lodges and cloisters, which was a blow to the tasavvuf (Sufi order) music (ibid., 58). In 1934, and for a period of 20 months, Turkish music was banned from radio broadcasts (Tekelioğlu 1996, 195).

At the same time, in order to promote Western music, other measures were taken such as: playing of Western music on Turkish Maritime Lines; government-sponsored ballroom dances; the sending of gifted musicians abroad for training and education; performances of polyphonic pieces in free-of-charge programs; free music classes at Halkevleri (People's Houses) (ibid.). Moreover, in the 1930s, through the advice and assistance of Béla Bartók, Hungarian composer and ethnomusicologist, the government initiated a program to collect and archive Turkish music, the archive being "intended as a fund of purely Turkish melodic and poetic elements which will eventually be recombined according to Western compositional techniques" (Stokes 1989, 29).

Upon transition to multiparty democracy in 1945, the country underwent significant political and sociological changes. A class of nouveau riche emerged. Rural populations migrated from their homes to big cities. With these changes, and over time, the music scene also changed, notably with the emergence of "Arabesk". Arabesk music marked the 1960s through to the 1990s. This is a music characterized by Arabic pop-influenced melodies and rhythms, Middle Eastern music including bağlama music, Turkish forms of oriental dance and Ottoman classical music in musical form (Arabesque 2010). The lyrics typically concern "an inferior world of turbulent and violent emotions, in which the ultimate symbol of the pervasive themes of alienation and powerlessness, is the junction of unrequited love and fate" (Stokes 1992a, 214). Arabesk was born in Turkey under the influence of the Egyptian films, which were popular in the 1940s. In 1948, the films were banned; however, Turkish musicians started to imitate their music (ibid., 215). In the 1970s and 1980s, Arabesk was banned from being broadcast via the state-owned media. In the 1980s, the state even tried to reform Arabesk by officially endorsing "acısız arabesk"—meaning "arabesk without pain"—in which the characteristically painful lyrics were replaced (ibid., 219); this turned out to be very unpopular.

Arabesk was regarded as a genre which oscillated between the East and the West but which carried the full characteristics of neither (Güngör 1990, 11). The mere existence of this music genre was a popular topic of discussion among the intelligentsia and it was seen as expressive of the identity problem of a country located between the East and the West but which could not integrate with either (Livaneli 1990, 7). This was a blow—almost a backlash—to the State's efforts in endorsing a Western musical taste.

Arabesk's popularity grew at the expense of Western-style pop music in the late 70s and early 80s, although Western-style pop music did not disappear entirely during this period and regained its popularity during the 1990s. By the 1980s, the country was undergoing liberalization, which changed society and the musical scene once again and set the context for the current situation. The 1990s marked the end of the state monopoly on TV and radio broadcasting and this made a huge difference to the development of musical style and expression. During this period, mainstream music was "corporate pop and arabesque genres." (Turkish Music 2010) My discussion continues with a view of current musical practice within the Turkish context, arguing that this historical concern with expression of a plural identity remains a strong element in this context.

Expression of Multiple Identities through Music in the Current Turkish Musical Scene

The topic of the expression of identity or identities through music has been the subject of several articles (Zagoria 2009; Saldanha 1998; Gazzah 2005; Torres 2008; Akrofi et al. 2007; Ilari 2006; Hargreaves et al. 2002; Gracyk 2004).[7] For example, according to Hargreaves et al., music is a means used to formulate and express one's individual identity. They suggest that we use music "to present ourselves to others in the way we prefer" (Hargreaves et al. 2002, 1). This works for the audience as well as the musicians. Just as our musical tastes and preferences indicate our values and attitudes, composers and performers may use their music to express their worldviews (ibid.). Gracyk (2004, 16) claims that "musical works offer a model of the intangible object that we seek when we seek ourselves."

Ilari talks about a "straight relationship" between music and identity and sees that music is important in the construction of personal, cultural and national identities (Ilari 2006, 123). In order to see how Eastern and Western elements are combined in contemporary Turkish music industry, examples will firstly be provided from the mainstream Turkish musical market. Then, as two platforms where Turkish music is put on the international stage, the examples of Turkish World Music and of the Eurovision Song Contest will be taken to show the reader that today Turkish artists use both Eastern and Western elements in their songs on both of these platforms.

Today's Turkish music scene is very eclectic. The state-sponsored West-East synthesis now seems to coexist with an East-West synthesis. The official policies on music during the early Republic years were partially successful in the sense that they instilled a Western taste in the Turkish audience just as intended. However, their goal was not completely fulfilled, as the Eastern roots were not eradicated and made a comeback, as described above, with the Arabesk. One can say that today a level of compromise has been reached. Today in Turkey there are various genres such as folk music, art music, pop music, fantasy music, rock music, heavy metal music, New Age music, world music, rap music, tavern music, and Arabesk. Moreover, regardless of their genres today, many songs in the musical market have both Eastern and Western musical characteristics, and a mainstream pop song in Turkey is generally expected to contain both.

For example, there are Westernized (modernized) folk songs. Artists such as Kubat, a male folk music artist, and Zara, a female folk music artist, often sing folk songs in Westernized fashion. Signaling this trend, an environmentalist NGO www.agaclar.net, inspired by the global movement Playing for Change,[8] started a campaign named Doğa İçin Çal (Play for Nature)[9] to increase environmental awareness in Turkey. The two songs they chose to perform, each of which they recorded as a video, are both Turkish folk songs, *Divane Aşık Gibi* and *Uzun İnce Bir Yoldayım* performed with a Western sound by 45 young Turkish musicians from different parts of the country, using mostly Western instruments such as acoustic, electric and bass guitars, various percussion instruments, keyboards, saxophone, flute, trumpet, harmonica, but sometimes also traditional Turkish instruments, such as *ney* (reed flute), *kemençe* (a small type of violin), *saz* (bağlama). One can follow the traces of Eastern and Western identities through the instruments being used; the sense of a wider identity is also reflected in the diversity of those in this group, such as Turkish people coming from different parts of Turkey in the first video and the Turks who live abroad, Greek people from Greece,

Armenian citizens of Turkey, as well as musicians with disabilities as seen in their second video.[10]

The sense of multiple identities in folk songs is not just limited to the coexistence of folk and Western elements. Brother and sister twins Öykü and Berk became popular after the release of their first album Kısmet, in December 2007, where they performed folk songs such as their hit "*Evlerinin Önü Boyalı Direk*" in flamenco style, which combines musical traditions from two distant corners of the Mediterranean.[11]

Another genre where Eastern and Western elements coexist is the rock scene, in sub-genres such as "Anatolian Rock" and "Arabesk Rock." Anatolian Rock was a genre that combined Turkish folk music with rock in the 1960-70s with leading artists and bands of that time.[12] Their foreign contemporaries in the 1968 spirit were influenced by Eastern mysticism, which in turn influenced the Turkish artists to combine rock with their own Turkish tunes (Anadolu Rock 2010). In the 1990s, some contemporary artists and bands, including for example Haluk Levent, a male rock artist, emerged and revived this genre.[13] Arabesk rock differs from Anatolian rock in the sense that the Eastern component there is not the Turkish folk tones, but the music form itself, or songs of Arabic origin (Arabesk Rock 2010).

Even hard rock and heavy metal bands use Eastern elements, such as the Nu Metal band MaNga, the Gothic Rock band Almora and the Heavy Metal band Pentagram. Nu Metal normally uses rap/hip-hop elements in lyrics and turntables but MaNga also uses *darbuka* (goblet drum), ney (reed flute) etc. in their instrumentation. Gothic Rock is based on epic lyrics with opera vocals in heavy metal and Almora, which in general follows a very Western sound, has a song named "Shehrazade" that contains slight Eastern tunes. Another band, Pentagram, has songs such as "Anatolia" with fragments played on the saz or "Şeytan Bunun Neresinde" which is a Turkish folk song, performed in heavy metal style.

A further category in which the expression of identities is apparent is that of Turkish world music. The record company Doublemoon Records states in its website that it is:

dedicated to spreading the cultural tapestry that is the city's (Istanbul's)[14] sound around the world. Doublemoon has made a name for itself that is synonymous with world fusion where global souls bring together jazz & world, acoustic & electronic, and occidental & oriental music… Ranging from Sufi-electronica to groove alla turca, from jazz to gypsy funk, from oriental hip hop to Anatolian blues the musical gems that emerge from recording sessions are documented and recorded by Doublemoon (About Us 2010).

This statement echoes Stokes' argument that "if anything is authentic now, it is hybrid genres, organically connected to the social life and cultural aspirations of particular localities" (Stokes 2004, 60). Stokes' concept of "hybrid genres" is very closely related to the notion of the musical expression of multiple identities; however, I would suggest that "hybridity" sees identities as fused into one another, while the concept of "multiple identities" instead allows us to see them as coexisting with one another. Stokes places Istanbul among those global cities where "multicultural energy and creativity is significantly freed from the dictates of the nation states to which they were formerly attached" (ibid., 64). This confirms Aytar and Keskin's (2003, 150) observations of Istanbul's being home to diverse kinds of music and a borrowing of musical types of different social and cultural groups from each other.

Doublemoon promotes several artists: Mercan Dede, Sultana, Laço Tayfa, Hüsnü Şenlendirici, Orient Expressions and Baba Zula among others. Mercan Dede is a punk DJ using electronic, rap and Sufi music with whirling dervishes in his stage performances. He also performs by the name of DJ Arkın Allen, a more Western musical persona than his Sufi inspired Mercan Dede persona. Sultana is a lady rapper who incorporates hip-hop style and Eastern elements. Laço Tayfa is a band of Roma musicians, which has collaborated with the New York based band Brooklyn Funk Essentials in one of their albums. Hüsnü Şenlendirici plays jazz with clarinet in Eastern tunes mostly of Roma music. Orient Expressions performs electronic music with Turkish ethnic music. Baba Zula is one of the most interesting examples. The band creates a sound of their own named "Oriental Dub" through mixing of oriental instruments such as the darbuka, electric saz, and spoons with electronics and modern sounds (Baba Zula 2010).

These world music artists are well known in Turkey and they also shoulder the Turkish contribution to world music. While doing so almost all of them use Eastern and Western elements, which is likely to reflect their multiple identities.

The Eurovision Song Contest has been perceived by every state and its musicians from the popular music genre as one of the most important steps in presenting themselves on the international platform (Kuyucu 2005, 20). According to Torres, the contest serves for identity formation at the Pan-European level, identity articulation at the national level and presents an arena for popular expressions of national contest and regional collusion. He sees the contest as "an arena for nations to establish a dialogue vis-à-vis Europe in terms of their position within it" (Torres 2006,

2-7). In that sense, Eurovision is a platform on which Turkey expresses its identity, and where it presents itself to its European counterparts.

Turkey has been participating in the contest since 1975. At first, the emphasis of the Turkish songs was almost always on Western elements. Turkey's preference was so much on its Western identity that during the contest in 1984, when an Arabian melody was used in advertising the Turkish songs, along with images of a fez (a type of hat with widespread use in the Ottoman Empire), this became a scandal. Turkey opposed the advertisement, arguing that Turkey was not an Arabic country and that it could not be represented by the fez. The directors of the contest responded that they regarded Turkey as a Middle Eastern country. The Eurovision contest was however perceived by Turkey as an opportunity to show the Europeans that the country was also part of the West (Kuyucu 2005, 123). This statement was therefore a great blow to Turkey. Moreover, every defeat was interpreted as a national failure. The common belief was that Turkish songs were rejected as Turkey was not fully perceived as European by the Europeans.

Livaneli (1990, 8) qualified Eurovision as the westward looking face of Turkey whereas Arabesk would represent the eastward looking face of Turkey. However, along with the liberalization that started in the 1980s, especially with the emergence of private media in the 1990s and the changing musical scene, the Turkish songs in Eurovision slowly started in the 1990s to divert from their Western-only sounds to sounds that incorporated both Eastern and Western elements. It is after this change that Turkey started to see positive results in the contest. In 1997 Şebnem Paker's "Dinle," an example of East-West synthesis, won third place. In 2003 Sertab Erener's—"Everyway That I Can," another song that reflected multiple identities, carried the trophy to Turkey. In the 2004 song "For Real" by Athena, in essence a ska-punk song, there were darbuka rhythms. In 2009 Hadise's "Düm Tek Tek" which won fourth place was again an East-West blend. In 2010, MaNga participated with a "Nu Metal" song where one can distinguish ney, darbuka and violins playing Eastern rhythms and melodies, winning second place. Even other songs such as Sibel Tüzün's "Superstar" in 2006 and Kenan Doğulu's "Shake It Up Şekerim" in 2007 had Eastern melodies incorporated into Western ones.

It is not only the musical elements of the songs, but also the performances of the artists that reflect their multiple identities. One example can be seen on the video clip prepared for the song "Everyway That I Can," which is about the pain of a favorite wife of the Sultan who fell from grace (Kuyucu 2005, 259). This clip was shot in the harem section of the Topkapı Palace, depicting the Harem life, a strongly exotic and orientalist scene to most Westerners. A second example is again by Sertab Erener when she performed her song "Leave" during the opening of the 2004 Eurovision song contest, which was hosted in Istanbul. The performance was based on a lightly dressed blond Turkish lady singing pop music with opera vocals with whirling dervishes in the background, reflecting both the Western character and the Eastern soul of the country.[15]

Conclusion

Ilari (2006, 129) qualifies music as "a democratic art form" and hopes it can encourage thinking along transnational lines. Embracing multiple identities would surely help this process of democratization. It is no coincidence that in Turkey, individuals chose to express the co-existence of their Eastern and Western identities more frequently as the country became liberalized and democratized. This does not mean that the existence of multiple identities and their expressions through music or otherwise could automatically create peaceful societies. However multiple identities can peacefully coexist, as exemplified in the account above by many of Turkey's musicians and by the population at large who make their work popular, even if these identities are on essentially different civilizational lines. Huntington's "clash of civilizations" thus seems to be questioned by Turkey's example, at least within the musical context. Seeing multiple identities as a threat to or as an asset for peace is a choice. Acknowledging multiple identities in ourselves and in others can be one of the paths towards creating relationships of solidarity within and beyond a country's borders. Music's role in this is potentially powerful, as shown in the case of Turkey.

Notes

1.   For more information on Hüsnü Şenlendirici visit the Wikipedia page, Accessed: August 16, 2010 from http://en.wikipedia.org/wiki/H%C3%BCsn%C3%BC_%C5%9Fenlendirici.
2.   Sen's article was also reached by following the link in the article on Multiple Identities on the page. Accessed: April 30, 2010 from http://www.facinghistory.org/resources/facingtoday/confronting-september-11-mul.
3.   Translated from the Turkish original by the author.
4.   Translated from the Turkish original by the author.
5.   Other torn countries Huntington cites are Mexico and Russia.
6.   Gökalp is a Turkish sociologist who influenced Turkish nationalism.
7.   It is noteworthy that most of these articles address the issue of multiple identities

    in migrants whereas this chapter tackles multiple identities of Turkish people who reside in Turkey. While spatial dislocation may facilitate adoption of multiple identities, it is not necessary as in the case of Turkey.

8.   Website: Playing for Change. Accessed: August 16, 2010 from http://www.playingforchange.com/.
9.   Website: Doğa İçin Çal
    http://www.dogaicincal.com/index.asp?l=2.
10. The video of Divane Aşık Gibi can be seen at: http://www.dogaicincal.com/index. asp?sayfa=caldiklarimiz&id=7, The video of Uzun İnce Bir Yoldayım can be seen at: http://www.dogaicincal.com/index.asp?sayfa=caldiklarimiz&id=32.
11. For more information on Öykü and Berk, visit their official website at: http://www. oykuberk.com/.
12. Cem Karaca, Barış Manço, Erkin Koray, Moğollar are among the examples of leading artists of the genre at the time.
13. Although in some sources, all the Turkish rock scene is called Anatolian rock, in this chapter the genre is taken as the very specific combination of Turkish folk and rock. Among other artists of Anatolian rock that emerged after the 1990s, Ayna and Kıraç can also be listed.
14. Author's clarification.
15. This performance created debates on the issue of the dancing of the whirling dervishes, especially the dancing of female and male dervishes together on stage, hinting at the religious character of the performance of "sema"—dance of whirling dervishes- in esence. The artist Sertab Erener did not back down and her choice prevailed in the end. For more information on the debate please see Kadın Semazen Krizi (Women Whirling Dervishes Crisis) http://www.tumgazeteler. com/?a=411318 where the source is shown as the Akşam newspaper http://www. aksam.com.tr , the issue from May 14th 2004. Accessed Nov. 1st 2010. To see the performance, follow link http://www.youtube.com/watch?v=s3i-CDDwF3Y.

References

"About Us." 2010. Accessed: April 30, 2010 from http://www.doublemoon.com.tr/English/Hakkimizda.aspx.

Akrofi, Eric. Smit, Maria. Thorsen, Stig-Magnus. 2007. *Music and Identity: Transformation and Negotiation.* SunPress.

Aksu, Sezen. 2000. "Oh Oh." *Deliveren.* Post Yapım. Music and lyrics by: Sezen Aksu.

"Anadolu Rock." 2010. Accessed: April 30, 2010 from http://tr.wikipedia.org/wiki/Anadolu_rock.

"Arabesque." 2010. Accessed: April 30, 2010 from http://en.wikipedia.org/wiki/Arabesque_(Turkish_music).

"Arabesk Rock." 2010. Accessed: April 30, 2010 from http://tr.wikipedia.org/wiki/Arabesk-rock.

Aytar, Volkan & Keskin, Azer. 2003. "Constructions of Spaces of Music in İstanbul: Scuffling and Intermingling Sounds in a Fragmented Metropolis." *Geocarrefour,* Numero Vol. 78/2, La Ville, le Bruit, Le Son; 147- 157.

Baba Zula. 2010. Accessed: April 30, 2010 from http://en.wikipedia.org/wiki/Baba_zula.

Belaiev, Viktor. 1935. "Turkish Music." *The Musical Quarterly.* Vol. 21. No. 3; 356-367.

Değirmenci, Koray. 2006. "On the Pursuit of a Nation: The Construction of Folk and Folk Music in the Founding Decades of the Turkish Republic," *International Review of the Aesthetics and Sociology of Music.* Vol. 37. No. 1; 47-65.

Gazzah, Miriam. 2005. Maroc-Hop Music and Youth Identities, *ISIM Review* 16, Autumn; 6-7.

Gracyk, Theodore. 2004. Does Everyone Have a Musical Identitiy?: Reflections on Musical Identities. *Action, Criticism & Theory for Music Education.* Vol. 3. No. 1, May. MayDay Group. Accessed: April 30, 2010 from http://act.maydaygroup. org/articles/Gracyk3_1.pdf.

Gopin, Marc. 2008. Confronting September 11: Introduction. Accessed: April 30, 2010 from http://www.facinghistory.org/node/244.

Güngör, Nazife. 1990. *Arabesk: Sosyokültürel Açıdan Arabesk Müzik.* (Arabesk: Arabesk Music From a Sociocultural Perspective). Bilgi Yayınevi. Istanbul.

Hargreaves, David J., Miell, Dorothy, Macdonald Raymond A.R. 2002. What Are Musical Identities and Why Are They Important? in *Musical Identities*, Oxford University Press, Ch. 1; 1-20. Accessed: April 30, 2010 from http://fds.oup.com/www.oup. com/pdf/13/9780198509325.pdf.

Huntington, Samuel P. 1993. A Clash of Civilizations. *Foreign Affairs.* Summer 1993. Vol. 72 No. 3.; 22-49.

Ilari Beatriz. 2006. "Music and Identity of Brazilian Dekasegi Children and Adults Living in Japan." *9th International Conference on Music Perception and Cognition, ICMPC9 Proceedings.* University of Bologna, August 22-26, 2006. Accessed: April 30, 2010 from http://www.marcocosta.it/icmpc2006/pdfs/129.pdf.

Livaneli Zülfü. 1990. Arabesk ve Biz. in Güngör, Nazife. 1990. *Arabesk: Sosyokültürel Açıdan Arabesk Müzik.* (Arabesk: Arabesk Music From a Sociocultural Perspective). Bilgi Yayınevi. İstanbul; 7-8.

Kargo. 1998. "Boğaziçi." *Yalnızlık Mevsimi.* Raks Müzik, Music by: Kargo, Lyrics by: M.Ş.Ş.

Kuyucu, Michael. 2005. *Eurovision: Türkiye'nin Serüveni* (Eurovision: Turkey's Adventure). Nokta Kitap, İstanbul.

Morrison, Cecily. 2003. "Not About Nationalism: The Role of Folk Song in Identity Process." Accessed: April 30, 2010 from http://www.fulbright.hu/book1/cecilymorrison.pdf.

Saldanha, Arun. 1998. "Music, Space, Identity Global Youth /Local Others in Bangalore India." Accessed: April 30, 2010 from http://www.snarl.org/youth/arun-msi.pdf.

Şenlendirici, Hüsnü. 2005. Hüsn-ü Klarinet. RH Pozitif Müzik.

Sen, Amarytha. 2001. "A World Not Neatly Divided." *The New York Times.* Op-Ed. 23 Nov.

Signell, Karl. 1980. Turkey's Classical Music: A Class Symbol. *Asian Music.* Vol. 12. No. 1. Symposium on Art Musics in Muslim Nations; 164-169.

Stokes, Martin. 1989. "Music, Fate and State: Turkey's Arabesk Debate." *Middle East Report.* No. 160: Turkey in the Age of Glasnost (Sep.-Oct.); 27-30.

Stokes, Martin. 1992a. "Islam, The Turkish State and Arabesk." *Popular Music*, Vol. 11. No. 2, A Changing Europe (May); 213-227.

Stokes, Martin. 1992b. "The Media and Reform: The Saz and Elektrosaz in Urban Turkish Folk Music." *British Journal of Ethnomusicology.* Vol. 1.; 89-102.

Stokes, Martin. 2004. Music and Global Order. *Annual Review of Anthropology.* Vol. 33; 47-72.

Tekelioğlu, Orhan. 1996. "The Rise of a Spontaneous Synthesis: The Historical Background of Turkish Popular Music." *Middle Eastern Studies.* Vol. 32. No. 2; 194-215.

"Turkish Music." 2010. Accessed: April 30, 2010 from http://en.wikipedia.org/wiki/ Turkish_music.

Torres, Cecilia A. R., 2008. "The Construction of Identity and Musical Identities: A literature Review." Accessed: April 30, 2010 from http://www-usr.rider.edu/~vrme/ v11n1/vision/Torres.Final.06.pdf.

Torres, Gonzalo. 2006. "Pan-European, Regional and National Identity in the Eurovision Song Contest." Accessed: April 30, 2010 from http://www.personal.ceu.hu/students/06/Nationalism_Media/Eurovision%20song%20contest.pdf.

Zagoria, Ilan. 2009. "Performing Glocal Identities: Codeswitching in African Songs Produced in Perth, Australia.", in Zhang L.J., Rubdy R. & Alsagoff, L. (eds.). *Englishes and Literatures-in-English in a Globalised World: Proceedings of the 13th International Conference on English in Southeast Asia*. Singapore: National Institute of Education, Nanyang Technological University; 83-93. Accessed: April 30, 2010 from http://www.ell.nie.edu.sg/esea2008/proceedings/7.Zagoria_I_%20Performing%20glocal%20identities.pdf.

Voices from the Living Heart:
Healing Australia's Dark Past

Elizabeth Bowen

Somewhere in the last century[1] white Australia developed the phrase and notion of "The Dead Heart." It was used to describe the arid interior of the country, which is anything but dead. At the centre stands Uluru, the great giver of life in the midst of that vast red interior. Whitefellas were scared of the emptiness, the loneliness, the silence. The blackfellas knew and loved every inch of their country intimately. This was a living heart not a dead one. They were deeply "within" their carefully-evolved Law, lore and "Dreaming" and the whitefellas were "outside," looking in, unable to see the hidden mysteries and the beauty of this ancient, tough but fragile ecology and cosmology. It was mainstream Australia which has carried a "dead heart."[2]

Introduction

Music is a powerful storyteller; it accompanies newsreels and films of war, glorifying it, and our own life-events, creating associations in the depth of our subconscious. Some music stands out because it both captures a time in history and spotlights the marginalized, heightening awareness of injustice. In Australia, such music exists in the form of many songs that relate the dark chapters in our history of the struggle for the very survival, as well as acknowledgment of the cultural identity, of the Indigenous[3] population. Since white settlement, a consistent backdrop to their existence and central to their story has been a discriminatory policy that has disastrously failed this population. In hopeful contrast, the current developing prominence of Indigenous music in mainstream rock, and recent collaborations with jazz music, are telling us about the resilience of hope in the face of a history of systemic violence and denial of human rights.

Despite an Indigenous history dating back some 40,000 years, white settlement in Australia nevertheless centered on the doctrine of *Terra*

Nullius or "Land that belongs to No-one." This was finally overturned with the Mabo[4] decision of 1992, and Indigenous lands rights and the way in which cultural identity was tied with custodianship of the land finally had a legal foundation. However, the rich cultural legacy of the traditional owners of the land has been slow to be acknowledged as enhancing cultural life not only for Indigenous but for all Australians. That this cultural spirit is still thriving and now being shared, in the face of the ravages wrought by deprivation and poverty, is a testament to its strength of spirit. Musical interchanges occurring between Indigenous and jazz musical traditions can be seen as a potential healing ground, further opening up a dialogue, and creating possibilities for a new vision of solidarity. Jazz, with its own traditional roots in raising awareness of black identity in the United States, has demonstrated its openness and has in its global diaspora absorbed the beauty of different cultural expressions.

This chapter offers a narrative that highlights musical collaboration as a potential force for healing and reconciliation in Australia's political and cultural landscape. In a case study of two innovative projects involving cultural exchanges and collaborations between white musicians and Indigenous musicians, I will describe how these have been significant in opening up a path of mutual commitment to cross cultural exchange, and instrumental in a healing process that is moving Australia closer towards reconciliation. These two projects have provided voice to the voiceless; they are The Australian Art Orchestra and Ngukkar musicians' *Crossing Roper Bar*, and The Black Arm Band's *The Hidden Republic* and *Murandak*.

I begin this discussion with an account of the historical background, which I hope will help establish and explain the context from which these projects have arisen.

Two Countries and "The Intervention"

Australia is two countries on the same continent. A broad sweep of one country's history is that of free white settlement with waves of multicultural immigration. This has driven dynamic, cultural, social and economic development for Australian citizens and a pride in the harmonious co-existence of various ethnicities. However, challenging experiences of resettlement for new immigrants, a poor record on treatment of some refugees and a widening gap between rich and poor as the middle class began to shrink in the 1980s cannot be denied. Australia, however, has fared very well during the recent global economic crisis. This Australia, albeit ironically, has been coined *The Lucky Country*, which is shackled only by the lack of imagination of a political bureaucracy "mired in mediocrity and manacled to its past."[5] This past is confined to a romantic connection to the "mother country" or its European heritage, and a rejection of its "black heart."[6]

The other country's history, lived in and experienced by Indigenous people, is a story of disenfranchisement, desolation and painful disintegration, with citizenship denied to these first Australians until a referendum in 1967. Populations have been all but wiped out by rifles and disease; families ravaged as children were taken away to live in white families in attempts at "assimilation," these children now recognized as the "stolen generation," and communities continue to be shattered by poverty, "sit down money,"[7] alcohol and child sexual abuse.[8] Radically lower than average life expectancy, poor literacy and educational attainment, squalid housing and health issues associated with the third world characterize the living conditions of these long-standing custodians of the land, and yet only very recent Australian citizens. Within the context of Australia's global reputation as an advanced economy, these indicators of basic well-being fall abysmally short and any kind of economic and social equality remain stubbornly out of reach.

The most recent response to these seemingly intractable conditions is referred to as "The intervention" or more officially, the "Northern Territory Emergency Response," which was implemented in 2007. This was a controversial response to the report, *The Little Children Are Sacred* (2007)[9] which documented child sexual abuse within the Indigenous population; but the resultant policy has been criticized for further stigmatizing and discriminating against Indigenous Australians for reasons cited below.[10] It is considered a paternalistic, top-down policy that contravenes Australia's international human rights commitment; and indeed its radical nature was epitomized in the need for Australia to revoke its Anti-Discrimination Act in order to implement this policy program. Jon Altman describes the outcome of this in his report in 2007:

> In the 183 days [to November 2007] since the intervention was declared—with its mobilisation of the armed forces, unprecedented powers for civilians and police, and recruitment of volunteer aid workers—there has been a frenzied level of media attention in indigenous affairs... And frenetic bursts of policy-making on the run. Blind faith defence of the intervention by politicians and their agents has usually been based on a seeming unassailable call to "save the children," a moral imperative that hides unstated, untested, but very evident ideological motivations far removed from concerns of child welfare.[11]

The policy can be seen as the most recent contribution to Australia's shameful track record on human rights, to which Irene Kahn, Secretary-General of Amnesty International, has recently drawn attention. She relates a story about Elsie:

> squatting in the raw dirt of an open field, surrounded by all her belongings, which bore the dents and scratches I have seen inflicted on scant possessions when people have to flee, for example from flood, war or forced evictions... I walked down the desert track, past the filthy and worn mattresses... past the wooden crate perched on a rough-hewn bench that is their kitchen, and stepped over the tangled extension cord that brought electricity to their single lamp.[12]

Khan then asks, "Did I meet Elsie in Sudan, Sri Lanka or Afghanistan? No. The political leaders responsible for Elsie's situation are not to be found in Khartoum, Colombo or Kabul. They are in Canberra and Darwin."[13] Khan relates her dismay at witnessing this abject poverty in one of the world's richest countries, citing its ranking in the top ten when measures such as health, longevity, community life, political stability and political freedom are added to GDP measures.[14] Elsie, through an interpreter, conveys the lived experience of poverty not captured by defining it only in relation to income: "Lady, I pay rent to the government for sleeping on a mattress in the desert. I have no home, I don't have a voice, no one is listening to me or my family."[15] For Khan poverty is "the stuff of real human insecurity; the stuff of marginalization, of voicelessness, of degradation, of inequality and injustice."[16]

Galtung defines cultural violence as those "aspects of culture, the symbolic sphere of our existence—exemplified by religion and ideology, language and art, empirical science and formal science (logic, mathematics)—that can be used to justify or legitimize direct or structural violence."[17] When examining his typology of violence, Indigenous Australians could be said to have had everything thrown at them. In Galtung's terms, cultural violence makes reality opaque, turning the moral color of actions from wrong to right or at least acceptable.

Rhetoric aside, too much has been accepted in Australia's history in terms of the poor living conditions for Indigenous Australians. One of the publicly stated motivations for maintaining the policies of the intervention was to close the gap in health and life expectancy for Indigenous Australians in comparison with the rest of Australia's citizens. For example, life expectancy is approximately twenty years lower and the prevalence of kidney disease is nine times higher, skyrocketing to thirty times higher in some regions of the Northern Territory.[18] Suicide, depression, incarceration and substance abuse are also at chronically higher levels than for the rest of the population.

Indigenous musicians are a public face to the stark reality of these health and social well-being indicators that are associated with chronic poverty, despair and disenfranchisement. Mandaway Yunupingui, frontman for Yothu Yindu, a band of Indigenous and Western musicians who combine Western with traditional Indigenous instrumentation, has a public battle with renal failure; and the singer Ruby Hunter (see below) passed away prematurely at the age of 54 in February of 2010. Paul Grabowsky, in tribute, describes her voice and unique cultural contribution:

> Her sound nursed somewhere at its heart a moan, a lament, which came from a deep place, a place outside of particularities of space and time, but a singularity, nonetheless. Occasionally I was reminded of Nina Simone, but more often it evoked the red earth of the interior, a vibration, a hum, an undulation on a distant horizon line.[19]

Both Ruby Hunter and Archie Roach were founding members of the collaboration with the Australian Art Orchestra (AAO) as well as the Black Arm Band project (both described below). They were life partners and members of the "stolen generation," who met each other while living on the street. Roach's song, "They took the children away" tells the heart wrenching tragedy of a previous policy bereft of human rights and compassion that was considered acceptable at the time, as the intervention appears to be now.

A Beginning of Reconciliation

Not long after the intervention was implemented in mid 2007, a change of government in late 2007 in Australia led to the symbolic gesture of a full parliamentary apology to Indigenous Australians in February of 2008. The apology was made to the stolen generation for the damage caused by government decisions leading to the removal of children from their families. Not conceivable by many generations of Indigenous Australians, it was cathartic for those of the stolen generation who were able to witness it, as well as applauded by most Australians. The intervention was, however, in place at the time of the apology and remains to date (July 2010). As Tracee Hutchinson says;

> With "Sorry" said we are now at one of the most important points in our nation's history to make good its intentions. And hope is the one thing that unites us.[20]

Throughout the long and ongoing struggle for rights, reconciliation and respect of their cultural heritage, much of this hope had been driven by Indigenous and white Australians, both prominent and ordinary Australians, who were committed to reconciliation. A powerfully symbolic expression of this will of the people occurred when between 200,000 to 250,000 Sydney-siders walked across the Harbour Bridge in the year 2000 in support of reconciliation and in protest of the prime minister of the time who stubbornly refused to apologize.

Preceding any political will, but reflecting an opposition to the dominant ideology of discrimination which has always been there, it is poets, artists, musicians who have been the spiritual bridge, continuously reaching out to raise awareness for the cause of justice through their artistic expression. I turn now to the two projects in which these strivings towards solidarity between two peoples are being expressed through their making of music together.

Ngukkar Musicians and The Australian Art Orchestra— *Crossing Roper Bar*

The Roper River flows from Mataranka, 100 kilometers south of Katherine and through the land of the Mangarayi and the Yumnman people. Before reaching the Gulf of Carpentaria it passes the town Ngukkar, which is located in the isolated region of Arnhem Land in the Northern Territory. For periods during the wet season Ngukurr is cut off completely and at other times only reachable at Roper Bar. This region and town, which brings together communities from outlying areas, is affected, like so many others, by the contemporary plight of Indigenous communities as described by Khan, and is subject to the intervention.

The musical heritage of Arnhem Land is one of the oldest on the planet, making it an ideal place to learn about traditional Indigenous music. But as the social system of kinship and respect for elders has continued to disintegrate, the Manikay (songs and song cycles) are being lost, and there is ongoing decline in "Bunggal" (ceremonies). Aaron Corn describes the nature of the Manikay:

> Manikay are typically performed in epic series of short songs. Each individual song ebbs into being with a gently hummed introduction, builds in intensity with the entry of the accompanying bilma [clap sticks] and yidaki [didjeridu], and flows out of being with a return to unaccompanied voice. This ebb-and-flow creates a natural sense of tension and release, just like breathing in and out or the lapping of the tide. Songs at the beginning of a Manikay series typically start slowly, and intensity builds as faster and faster songs are gradually introduced with greater frequency.[21]

It is feared by community elders as well as those who have an appreciation of the significance of the cultural artifacts of this region, as community infrastructure breaks down beyond a certain point—that the pride and dignity in performing traditional cultural practices will be in danger of being lost altogether. Whereas hip-hop, reggae and rock music have been used to engage a marginalized younger generation, a renewed interest and pride is being fostered in the preservation of traditional music as a result of the collaboration with these accomplished jazz musicians—giving respect and new voice to a spiritual ancestry dating back 40,000 years.

The Australian Art Orchestra (AAO) is an ensemble of twenty improvising musicians from around Australia. Since forming in 1994, they have brought diverse individual expressions together for musical projects with the aim of creating opportunities for "free and open exchange of musical and dramatic ideas between different cultures and traditions."[22] Paul Grabowsky, its musical director, states the belief which drives its existence, and which resonates with the theme of music for a global consciousness of solidarity:

> Music is a language which establishes and builds connections between people, whether as individuals, societies, cultures or as nations.[23]

Crossing Roper Bar is an ongoing collaboration between the AAO and Indigenous musicians from Ngukurr. The project's title is a metaphor for a musical dialogue aimed at bridging the gap between two cultures through an interchange of learning about each other's musical traditions. Also, it symbolizes the desire for reconciliation within the context of seemingly impassable social, economic and political divides. Its aims are described as follows:

> *Crossing Roper Bar* is a collaboration based on an equal exchange of knowledge through a dialogue centered on music. It also soon came to extend to social interconnectedness as ways of organizing how to work together became clearer. An important part of *Crossing Roper Bar* is that the crossing is both ways and exchange visits between Ngukkur and Melbourne are a feature of the project.[24]

As it states above, the project is not only limited to performance. Social interconnectedness is an emphasis and exchanges "both ways" are integral components of the project. This has involved members of the AAO visiting Ngukkur to learn about the traditional Manikay and give workshops on jazz and contemporary improvised music. A question from an elder to one of the participants on the first visit was, "Are you coming back?" The question implies the desire for ongoing commitment, but it can also be read as an expression of weariness toward "flash in the pan" policies to fix the "aboriginal problem" that have been imposed so often (and so blatantly in the case of the intervention) with little consultation or authentic interchange. And indeed, this project has continued from its inception in 2004, with ongoing regional touring and cultural exchanges held in Melbourne and Ngukkar.

The public performances of *Crossing Roper Bar* begin with a traditional welcome followed by a series of Manikay by traditionally dressed Ngukkar musicians who have grown up learning the stories, song and dance from community elders. The AAO musicians then begin to accompany, layering the traditional music with improvised sounds characteristic of jazz on keyboard, saxophone, bass, and percussion. When she was alive, Ruby Hunter (see above) would perform original songs, relating her experiences of being homeless, for example in *Down City Streets*, and her childhood playing on the riverbeds of the river Murray Darling, captured in the catchy tune *Daisy Chains, String Games and Knucklebones*. Then would come an improvised jazz instrumental *Hot Tin Roof* leading into the finale. The audiences are engaged in clapping to a rhythm driven by the didjeridu and all the collaborating musicians join a finale that fuses Indigenous traditional, jazz and contemporary improvisation in a unique interchange of musical ideas.

Reviews of such performances highlight the caliber of the project as being "not a superficial fusion of two musical cultures, but the beginnings of a mutually respectful and heartfelt understanding."[25] Kelly Curran asks in her review:

> So, how does one rate the success of such an adventurous project—in the process, the result, or both? Certainly, each musician has learnt a great deal from others, and gaps have been bridged. Audiences from Darwin to Perth, and in many remote places in between, have been exposed not only to an interesting mix of musical styles, but have witnessed an ancient and unique musical culture.[26]

From ethno-musicologists come the following insights into the unique nature of this project, Aaron Corn noting that:

> It is difficult to comprehend how only nine musicians can create such an effect. But again, this is the beauty of the Manikay tradition, which weaves individual lines into a unified whole creating one voice made of many that seems to dissolve the shroud of reality itself. Here, there is no complacency to simply accompany the Wagilak Manikay with a conventional progression of chords, to insist that it conforms to Western ideals of tuning and timing. Nor is there any musical apartheid where the Wagilak and the AAO take turns to play their respective bits because of some assumed incompatibility. Through deep listening, they have cracked each other's codes to create a work that gels musically at a deep structural level.[27]

Also saying:

> Let's put it this way, with my music hat on, as a person with a PhD in music, these people have achieved something that no Australian composer has ever achieved be-

fore; they have never achieved a real collaboration where two groups of people with two musical backgrounds get together and really collaborate other than the normal ripping off and recorded material that goes on.[28]

And from Adrian Walter:

What really impressed me is the organic way it's happening. There's no preconceived idea about what's got to come out of it; just letting the whole thing develop. I notice they are very gentle the way they were making themselves a delicate texture; they weren't dominating, just letting themselves supply a line within the music which is a very nice thing to see.[29]

The approach of this project supports the notion of a dialogue through music as a powerful creative force for solidarity. It celebrates cultural differences, and the diversity and identity of the performers, as well as social interconnectedness in the community. These are all developed through an equal exchange of learning from each tradition of Indigenous and jazz music and—very importantly, as Corn highlights, deep listening. In stark contrast to the glossing over of cultural identity and lack of consultation characterizing the intervention, this project has not only created a cultural link with the past but also opened up possibilities for creative paths forward. A positive outcome of the interaction of this project is that young people in the Ngukkar community have become interested in the musical instruments of Jazz-brass and other acoustic instruments. Rock music instruments, relying as they do upon heavy amplifying equipment that is not easily transportable, often break down, and becomes neglected and worn by red-earth dust. This awareness of jazz as an intricate musical form is also providing a possibility of improving skills and musical vocabulary that is reigniting appreciation of their own traditional music. As Adrian Walter says:

the traditional music is about eight rungs higher up the ladder than the popular music most of the (local) bands are playing.

Importantly, engaging in an *equal* exchange of learning, and the ongoing commitment by the AAO and the people of Ngukkar, has created hope that the precious cultural artifacts of traditional music of this region will not be lost. A significant part of Australia's heritage will be preserved for future generations. With this crossing over of cultures both ways, a truly unique cultural expression of two musical traditions, built on respecting each other's cultural identity, has great potential to bring to the fore a consciousness of a common shared humanity.

The second project is similarly compelling in its celebration of what can be shared and in the rebuilding of hope.

The Black Arm Band—*Murandak* and *The Hidden Republic*

The Black Arm Band chronicles the journey of contemporary Indigenous music. Backed by a large jazz orchestra, its members are black and white Australian musicians. High profile Indigenous musicians include Archie Roach, Ruby Hunter (1956-2010), Rachel Maza Long, Kev Carmody and Lou Bennett. White musicians who collaborated on this project, such as Shane Howard and Paul Kelly, have supported the cause of Indigenous music and have produced iconic songs raising awareness of the lack of human rights experienced by Indigenous Australians. The mission of the Black Arm Band is stated as:

> to perform, promote and celebrate contemporary Australian indigenous music to the highest possible professional standard as a symbol of resilience and hope in the spirit and action of reconciliation. The long-term vision for the Black Arm Band is as an ongoing organized presence.[30]

The Black Arm Band has put together two large projects, *Murundak* and *The Hidden Republic*; both have been showcased at large festivals and have toured in regional areas.

Murundak was premiered at the Melbourne Arts Festival in 2006. A record of the last thirty years of Indigenous music, it consists of a weaving together of three decades of protest songs of Indigenous Australian's struggle for rights—land, human, political, social and cultural. Likening these to the songs of the civil rights movement in the United States, a review stated that "in spite of a shared orientation towards political struggle, this galaxy of stars and styles was like listening to a gathering of Baez, Dylan, Judy Collins, Eric Clapton and Odetta... an 11-piece band... as loud and brassy as Stan Kenton's '40s ensemble."[31] *Murundak* is described as a "long story without an end. A tale of guitars and dusty roads, of struggle and identity, sweat and blood and more guitars, it's a yarn we can't possibly tell in its entirety."[32]

Whereas *Murundak* focuses on the past, the struggles and the protest, *The Hidden Republic* turns towards the future in a concert themed around a renewed hope for healing the past in a post-apology Australia. *The Hidden Republic* opened the 2010 Sydney Festival to an enthusiastically receptive crowd of over 100,000 people. As in *Murundak*, the lineup includes prominent Indigenous singers accompanied by both a classical orchestra as well as a jazz section with approximately 40 musicians in total. In this case, the largesse of the musical accompanists and collaboration of contemporary, classical and jazz formed a dynamic concert experience reminiscent of the big-band era of jazz. Jimmy Little, one of the first Indigenous singers who rose to fame in the 1950s with a popular song, "The Royal Telephone" began the performance by reading from Oodgeroo Noonuccal's poem "Song of Hope." A pivotal poem written at the time of the struggle for Indigenous suffrage in the 1960s, the first stanza reads:

> Look up my people,
> The dawn is breaking,
> The world is waking,
> To a new bright day,
> When none defame us,
> Nor color shame us,
> Nor sneer dismay.[33]

Throughout the piece, segments of this poem constitute a thread that sews together the theme of hope and a movement toward a bright future. This is whilst urging the need for healing by acknowledging, but not holding on to, the sorrow of the past. And although it does not ignore these painful experiences in its repertoire, the show is both energetic and poignant. It moves between powerful anthems and songs highlighting the resilience and unbroken spirit of the men and women integral to the story of Indigenous struggle, with its themes of embracing hope, healing and the need for reconciliation for future generations.

A compelling component of the program is the inclusion of dynamic Indigenous women singers, including the all female group the Tiddas. Lou Bennett of the Tiddas has described writing *Inside my kitchen*, of which part of the songline is; "come inside into my kitchen and I will listen." It was after her partner of the time had a psychotic episode and she goes on to say: "We created many of our songs around the kitchen table together."[34] The late Ruby Hunter sang "Ngarrindjeri Woman" in "The Hidden Republic"; this was a song about being proud to be an Indigenous woman. The pain of women's experience when their children were taken away, (to become the "stolen generation" described above), is captured in *Lighthouse*, written by Archie Roach. It tells of the trauma of two mothers—one white adopting mother and one black birth mother—of a young male who was brutally murdered in a racist attack in Perth in 1992.

The themes of anthems calling for social justice for Indigenous people can be perceived from their titles; "Solid Rock," "Dead Heart" and "Blackfella/Whitefella"—this song described by Hutchinson as the ultimate song of reconciliation.

In the lead-up to the finale there is an outstanding improvised didjeridu performance by world-renowned Indigenous artist, Mark Atkins. The finale is the song "Treaty," arguably the most famous anthem of protest, which was originally composed by Yothu Yindi in collaboration with Paul Kelly and Midnight Oil[35] after yet another unrealized promise. This promise made in 1988, the year in which the bicentenary was celebrated by Australia, by the prime minister of the time was to enter a treaty with Indigenous Australians by 1990. A remixed version of the song performed by Yothu Yindi became a number one hit on the Australian charts in 1992.

In summary, I invoke Hutchinson's words in which she endeavors to capture the spirit of hope within this project:

> Once again it is possible to believe that past wounds can be healed. That forgiveness and understanding is achievable. That we be the kind of country we all want to live in. A country that acknowledges it has a proud black heart and a proud black history. That we can, with open hearts, embrace a meeting of old way and new way, a caring way, to find a way forward for us all.[36]

Both *Maranduk* and *The Hidden Republic* express the spirit of resilience, the long struggle for recognition of their cultural identity linked to the land, and the desire for reconciliation with "the other country" by Indigenous people. Reviews of the *Black Arm Band* performances include comments on the contribution this project makes in terms of healing and solidarity:

> Audiences received (the band) so well that you know that something healed, it just did.[37]

And (that it is):

> an uplifting experience that said more about black and white solidarity than a million parliamentary speeches.[38]

It is significant that some of the songs of hope in this repertoire have been written in collaboration with well-established white Australian artists. Hutchinson points out that these partnerships have often preceded political attention to Indigenous issues. These include "From little things big things grow," a song of hope and perseverance in the long, painfully slow process leading up to the Mabo decision.[39] Acknowledging the past while calling for a hopeful future has been achieved once again through a unique collaboration of musicians performing jazz and Indigenous contemporary music. These performances have paved the way for a consciousness of solidarity by raising awareness and offering the possibility of healing as a starting point for reconciliation.

As the Indigenous musician Archie Roach says of his work in this project:

> The Black Arm Band reminds me of the long struggle and the long journey we've been on. 30 years ago we were marching for justice down the city streets, but now we're telling our stories in the concert halls.[40]

The final passage of Oodgeroo of the tribe Noonuccal read by Jimmy Little poignantly expresses the juxtaposition of remembering the sorrow of the past while moving forward from it by creating a hopeful future:

> To our father's fathers
> The pain, the sorrow;
> To our children's children
> The glad tomorrow.[41]

Music for Envisioning a Culture of Peace

These innovative projects highlight the role of music as a force for creating a universal consciousness of solidarity. But such projects are rare. Marcus Westbury, a critic of the current and classical music-oriented distribution of arts funding, calls for a shift in the debate: "Rather than ask how to make the Australian community more interested in opera, we should perhaps ask the unaskable about the cultural traditions Australians actually value and how we might best support and resource them."[42]

In systemizing violence to include cultural violence, Galtung asks us to try to envision the opposite—"cultural peace": "meaning aspects of a culture that serve to justify and legitimize direct peace and structural peace."[43] In Australia a vision of cultural peace needs to include a healing of past wounds wrought by systemic violence and paternalistic policies endlessly heaped on Indigenous Australians since white settlement. Although progress has been made, and the intervention may turn out to be a strange and regressive moment, soon to pass, healing would seem to begin with celebrating both cultural difference and shared humanity. This seems to be what is possible to express in music, for the best musicianship requires deep listening, and through collaborative projects such as the ones described here, Indigenous musicians have been enabled, in Roach's words, "to take their struggle from the street to the concert halls."

These two projects have in different ways highlighted the voices of Indigenous culture, both in its traditional and contemporary expression, supported by the improvising sounds of jazz. Through musical interaction there are new and old stories being told and an audience is listening—a crucial aspect of healing Australia's dark past and of creating a catalyst for a consciousness of solidarity that, if successful, may be global in its implications.

Notes

1. Dead heart is a phrase coined by early twentieth century explorer Cecil Madigan, referring to early European exploration into Australia's interior, which was regarded as a desolate and empty space.
2. Shane Howard, songwriter and artist, Melbourne International Arts Festival Program for The Black Arm Band, (2008) Hidden Republic performance.
3. Indigenous is the preferred and more accepted term used as opposed to Aboriginal in reference to the original inhabitants of Australia. It is become an accepted practice to capitalize when referring to Indigenous Australians as a mark of respect.
4. *Mabo v. Queensland.* 1992. A landmark decision by the High Court of Australia to overturn the doctrine of Terra Nullius, which was the premise of European settlement and to recognize native title to land can continue to exist.
5. Mackay, Hugh. Introduction to Horne, D. (2008). *The Lucky Country.* Penguin Modern Classics, Australia.
6. Hutchison, Tracee. 2008. An Essay by Tracee Hutchison to accompany The Black Arm Band's "Hidden Republic."
7. Refers to the concept of welfare dependency, which some Indigenous leaders such as Noel Pearson argue, rather than contributing to improving conditions, is continuing the cycle of dependency.
8. Northern Territory Government Inquiry into the Protection of Aboriginal Children from Child Sex Abuse (2007) The Little Children are Sacred.
9. Northern Territory Government Inquiry into the Protection of Aboriginal Children from Child Sex Abuse (2007) The Little Children are Sacred.
10. Streich, Michel. 2009. "Does International Law Matter on Remote Communities?" Accessed: January 8, 2010 from http://newmatilda.com/2009/09/21/.
11. Altman, Jon. 2007. The Howard Government's Northern Territory Intervention: Are Neo-Paternalism and Indigenous Development Compatible? Centre for Aboriginal Economic Policy Research, Topical Issue No. 16/2007.
12. Khan, Irene. 2009. "Money won't fix poverty," The Age, 23 November; 13. Quoting from Address to National Press Gallery in Canberra.
13. Ibid.
14. Ibid.
15. Ibid.
16. Ibid.
17. Galtung, Johan. 1990. "Cultural Violence," *Journal of Peace Research*, Vol. 27, No. 3; 291.
18. Fred Hollows Foundation (2004) Annual Report. Accessed, January 6, 2010 from www.hollows.org.au.
19. Accessed: January 19, 2010 from http//www.aao.com.au/people/musicians/bio/ruby-hunter/?tag_phrase=guest%20artists.
20. Hutchinson, T. op. cit.; 1.
21. Corn, Aaron. "A Work of Rare Integrity." Accessed: January 19, 2010 from http://aao.com.au/projects/programs/review/crossing-roper-bar/2/.
22. Grabowsky, Paul, The Australian Art Orchestra official website. Accessed: January 19, 2010 from http://aao.com.au/about.
23. Ibid. Accessed: January 19, 2010 from http://aao.com.au/projects/programs/program/into-the-fire.

24. The Australian Art Orchestra "Crossing Roper Bar-An Introduction." Accessed: January 19, 2010 from http://aao.com.au/projects/programs/review/crossing-roper-bar/6/.
25. Nicholas, Jessica. 2007. "Earth, Wind and Song Cycles Performing in Concert." The Age, 22 March.
26. Curran, Kelly. 2008. "Very Old Meets Very New in Quest for Mutual Understanding," 25 September. Accessed: January 19, 2010 from www.resonatemagazine. com.au.
27. Corn, Aaron. A Work of Rare Integrity. Accessed: January 19, 2010 from http://aao. com.au/projects/programs/review/crossing-roperbar/6.
28. Corn, Aaron. ibid.
29. Walter, Adrian. The Australian Art Orchestra "Crossing Roper Bar—An Introduction." Accessed: January 1, 2010 from http://aao.com.au/projects/programs/review/crossing-roper-bar/6/.
30. Accessed: January 6, 2010 from http://www.blackarmband.com.au/about-the-black-arm-band.
31. Slaven, John. 2006. "Spirited fold a call to arms," 30 October. Accessed: January 6, 2010 from http://www.theage.com.au/news/music/.
32. Accessed: January 6, 2010 from http://www.blackarmband.com.au/about-murundak.
33. Oodgeroo of the tribe Noonuccal, from My People, reproduced in the Melbourne International Arts Festival Program for The Black Arm Band, (2008) Hidden Republic show.
34. Op.cit Melbourne International Arts Festival Program for The Black Arm Band, Hidden Republic show.
35. Paul Kelly is a popular singer/songwriter and Midnight Oil is a band that who wrote many protest songs throughout the 1980s and 1990s. The lead singer, Peter Garrett, is now Minister for Environment Protection, Heritage and the Arts.
36. Huthinson, Tracee. 2008. op. cit.
37. Coslovich, Gabriella. 2006. "Prizes and party make for fitting end to arts festival." The Age, 30 Oct.
38. Quoted from http://www.blackarmband.com.au/about-the-black-arm-band, accessed: January 6, 2010.
39. Op cit. Mabo v. Queensland (1992).
40. Quoted from http://www.blackarmband.com.au/about-the-black-arm-band, accessed: January 6, 2010.
41. Oodgeroo of the tribe Noonuccal, op. cit.
42. Westbury, Marcus. The Age, 23 November 2009; 23.
43. Galtung, Johan. op cit.; 291.

References

Altman, Jon C. 2007. "The Howard Government's Northern Territory Intervention: Are Neo-Paternalism and Indigenous Development Compatible?" Centre for Aboriginal Economic Policy Research," Topical Issue No. 16/2007.

Australian Art Orchestra. Accessed: January 19, 2010 from http//www.aao.com.au.

Black Arm Band. Accessed: January 6, 2010 from http://www.blackarmband.com.au/about-the-black-arm-band.

Corn, Aaron. "A Work of Rare Integrity." Accessed: January 19, 2010 from http://aao.com.au/projects/programs/review/crossing-roper-bar/2/.

Coslovich, Gabriella. 2006. "Prizes and party make for fitting end to arts festival." *The Age*, 30 Oct. Accessed: January 6, 2010 from http://newsstore.theage.com.au/apps/

viewDocument.ac?page=1&sy=age&kw=Coslovich&pb=all_ffx&dt=enterRange&
dr=5years&sd=1%2F1%2F2006&ed=1%2F12%2F2006&so=relevance&sf=text&
sf=author&sf=headline&rc=10&rm=200&sp=adv&clsPage=1&docID=AGE0610
30F84T53F27P.

Curran, Kelly. 2008. "Very Old Meets Very New in Quest for Mutual Understanding"
Accessed: January 19, 2010 from www.resonatemagazine.com.au, 25 September.

Fred Hollows Foundation. 2004. Annual Report. Accessed: January 19, 2010 from www.
hollows.org.au.

Galtung, Johan. 1990 "Cultural Violence," *Journal of Peace Research*, Vol. 27, No. 3;
291.

Grabowsky, Paul. 2010 Australian Art Orchestra. Accessed: January 19, 2010 from
http//www.aao.com.au.

High Court of Australia. *Mabo v. Queensland* (1992).

Howard, Shane. 2008. Melbourne International Arts Festival Program for the Black Arm
Band Hidden Republic Performance.

Hutchison, Tracee. 2008. An Essay by Tracee Hutchison to Accompany The Black Arm
Band's Hidden Republic.

Khan, Irene. 2009. "Money won't fix poverty," *The Age*, 23 November; 13.

Mackay, H. 2008. Introduction to Horne, D, The Lucky Country Penguin Modern Classics, Australia.

Melbourne International Arts Festival Program for The Black Arm Band. (2008). Hidden Republic show.

Nicholas, Jessica. 2007. "Earth, Wind and Song Cycles Performing in Concert." *The
Age*, 22 March.

Northern Territory Government Inquiry into the Protection of Aboriginal Children from
Child Sex Abuse (2007). The Little Children are Sacred.

Oodgeroo of the tribe Noonuccal, excerpt from the poem My People, reproduced in
the Melbourne International Arts Festival Program for The Black Arm Band, 2008.
Hidden Republic show.

Roach, Archie. Accessed: January 6, 2010 from http://www.blackarmband.com.au/about-
the-black-arm-band.

Slaven, John. 2006. "Spirited fold a call to arms." Accessed: January 6, 2010 from
http://www.theage.com.au/news/music/30 October.

Streich, Michel. 2009. "Does International Law Matter on Remote Communities?" Accessed: January 8, 2010 from http://newmatilda.com/2009/09/21/.

Walter, Aaron. The Australian Art Orchestra "Crossing Roper Bar—An Introduction."
Accessed: January 19, 2010 from http://aao.com.au/projects/programs/review/cross-
ing-roper-bar/6/.

Westbury, Marcus. 2009. "Australia is long overdue for a serious discussion about cultural
priorities" *The Age*, 23 November. Accessed January 6, 2010 from http://newstore.
theage.com.au/apps/viewDocument.ac?page=1.

Music and Human Rights: Towards a Paradoxical Approach

María Elisa Pinto García

Introduction

A growing corpus of international experiences has shown the intersection between the arts and peacebuilding; nevertheless, within the academic literature, there is not a wide range of research on arts-based peacebuilding[1] or, more specifically, on the potential links between the arts and human rights. Ranging from Picasso and his painting "Guernica"—which portrayed one of the bombings of the Spanish civil war—to contemporary nonprofit organizations such as "Artists For Human Rights" and "Art for Humanity," which bring together multiple artists who have a special interest in the issues of peace and human rights,[2] there are various examples that illustrate how art can be used to raise human rights awareness, to transform the audience view regarding human rights violations and, in general, to propagate and to promote the respect of human rights. These endeavors can be seen as the "traditional" or most common uses of art within the human rights field. However, are there alternative paths that could converge in the fruitful intersection between human rights and art?

In this chapter I will argue that there are indeed alternative experiences that stand out, not only because the outcome of the work connects to the field of human rights, but also because the actors involved in the process of production are individuals implicated in past abuses of human rights. To support this argument, the chapter focuses on the link between music and historical memory of human rights abuse by presenting some cases in Colombia that involve persons who recently were either victims or perpetrators of human rights violations in the internal armed conflict of that country.

Colombia has faced an intense violent conflict since the 1980s, with the presence of guerrillas, paramilitary groups, drug dealers and other criminal mafias; all of them have committed serious violations of human rights. In 2003, after the signature of the "Santa Fe de Ralito Agreement,"[3] the Colombian government started a Disarmament, Demobilization and Reintegration process (DDR) with the paramilitary groups, and from 2005, the "Justice and Peace Law" has been acting as the main legal framework for transitional justice in the country. The general objectives of these processes are to reintegrate demobilized ex-combatants of illegal armed groups—paramilitary and guerrilla groups—back into civilian life, and to fulfill the victims' rights to know the truth, to find justice, and to be awarded reparations. It is in this context that victims and perpetrators have used lyrics set to music as a storytelling tool to describe past abuses of human rights and the emotions related to them, and also to express their thoughts about the current DDR process and what will come next in the future.

In his book "Preparing for Peace: Conflict Transformation across Cultures," John Paul Lederach suggests that peacemaking may be understood as containing values which tend to be in opposition to each other, what he terms as "paradoxical values" (Lederach 1995, 19).[4] He suggests here "at least" four such paradoxes, one of which is what he calls *The Gandhi Dilemma: The Paradox of Process and Outcome*. Here, there is a tension between the crucial importance of taking real care of the *process* of mediation in conflict, and a corresponding but nevertheless simultaneously paradoxical imperative to concentrate on *outcome*.[5] Each goal dictates a different course of action, and these may in fact be, at least at first view, incompatible. In those initiatives in Colombia where music is seen as integral, I suggest that there may be found such a "paradox," where the message and the positive effects, of the lyrics themselves, can be understood as the *outcome* of these initiatives, while the activity of people, earlier involved in the conflict, may be understood as constituting the *process* taking place in the making and performing of the songs.

In the first section, I will expand on the outlined paradox of process and outcome, articulating the paradox in reference to the nature of peacebuilding in general, and to the historical memory of human rights abuse in particular. In the second section, some cases of victims of human rights violations using music are outlined. In the third section, the project *Canta conmigo por la reintegración*[6] is analyzed, and ex-combatants' experiences with music are illustrated. I conclude with the main findings, in order to gain an insight into the nature of paradoxical but also fruitful intersections of music and human rights.

Theoretical Framework: The Paradox of Process and Outcome

Peacebuilding is a complex venture which takes place in different levels and instances and often implies the promotion of opposite or even exclusive values. This is the reason why John Paul Lederach suggests the use of *paradoxes* to describe the key values of peacemaking and the complex transformation processes inherent to peacebuilding. Paradox is defined as "a statement that seems impossible because it contains two opposing ideas that are both true."[7] Lederach explains that this apparent irreconcilable opposition "emerges from a tendency to understand contrary ideas in an either/or frame of reference in which one must be chosen over the other (...) A paradoxical approach suggests the energy of the ideas is enhanced if they are held together, like two sides of the coin."[8] Moreover, he goes further in the definition by highlighting its etymological root, where the Greek word *para* refers to "something that is outside or beyond common belief" and "suggests that truth lies in but also beyond what is initially perceived (...) Paradox holds together seemingly contradictory truths in order to locate a greater truth."[9]

Lederach suggests transcending the tendency in peacebuilding to judge apparently contradictory ideas as being exclusive. As described, he proposes, rather, moving to a *paradoxical approach* which holds them together and offers an account that goes constructively beyond the expected in four areas: these are *the paradox of personal and systemic change*, *the paradox of justice and mercy*, *the paradox of empowerment and interdependence*, and finally, *the paradox of process and outcome*. It is this last example that indicates the importance of stressing *both* the end *and* the means in transformative peacebuilding.

Lederach explains that in conflict and post-conflict situations the process is often overlooked. Due to the need of generating prompt responses to the inherent problems of peacebuilding scenarios, too little attention may be given to the way issues are to be approached or implemented.[10] On the other hand, it may be the outcome that is overlooked. For instance, critics of mediation argue that it gives too much emphasis to the methodology of the process, with mediators tending to place the final outcome in the background.[11] Nevertheless, the general idea of using paradoxes is precisely to *avoid* this dualistic vision. By focusing attention both on the results and on the means and processes to attain them, Lederach suggests that the outcome will not only be enhanced but that these therefore "paradoxical" results will go constructively beyond the "common belief" referred to above.

I argue here that the paradox of process and outcome may be applied to historical memory efforts in societies affected by widespread or systematic human rights abuse. Historical memory is an area that has developed in parallel with transitional justice, which is defined by the International Center for Transitional Justice as justice adapted to societies transforming themselves after a period of pervasive human rights abuse.[12] Given the complexity of this task, transitional justice incorporates diverse "basic approaches" including criminal prosecutions, truth commissions, and memorialization efforts, among others.[13] To show how we might apply the concept of this paradox, I am looking here at those approaches to historical memory, within Colombia, which are intended both to preserve public memory of past human right abuse, and to raise moral consciousness about this abuse through a collective representation and reconstruction of the past.[14]

Predominant initiatives include museums, public memorials, and monuments which consist of physical spaces that may be "valuable components of a comprehensive transitional justice approach by helping to create a healthy and democratic dialogue about the past; promote healing and reconciliation; and strengthen historical memory about past atrocities."[15] In the case of Colombia, the "Center of Memory, Peace and Reconciliation" (under construction at the time of writing, July 2010) is the most remarkable example. It seeks to commemorate the victims of the Colombian internal conflict through a physical and virtual center, as well as to promote a culture of peace and respect of human rights.[16]

However, there are some cases where the inherent process of these initiatives may have worked counter to the desired outcome. For instance, in the process of construction of the Peace Memorial Park at Hiroshima, opened to the public in 1954, the 20,000 Korean victims were not acknowledged. It was not until 1970 that the *Cenotaph for Korean Victims* was erected to honor both Korean victims and survivors. Although the initial outcome of the construction of the Peace Memorial Park was to commemorate all victims of the bomb and promote world peace, ignoring Korean victims in the process might in fact have exacerbated the existing tensions between the Korean and the Japanese populations. The plaque of the Korean cenotaph reminds the reader how Koreans were "brought to misery through force" in the time of war, and states: "We pray of course for the solace of those lost souls longing for their homeland, but killed in foreign soil. However, we also pray that the

plight of Korean survivors, poorly understood even today, will emerge
into public awareness and that reasonable assistance for these survivors
will be provided immediately." This demonstrates the fundamental need
to understand process and outcome in dialectic relationship, rather than
privileging one over the other.

Music has played an important role in the historical memory of conflict. Ana María Ochoa, director of the Center for Ethnomusicology at
Columbia University, affirms that music has significantly contributed
to the building of historical memory in some wars of Central America,
Africa, and the countries of the former Yugoslavia.[17] Hip-hop music and
the "corridos" in Mexico constitute a good example of how music may
be an important storytelling tool in narrating events through long and
meaningful lyrics.[18]

As in the processes and outcomes of designing memorials and museums, as described above, some contradictions may also emerge between
the processes and outcomes of composing human rights related songs.
For instance, if the outcome of the song is to be the ultimate inculcation
of respect for human rights within the individuals who have committed
crimes, cultural factors as language, social condition and musical taste
should be taken into account during the process, so that the message
actually succeeds in getting through to the desired audience. However,
when these factors are overlooked, the music cannot reach this public
and so the original outcome is not achieved. That may happen with some
musicians in Colombia who have become sensitive to human rights issues but unfortunately, have not taken into account the musical taste,
type of language and general conditions of the desired audience during
the process of composition.

This is why this chapter focuses upon musical projects where the process of writing and composing songs directly involves the participation of
victims and perpetrators of human rights abuse. This emphasis on the process
not only facilitates the positive effect of its final outcome, but also can give rise
to other constructive developments that will be presented in some case studies
in Colombia in the following section. By studying these cases, significant
and paradoxical results may be found that might in turn be employed
as useful inputs in the extremely difficult task of rebuilding trust and
relationships in a society that has faced a protracted armed conflict.

The Music of the Victims

The Atlantic and Pacific coast regions of Colombia are well known
for their musical tradition. Outstanding Colombian rhythms like *cumbia*,

vallenato, paseo, porro, puya, and *currulao* originate in these areas, where the African descendants of the slave communities profoundly influenced the creation and fusion of music.[19] Yet these regions have also been extremely affected by the internal conflict. Being strategic zones to establish connections with Pacific and Atlantic consumer countries of narcotic drugs, both regions have faced the presence of drug dealers, paramilitary groups and guerrillas whose main source of finance is the illegal business of drug trafficking.[20]

In addition, both areas relied on a partial presence of the State, which allowed the guerrilla and paramilitary groups to exert control over the territory, as well as to fight against each other to maintain or increase that territorial control.[21] The methods to exert this power included most of the internationally catalogued "crimes against humanity" and "war crimes" (Rome Statute of the International Criminal Court, Article 7 and Article 8), such as murder, extermination, inhuman treatment, rape, taking of hostages, and systematic persecution against community leaders and politicians.[22]

In the context of the transitional justice process mentioned above—which has mainly involved ex-combatants of the demobilized paramilitary groups—some victims who still live in these regions, or who were displaced from the area, have composed an important collection of songs related to past abuses of human rights. The compilation of these works has been mostly carried out by the "Historical Memory Group" under the "National Commission on Reparation and Reconciliation" in Colombia, an organism created by the "Justice and Peace Law" which undertakes the task of historical memory reconstruction.[23]

There have been two violent tragedies that are notable for having generated the major number of songs composed by the victims.[24] The first one is the three-day-long massacre of El Salado from February 16th to February 19th in 2000; this genocide was the largest slaughter committed by the paramilitary groups in Colombian history, according to the Public Prosecutor Office. In this small town located in Bolivar (on the Atlantic Coast) more than 100 persons were tortured, raped, decapitated, and assassinated in terrible ways, while the perpetrators drank liquor looted from the stores and played loudly *vallenato* music—a popular rhythm in the region.[25]

The second tragedy was the Bojayá massacre. In this small town located in Chocó (a Colombian province on the Pacific coast), civilians were trapped in crossfire between the FARC-EP guerrilla—*Fuerzas Armadas Revolucionarias de Colombia-Ejército del Pueblo*[26]—and the

AUC paramilitary group—*Autodefensas Unidas de Colombia.*[27] Although the families fled their homes and ran into the church, FARC-EP members decided to attack the structure with an improvised homemade bomb assembled with gas cylinders parts (known in Spanish as *pipeta* or *cilindro bomba*), causing the death of 119 civilians on May 2, 2002.

In more recent times, the DDR process with the paramilitary groups and the legal framework given by the "Justice and Reparation Law" have given the victims a sense of security in being able to express their thoughts and feelings. Within this context, those victims have used different expressive means, including musical forms and activities to narrate violations of human rights committed in the past. A special report of the Colombian magazine *Cambio* illustrated some of these experiences, taking as an example the case of Noel Palacios, known in the artistic world as *Javimán,* a survivor of the Bojayá massacre, who reconstructs the memory of the tragedy through a fusion of *champeta* (a Caribbean dance music) and rap in his song named *Lo Ocurrido en Bojayá.*[28] His song narrates:

> It was 6 in the morning buddy/ when a very serious case happened/ it was the sound of a rifle hu! it was an AK/ it was the sound of a gun and the *paras*[29] responded/ they came to Bojaya and the thing got even worse/the shooting started its spinning and the scared people had the idea to run to the church/since they were safe there/ since nothing would happen to them there/ since it was God's place/ the Lord would help them/ The FARC threw the *pipeta* when they least expected it/ it drop right into the church/ending many lives.[30]

The initiative of *Javimán* has not been a unique case. In the case of the tragedy of Bojayá, the victims have composed more than 100 musical pieces, including *alabaos, champeta,* reggae and rap rhythms.[31] Similarly, the El Salado massacre has also generated several songs. One example is *Retorno Histórico,*[32] created by the internally displaced woman Darly Cárdenas who composed it not only to honor the memory of the victims and reconstruct what happened, but also to demand a response from the government regarding the still unattended and forgotten town she found when she came back in 2003.[33] One of the fragments of her song, which is a fusion of *puya* and *paseo* rhythms, angrily expresses:

> What I am telling you is genuine reality/ now the people of this town don't even want to come back/ The cars cannot get in, the situation is messed up/ (...) We have no teachers, our kids grow up dumb/ so what are we going to do with this huge discontent?/ Neither a single nurse, nor a social service officer comes to this town/ and then, what is it going to happen with us?/ Now the road is damaged, we are unconnected/ and then, what do you people pretend with this worn-out town?/ I ask the President to bear in mind this town/ this town that has been displaced by that damned people.[34]

Both songs constitute a valuable testimony of serious human rights violation. They raise moral consciousness about these events and offer an important account for the historical memory of the Colombian conflict. On the other hand, and going beyond the meaning and purpose of the lyrics, victims also highlight in the special report of *Cambio* magazine how music may be a cathartic process which gives them another perspective to overcome the pain, forget the hate and start a new life.

For instance, the report illustrates how a young internally displaced musician from Cauca (a Colombian area in the Pacific region) affirms that: "music allows us to reconcile and cling to life. It is not only about entertainment but also a sort of pacific resistance."[35] Likewise, *Javimán* declares: "We sing to forget the hatred, because, as the song of the famous salsa artist Ruben Blades states, 'sing and forget your pain because the one who sings says more and suffers less'."[36]

These inner transformations may be also understood as outcomes generated in the process of writing and composing historical music related to human rights' abuse. In Lederach's terms, the outcome is enhanced when victims are involved in the process of making songs for the historical memory.

The Music of Ex-Combatants

In the case of ex-combatants, the Project of the High Counselor for the Social and Economic Reintegration named "Sing with me for the Reintegration," which took place in 2009, constitutes a very interesting case. The project started with an open call for beneficiaries of the Colombian DDR process (ex-combatants), as well as for members of the communities affected by the violence, who thought they were talented for singing. More than 141 people auditioned. In a process similar to a TV reality show, participants were progressively eliminated by a jury which took the final decision of selecting 12 people, 8 of them former combatants of guerrilla and paramilitary groups, and 4 of them community members.

The selected participants were trained for two months in vocal technique and expression, repertoire and text analysis, interpretation, mise-en-scene, improvisation techniques, composition, choral practice, ear training, performing arts, and the entertainment and creative business. These activities were carried out in a house where all participants received daily training during two months. After its completion, the 12 beneficiaries received a diploma in April 2009 certifying the preparation on "Comprehensive artistic training" with emphasis on vocal technique by the Santiago de Cali University.[37] In addition, they recorded a disc that uses different popular rhythms including *vallenato, ranchera,* and pop music.

Most of the themes deal with happy and unhappy love stories. However, there are two songs referring to the armed conflict that were composed by former combatants of the AUC, Ferley López and Daner David Martínez. López created the song *No Más Violencia,*[38] which briefly narrates how hard it was for his family to live in a context of armed conflict, making a special appeal for the end of violence with a cheerful rhythm:

> How sad it is to live with violence/ in my town only the sound of guns could be heard/ When the guns were shot/ In a corner I began to shiver/ And lots of fear among my brothers and me/ and our parents that did know how to comfort us/ see how sad it is to live what we live today/ in my song I want to demand from you/ no more violence no more violence please, I beg you/ make peace and forget about the guns right now/ let's make today a world of illusion/ I want to come back there, against the fear/ I want to come back to sing and see my hometown happy/ and voices instead of arms I wish they hear in me/ and I wish the violent people listen to my song and say/ peace and love are back again/warrior men listen to my song/ and a cease fire and a better world will come.[39]

Daner David Martínez composed *Saca La Guerra de tu Corazón,*[40] a *vallenato*[41] song with many lyrics expressing acknowledgment of the past mistakes. The words appeal for a new beginning and reconciliation, and also add to memory by expressing how the author joined the armed group. The following is a compilation of different excerpts from his song:

> And I am also the one that found the wrong solution there/ because I felt intimidated, ill-treated and persecuted and I had to defend myself/ and I am aware of the fact that I have made mistakes (…) I sing for war to stop/ because I lived in the middle of it/ and there I understood that/ the problem is not outside if it still lives in inside you/ and this message goes to the one who wants/ to leave now the past and to begin a new life/ I invite you, come! And sing with me here/ and I was able to change my trench for a stage/ and that gun that shared so much time along with me/ I changed it for my guitar which I used to make this song.[42]

These two songs composed by former paramilitary combatants also constitute valuable inputs for the historical memory of the Colombian conflict. Although the events are not described with the same accuracy as the ones of the victims, the songs constitute a testimony of how there is little option for a person who lives in a context of violence to remain outside the conflict. In addition, there is an explicit reference to reconciliation, which in the case of the victims however may have been rather more of an inner process.

As in the process, and going beyond the outcome of the lyrics, the implementation of the project itself constitutes a valuable example of reconciliation, and of the use of music in this. Guerrilla and paramilitary ex-combatants worked together in musical activities with members of communities affected by the conflict. "During the process, they knew each other, they forgave each other and discovered that they could join their voices to transmit the message of hope and reconciliation that Colombia needs for starting to change history."[43]

Conclusions

The musical activities described in this chapter have contributed to peacebuilding for two reasons. Firstly, the lyrics—understood as the outcome—have provided for both groups a storytelling tool to describe past abuses of human rights and the emotions related to them. Secondly, the composition of the music by actors implicated in the conflict—understood as the process—has contributed to acknowledging the pain, getting it acknowledged by others, and also starting to overcome it.

It is difficult to imagine a more paradoxical situation than this sharing of interests and feelings by former victims of violence, and its perpetrators. However, this is the most valuable conclusion of this chapter. By studying the cases presented here in the light of the paradox of outcome and process, we can see that it is possible for victims and past perpetrators of human rights violations in Colombia to learn to find common ground. They have both used music with the same purposes of reconstructing the historical memory, promoting reconciliation and expressing their feelings about the human rights abuses they experienced—as the abusers or as the victims. Similarly, music as a personal experience has enlarged their vision, giving them a prism that has allowed them to view the world through a new lens[44] and to give them a new beginning.

As described above, Lederach conceives "paradoxical" results that might take us outside, or ahead of, what is normally understood to be possible and in this way enable us to "locate a greater truth." Having found common spaces and interests between former abusers and abused not only goes beyond the expected, but also constitutes a valuable tool for rebuilding trust and relationships in a society that has faced a protracted armed conflict.

Finally, the intersection between human rights and art is complex and rich, and offers a large cluster of possibilities. There remain numerous areas for further research and development; these stories can offer convincing cases for both peacebuilding practitioners and theorists, in order to further explore the role of the arts in this field, and perhaps to grant them the place they deserve therein. The dualistic division that might exist between "hard" issues of peacebuilding studies (security, disarmament, justice, etc.) and "soft" issues (aesthetics, trust, compassion, etc.) needs to be transcended through paradoxical approaches.

Notes

1. Shank, Michael, and Schirch, Lisa. 2008. "Strategic Arts-Based Peacebuilding." *Peace & Change Journal*, Vol. 33, Issue 2; 217-242. Accessed: June, 2010 from http://www.michaelshank.net/publications/pcartspeacebuilding.html.
2. Accessed: June, 2010 from http://www.artistsforhumanrights.org/ and from http://www.afh.org.za/.
3. "Santa Fe de Ralito Accord to contribute to peace in Colombia" (Conciliation Resources web site). Accessed: July 15, 2010 from http://www.c-r.org/our-work/accord/colombia/santafederalito-accord.php.
4. In his subsequent work *Building Peace: Sustainable Reconciliation in Divided Societies*, Lederach proposes further paradoxes for reconciliation; these are the paradox of past and future, the paradox of truth and mercy, and the paradox of justice and peace. In Lederach, John Paul. 1997. *Building Peace: Sustainable Reconciliation in Divided Societies*. Washington DC: United States Institute of Peace Press; 20.
5. Lederach, John Paul. 1995. *Preparing for Peace: Conflict Transformation across Cultures*. New York: Syracuse University Press; 19-23.
6. In English, Sing with me for the Reintegration.
7. Definition of paradox in *Longman Dictionary of Contemporary English*, updated edition CD-ROM.
8. Lederach, John Paul. op. cit.; 19.
9. Lederach, John Paul. 2005. *The Moral Imagination. The Art and Soul of Building Peace*. Oxford: Oxford University Press; 36.
10. Lederach, John Paul. 1995. op. cit.
11. Ibid.
12. "What is Transitional Justice?" (International Center for Transitional Justice web site). Accessed: June 10, 2010 from http://www.ictj.org/en/tj/.
13. Ibid.
14. Ibid.
15. Ibid.
16. (Centro de Memoria, Paz y Reconciliación Web site). Accessed: June 10, 2010 from http://www.centromemoria.gov.co/el-centro-de-memoria.
17. "Víctimas del conflicto hacen memoria de sus tragedias al ritmo de alabaos, vallenato y champeta," in *Revista Cambio*, Vol. 855 (November 2009). Accessed: June 10, 2010 from http://www.cambio.com.co/informeespecialcambio/855/AR-TICULO-WEB-NOTA_INTERIOR_CAMBIO-6610747.html.
18. "Cantando la Revolución." Accessed: June 10, 2010 from http://redescolar.ilce.edu.mx/redescolar/act_permanentes/historia/html/cantando_revolucion/revolucion.htm.
19. "Al Son de la Tierra: Músicas Tradicionales de Colombia" (Colombian Minister of Culture website). Accessed: July 10, 2010 from http://www.mincultura.gov.co/recursos_user/documentos/migracion/library/documents/DocNewsNo822D-ocumentNo1049.PDF.

20. For more information about the territorial and economic dynamics of the Colombian armed conflict see Echandia, Camilo, *Dos décadas de Escalamiento del Conflicto Armado Colombiano*, Bogota: Universidad Externado de Colombia, Facultad de Finanzas, Gobierno y Relaciones Internacionales, 2006.
21. Ibid.
22. Diaz, Catalina. 2007. "Colombia's Bid for Justice and Peace." Study "Workshop 5—Lessons from Negotiated Justice Options in South Africa and Colombia," May 2007, International Center for Transitional Justice. Accessed: December 10, 2009 from http://www.humansecuritygateway.com/documents/PJC_Colombia_bidforjusticeandpeace.pdf.
23. "The Group of Historical Memory is a research group whose objective is to elaborate and release a narrative about the Colombian armed conflict in order to identify 'the reasons for the upsurge and evolution of illegal armed groups' (Law 975 of 2005), as well as the different truths and memories of violence, with a differentiated approach and a preference for the suppressed or silenced voice of its victims (…) Given the nature of its mandate, the Historical Memory Group enjoys academic and operational autonomy to perform its task with scientific rigor and veracity." (National Commission on Reparation and Reconciliation web site). Accessed: July 15, 2010 from http://memoriahistorica-cnrr.org.co/archivos/arc_quees/what_is_MH.pdf.
24. "Víctimas del conflicto hacen memoria de sus tragedias al ritmo de alabaos, vallenato y champeta," op. cit.
25. "Más de 100 fueron las personas asesinadas por 'paras' en masacre del Salado, revela la Fiscalía" in *El Tiempo*. Accessed: December 4, 2009 from http://www.eltiempo.com/colombia/justicia_c/2008-06-23/mas-de-100-fueron-las-personas-asesinadas-por-paras-en-masacre-del-salado-revela-la-fiscalia_4341911-1.
26. In English, the Revolutionary Armed Forces of Colombia—People's Army.
27. In English, the United Self-defense Forces of Colombia.
28. In English, What happened in Bojayá.
29. Paras is a coloquial way of naming the paramilitary groups.
30. "Víctimas del conflicto hacen memoria de sus tragedias al ritmo de alabaos, vallenato y champeta," op. cit. (Translation made by the author).
31. Ibid.
32. In English, Historical Return.
33. Ibid.
34. Ibid. (Translation made by the author).
35. Ibid.
36. Ibid.
37. Contreras Fajardo, Lilián, "Integrantes de 'Canta conmigo por la reintegración' se gradúan este sábado," April 24th, 2009, in *El Espectador*. Accessed: December 15, 2009 from http://www.elespectador.com/articulo137628-integrantes-de-canta-conmigo-reintegracion-se-graduan-sabado.
38. In English, No More Violence.
39. López, Ferley. 2009. No más Violencia, on *Canta Conmigo por la Reintegración* [CD]. Bogota, Colombia: High Counselor for the Social and Economic Reintegration. (Translation made by the author).
40. In English, Take the War out of Your Heart.
41. Vallenato is a folk music of Colombia played with accordion and other instruments.
42. Martínez López, Daner David. 2009. Saca la Guerra de tu Corazón, on Canta Conmigo por la Reintegración [CD]. Bogota, Colombia: High Counselor for the Social and Economic Reintegration. (Translation made by the author).

43.   "12 Colombianos unen sus voces por la reintegración" (Special Report of the "Sing with Me for the Reintegration" Project). Accessed: December 15, 2009 from http://www.reintegracion.gov.co/Es/prensa/reportajes/Paginas/cantaconmigo. aspx.
44.   Shank, Michael and Schirch, Lisa, op. cit.; 237.

References

Alta Consejería Presidencial para la Reintegración (High Presidential Office for the Reintegration): http://www.reintegracion.gov.co.

Artist for Human Rights: http://www.artistsforhumanrights.org/.

Art for Humanity: http://www.afh.org.za/.

"Canta Conmigo por la Reintegración" project. Accessed: from http://www.reintegracion. gov.co/prensa/reportajes/mayo/canta_conmigo.html.

"Cantando la Revolución." Accessed: June 10, 2010 from http://redescolar.ilce.edu. mx/redescolar/act_permanentes/historia/html/cantando_revolucion/revolucion.htm.

Centro de Memoria, Paz y Reconciliación: http://www.centromemoria.gov.co/el-centro-de-memoria.

Contreras Fajardo, Lilián, "Integrantes de 'Canta conmigo por la reintegración' se gradúan este sábado." Accessed: April 24, 2009 from http://www.elespectador. com/articulo137628-integrantes-de-canta-conmigo-reintegracion-se-graduan-sabado.

Diaz, Catalina, "Colombia's Bid for Justice and Peace." Study "Workshop 5—Lessons from Negotiated Justice Options in South Africa and Colombia." May 2007, International Center for Transitional Justice. Accessed: June 10, 2010 from http://www. humansecuritygateway.com/documents/PJC_Colombia_bidforjusticeandpeace.pdf.

Echandia, Camilo. 2006. *Dos décadas de Escalamiento del Conflicto Armado Colombiano*. Bogota: Universidad Externado de Colombia, Facultad de Finanzas, Gobierno y Relaciones Internacionales.

"El Tiempo" newspaper: www.eltiempo.com.

"El Espectador" newspaper: www.elespectador.com.

International Center for Transitional Justice: http://www.ictj.org/en/tj/.

Kees Epskamp. 1999. "Introduction. Healing Divided Societies" in People Building Peace, 35 Inspiring Stories from Around the World, a publication of the European Center for Conflict Prevention in cooperation with IFOR and the Coexistence Initiative of State of the World Forum.

Law 975 of 2005. Accessed: from http://www.secretariasenado.gov.co/senado/basedoc/ ley/2005/ley_0975_2005.html.

Lederach, John Paul. 1995. *Preparing for Peace. Conflict Transformation across Cultures*. Syracuse: Syracuse University Press.

Lederach, John Paul. 1997. *Building Peace: Sustainable Reconciliation in Divided Societies*. Washington DC: United States Institute of Peace Press.

Lederach, John Paul. 2005. *The Moral Imagination. The Art and Soul of Building Peace*. Oxford: Oxford University Press.

Longman Dictionary of Contemporary English, updated edition CD Room.

López, Ferley. 2009. "No Mas Violencia," on *Canta Conmigo por la Reintegración* [CD]. Bogota, Columbia: High Counselor for the Social and Economic Reintegration.

Martínez López, Daner David. 2009. "Saca la Guerra de tu Corazón," on *Canta Conmigo por la Reintegración* [CD]. Bogota, Colombia: High Counselor for the Social and Economic Reintegration.

National Commission on Reparation and Reconciliation. Accessed: June 10, 2010 from http://memoriahistorica-cnrr.org.co/archivos/arc_quees/what_is_MH.pdf.

Shank, Michael and Schirch, Lisa, "Strategic Arts-Based Peacebuilding," Peace & Change Journal, volume 33, issue 2 (April 2008). Accessed: June 10, 2010 from http://www.michaelshank.net/publications/pcartspeacebuilding.html.

The Institute of Democracy and Human Rights from the Catholic University of Peru, CERI—Sciences Po/CNRS Paris, France, "The Theater and the Conflicts Transformation in Peru." Accessed: June 10, 2010 from http://www.ceri-sciencespo.com/themes/re-imaginingpeace/va/resources/enquetes/theatre_perou.pdf.

"Víctimas del conflicto hacen memoria de sus tragedias al ritmo de alabaos, vallenato y champeta," *Cambio* Magazine, Vol. 855 (November 2009). Accessed: June 10, 2010 from http://www.cambio.com.co/informeespecialcambio/855/ARTICULO-WEB-NOTA_INTERIOR_CAMBIO-6610747.html.

Zelizer, Craig. 2003. "The Role of Artistic Processes in Peacebuilding in Bosnia-Herzegovina," September. Accessed: June 10, 2010 from http://www.pangea.org/unesco-pau/castellano/programas/musica.htm.

Music Therapy: Connecting through Music

Barbara Dunn

Introduction

Music has the potential to inspire foundational connections on a very human level. It can reach a person's heart in a matter of a few notes in a song. I have experienced this time and again through my more than 25 years as a music therapist. I have seen families unable to communicate with each other yet able to express their feelings through musical instruments. I have seen hardened faces brighten as they heard a distant flute—as if that flute were sending a direct line to their embroiled emotions. The lessons from the field of music therapy are great; they offer a window to possibilities for increasing a consciousness of our interconnectedness and inspiring solidarity as human beings.

Conflict transformation theory suggests that rather than focusing solely on the problem at hand, increased work on improving the *relationships* of those involved in conflict can be a more effective approach. This is true for many settings where conflict might arise, from the workplace, to marriage, to the community (Bush and Folger 2005; Lederach 2003). In music therapy, music can be used to address relationship issues and nonmusical goals, and the musical activity can provide on overarching approach that helps to heal and enhance relationships as well as address physical or emotional needs. Music therapists have a wide array of musical tools they can use, from composing a song for a client, to teaching her/him to play a musical instrument, to helping with relaxation and pain management with recorded music. In my work, I frequently refer to these tools figuratively as my "musical bag of tricks." This bag is always with me and can be used whenever and wherever needed. It holds *all* of my musical experiences, e.g., the songs I learned as a child, the Celtic music I learned to play on the pennywhistle, the classical art songs I sang in college… All of this music is available to me and within the realm of possibility for me to use in my work; and while this work is based in the field of music therapy, I have also always maintained a musical presence in my community, family, and just about everywhere else I have been. This might include offering a new song to sing before a meal, organizing a community drum circle, bringing different groups of people together to perform a benefit concert, leading a community sing along, and jamming with friends and family whenever an opportunity presents itself. Thus my "bag of tricks" is constantly replenished.

Music therapy had its very early beginnings in the 1920s and 1930s in the United States with music used to help patients in hospitals (Davis, Gfeller, and Thaut 2008). Today there are academic degrees in music therapy and professional organizations all over the world. In general, the training is weighted heavily on musical skills, and also includes studies in psychology, neurology/physiology, and music therapy techniques.

In this chapter, I will bring the reader into scenes and stories from music therapy that highlight connections made and felt on a deeply human level—connections made or supported expressly through the use of music. Additionally, I will describe some of the specific techniques used by music therapists, and conclude with some thoughts on the implications for global solidarity inspired by the practice and principles of music therapy.

Scenes and Stories

At the very core of music therapy and using music to help people is the human connection made with music. It is a mindfulness-based experience that helps to give pause to everything but the sounds at hand. Before I walk into a patient's room with my guitar, I stop and bring myself to full awareness of the present situation and my patient's needs. I enter the room and am completely cognizant of everything happening there, from the IV drip to the family or friends gathered with the patient. I focus on my patient, using the music to connect with him or her while, at the same time, keeping all the other particulars in my purview. I stay "in the moment" throughout the session, changing and adapting the music as needed throughout the session.

The Setting

The primary setting for these stories is from my work in a community hospital on an island in the Pacific Northwest region of the United States.

It is a rural hospital where our patients get help for a wide variety of concerns. Examples include patients coming in for outpatient surgery, mothers coming in to birth their babies, patients receiving chemotherapy for cancer, and children with autism coming in to work on speech or motor challenges. We also serve patients in their homes with home health needs and hospice care. Our music therapy program provides services to all these departments. On any given day I could see a patient with a new diagnosis of cancer on the medical unit, then go in to a session with a young child who has a developmental disability on the rehabilitation unit, and then end my day making a hospice visit to a dying patient in his or her home.

An interesting point about our hospital is that it is in the middle of two very different parts of a long island. In the north there is a military base and a town that tends to be more politically conservative. The south part of the island has a greater percentage of artists and organic farmers; it tends to be more politically progressive. Stereotypes abound about the demographics of people in each of these regions. Everyone comes together at the hospital and, for the most part, political differences take a back seat. This helps to create the perfect setting to bring music in to further help people connect in a non-divisive setting.

The stories I will highlight come from several of the different programs I coordinate and supervise at the hospital and home health and hospice program. These include the direct patient music therapy work done by myself and our music therapy interns and community musicians who are involved in our "Live Music Program." With these stories I hope to paint a picture of the power of music to enable one person to reach another and form connections on a level that is separate from their physical or mental challenges. It is the place where music weaves into our inner being and helps us realize how connected we really are.

Music Therapy with Patients

In some of my hospice work, the human connections made through music are almost palpable. I recall being in the home of one patient and she had a good friend over. We were having a relatively upbeat conversation. When it came time for me to sing, I was not into the song but for three notes when the friend began to cry. My patient had her eyes closed and was responding to the music with the soft rocking of her body. The tenderness of the moment was in the air and there was a felt connection between all present. No spoken words were needed; eye contact was even unnecessary. In those moments we were in a place where the music seemed to hold us together. It gave breath and release to the very real emotions of the situation and setting.

One family I worked with on our rehabilitation unit had two very challenging adolescent boys. The boys had behavior challenges in addition to their autism. The parents were stressed and there was much negative communication occurring between family members. Verbally we worked on some of the issues at hand. Musically we worked on finding a connection that allowed for self-expression and healthy communication and we found that around a drum. We began and ended each session gathered around our big drum and used only bare hands to feel and play the beat. Often the beginning of this playing was disconnected, with the boys distracted, and looking around the room. I used the music to inspire and engage the boys, rather than instructing them to "pay attention and play along." It usually took only about one or two minutes for the drumming to "bring them in" and engage them fully in the music making. By the end of the drumming there were frequently big smiles from the boys, laughing, and some wild and creative drumming.

The drum served as a gathering tool to allow for new ways to communicate. Both of the boys demonstrated limited ability or interest in using words to communicate. The parents frequently spoke to the boys with harsh voices and short commands telling them what to do. Drumming put the family members on an equal footing in expressing themselves with improvised rhythmic drumming patterns and varying tones made by hitting the drum. My part was to set the stage to invite this type of musical expression and communication to occur. The family both listened and responded to each other's drumming. It was a way for them to have a kind of conversation that was verbally unattainable. They also had moments of playing all together in such a way that their rhythms joined in a unified beat.

In another case, I worked with a woman in the hospital who was admitted while vacationing from another state. Her sudden illness was confounding our doctors and she had an unusually long hospital stay while they tried to ascertain her diagnosis. Needless to say, she was extremely disheartened with this process, and with the pain she was experiencing due to her illness. I worked with her for several weeks, using imagery and various relaxation exercises with music in efforts to help ease her pain. We talked about her life and sang some songs together. One day, as I was coming in to work, I had a sudden thought that I should sing the Holly Near song "I Am Willing" to her. I knew intuitively that it would be a powerful song for her. The words to the song poetically inspire an open and willing approach to change. Near suggests that having hope and being open to change is a way to honor the people who have walked on roads similar to ours (Near 2006). When I began singing it to her, her jaw dropped. It was indeed a powerful song for her. She had heard it during a church service about a year ago, and it had moved her so much she had then spent about 6 months trying to find the song. For many reasons, some I knew others I did not know, this song spoke to her in a very profound way. Of all the songs I could have picked to sing to her it is interesting that this one also called out to me with her name in it. It seemed to mean a lot to her that I would bring this song to her. It highlighted and expanded the musical connection we had already established with our singing together and with my using music to help her with her pain. When we sang this Holly Near song, there was an unspoken understanding of the power of the music and lyrics to "lift [us] up to the light of change"—that even though times could be tough, there was hope and we needed to keep moving. The singing allowed us to experience the message on a level apart from just the lyrics alone, a level that included the physiological experience of singing and harmony. This joined nicely with a global conscious-ness that includes "those who go before us" and others who also have challenges in their lives.

The "Live Music Program"

Our *Live Music Program* brings volunteer musicians in from the community to play instrumental music in various places around the hospital. The musicians audition for the program, and all have advanced musical abilities. They join our program with a commitment to play two hours per week. We have an initial orientation and training that helps them with ideas and selection of repertoire, volume levels, and musical responsiveness to the patients in the milieu in which they are playing. Several volunteers have noted they feel they are probably getting more benefit from playing than the patients.

A particularly challenging part of this program is that the volunteer musicians are playing for a general audience, such as people waiting in the lobby, as opposed to the music therapy I do with patients on an individual basis. Thus, their music has to respond to the overall feeling in the room, knowing that some patients will be feeling very poorly or discouraged (e.g., progressing illness) while others may be in better spirits (e.g., news they are cancer-free). They need to be able to read the energy of the room; often this is the main lobby where there are patients and staff, all with differing situations and needs. The music needs to be responsive when tension is high as well as when the energy is low. Matching music to the energy of the room is often referred to in music therapy as the *iso principle* (see description in next section). The music provides a way for the patients to be engaged in communication without direct speaking. They can feel the music and experience the connections made between the musician and themselves.

It is of crucial importance that the music is brought into this setting with great care and cognizance of the effect it is having on the people there. If the musicians are making music in a way that is not responsive to the needs of both patients and staff, this can actually hinder the creation of a healing atmosphere. For example, if the music is too loud, it can make it hard for staff to do their job of talking with patients and other medical staff. If it is frenetic it can make things tenser for patients. If it is too slow and morose it can increase the sadness that someone might already be feeling. The musicians and I work closely to find the right balance in their playing and music for the setting. Sometimes this means working with specific repertoire or it might involve adjusting where they are physically playing in the room.

We offer patients and staff an opportunity to comment on their experience of the music. The following comments indicate some of the effects of the musicians' work, perhaps thus confirming the human-to-human connection made between the musician and patient through the music:

- It really soothes the hurt.
- How soothing to listen to this beautiful pianist. Coming to the hospital can be an anxious time and I found her music very relaxing.
- The live music was very comforting under the current stressful situation.
- Over the past 3 months the music has soothed my times at the hospital—made me dream, smile, laugh at memories, made me miss my husband, made me better for the musician's efforts.

One of the patients even suggested using music to directly address tension in other settings.

- Extremely enjoyable!! Whoever on the staff came up with this gem is (or should be) retained and encouraged at all cost! Sincerely—such "creative and progressive thinking," especially in the "healing arts," is extremely valuable. I witnessed a noticeable improvement in the attitudes of both patients and staff alike. If I could bring a harpist to a housing development or a meeting with the Coupeville "Hysterical"

> Society and get the results your musicians do…I would have fewer
> grey hairs…

A distinction needs to be made between recorded music and live music. The musicians who volunteer for our *Live Music Program* provide a human service that can respond to the needs of the present moment. The music can be adjusted, the patients see and sense the presence of a person who is playing music so that they will have a better experience. Patients seem to be genuinely touched to see and hear the care put into the music, not to mention the notion that someone is giving so freely of their time. This is a very different experience from recorded music. One patient commented,

- Surprise and pleasure hearing "live" music performed at reasonable sound levels and sensitive to the vulnerable people who come here. Personally, I find "canned" music annoying and this is so lovely.

Related to this is an experience I have frequently in the hospital. I like to carry my guitar on a strap over my shoulder (just as if I am ready to play) when I walk around the hospital. I see the expression in peoples faces change when they see the guitar. They may be holding tension related to their medical condition, then they see the guitar and look up to speak to me saying something like "you gonna play that?" or "is that a Martin [guitar]?" They seem surprised to see a musical instrument in the hospital setting. So even the presence of the musical instrument and the musician can create a connection before a single note is even played!

Music Therapy Techniques

As I stated in the beginning of this chapter, music therapists use a wide array of techniques and tools. This section will highlight a few vital techniques commonly used by music therapists. They include Improvisation, Iso Principle, and Entrainment.

Improvisation

Improvisation is a vital tool for music therapists. A well-known model of music therapy, called Nordoff-Robbin's Creative Music Therapy, relies heavily on piano and vocal improvisation. It uses all the breadth of musical offerings, including modes, dissonance, different meters and scales, and a variety of styles. This model was developed through Paul Nordoff and Clive Robbin's music therapy with children who were profoundly disabled and, essentially, not otherwise responsive.

Nordoff-Robbins creative music therapy focuses on working with those parts of the client that are essentially human and non-exceptional. There is a great emphasis on the power of music to awaken emotional responses" (Peters 2000, 388).

Improvisational music provides an avenue for connecting on what I conceive as a "heartfelt" level. The music therapist must be skilled in creating the musical experience. Sometimes this means accompanying with a specific chord structure, such as the 12-bar blues. This helps lend comfort to the player by giving a framework to the music. It also opens up possibilities for expression of feelings in the way that melodies are created above the chords. Another very common improvisational tool used by music therapists is the pentatonic scale. This can be used with or without the rhythmic structure. The five notes used in a pentatonic scale create an open sound that lends itself to many possibilities; all the notes sound good in any sequence of playing.

In the situation mentioned earlier of the two boys with autism, I often used a xylophone and tone bells that were tuned to a pentatonic scale. One of the boys was significantly more challenged in his very limited use of words. I would set up an improvisational experience for him with an array of instruments. This included the xylophone, tone bells, and a few percussion instruments. He appeared delighted to be able to express himself through the varied musical choices. This was significant because he had very few other avenues for self-expression.

Iso Principle and Entrainment

The iso principle concerns the matching of music with a client's mood and/or physiological response. The music is then altered by the therapist in degrees to effect changes in the client (Davis, Gfeller, and Thaut 2008). The iso principle was first developed in the mid-twentieth century by Dr. Ira M. Altshuler who theorized that "music bypassed cerebral interpretive relays and appealed directly to the seat of aesthetic reactions" (Peters 2000, 36). The iso principle is a foundational underpinning of *musical entrainment,* which is a technique used by many music therapists.

Entrainment can be used to alter the physiological state of a patient. It involves matching music to a patient's observable physiological behavior and then altering the music to create change in the patient. For example, when used to address pain, the music can entrain to the intensity of the pain through matched tension and perhaps some musical dissonance. Once the pain and music are locked in with matched intensity the musician can gradually shift toward more consonant and relaxed music. The intensity of pain felt by the patient will then also move along toward a more relaxed state (Peters 2000).

Rhythmic entrainment identifies the concept of "timing" to the use of entrainment. It goes beyond matching a downbeat by addressing the distance between the beats, i.e., the rhythmic flow between beats. As explained by Davis et al.:

> Rhythmic entrainment occurs when the frequency and pattern sequence of movements become locked to the frequency and pattern of an auditory rhythmic stimulus, such as in metronome pulses or the metric and rhythmic patterns in music... Auditory rhythm enhances time stability and movement planning and execution during the whole duration of the movement (Davis, Gfeller, and Thaut, 2008, 286-287).

In reference to its applications for music therapists, the iso principle generally describes a process of matching and moving a patient's experience to a different level. This can be done in various ways and does not always translate into the more physiological "lock-in" of entrainment. For example, our volunteers with the Live Music Program use the iso principle by matching and altering the energy of the people in the lobby but they do not "entrain" with the individuals present.

Music for entrainment is best done with *live* music that can be adapted to match the immediate experience of the patient. For example, one of my hospice patients was experiencing intense pain. His body was shaking very badly and his face grimacing. He was unable to verbally communicate with me and seemed to be in and out of consciousness. I began by playing improvisational guitar music that was moving at just under the tempo and intensity of his bodily movements. I played this way for about ten minutes until we were locked in to the same rhythm and intensity. Once we arrived at that place I began to very gradually change my rhythm and intensity. He was able to follow me to a level that was less intense and he appeared to be physically more comfortable. He did not regain consciousness for us to talk about the experience. I can only go by his physical movements and facial expression that seemed to respond to my music. The human connection we had through music seemed to provide the comfort and support needed at that time.

Building Connection and Solidarity

Breaking down barriers and helping people relate to each other is a fundamental component of transformative approaches to addressing conflict (Bush and Folger 2005). By and large this means helping people see the humanity in each other. It means recognizing that at times we all have feelings of anger, sadness, passion, pride, jealousy, loneliness, etc.

Having these feelings helps us to appreciate being human (Stone, Patton, and Heen 1999). Creating a feeling of solidarity towards others through our ability to relate to one another on a purely human level can serve as a stepping-stone toward transforming our conflicts (Lederach 2005). Examples from music therapy, as glimpsed in the accounts above, can begin to demonstrate how music can help us reach that understanding and the sense of connection with the other which underpins the notion of solidarity.

Use of techniques such as improvisation and entrainment allow for the music to inspire movement or create change in a variety of distressing situations, be it pain due to illness, or pain and angst over interpersonal conflict. As discussed in many authors' work, music provides a way to move beyond language as a primary means of communication; and examples from music therapy may show some ways in which this can happen.

These are some of the lessons that can be gleaned from the field of music therapy, and the following chapter by my fellow music therapist Vanessa Contopulos continues this "story" with one from the field in which music therapy techniques, in this case focusing upon their potential to strengthen dialogic processes, were indeed used to help people in a situation of longstanding, culturally-based conflict, to reduce the tension between them.

We need to spread the word that music making is in fact a tool that can be utilized in many ways, including increasing our understanding of each other, helping us simply be together even if we disagree, and actually helping us work through our challenges together.

And we need to enable people to experience music and understand how it can alter physiological and emotional experiences. This requires stopping and *paying attention to* how the music is affecting us. For me, my work in music therapy helps me to stop the "busyness" of the rest of my work (e.g., chart writing, staff meetings...) and simply "be with" another human being in music. Even in the short span of a 3-minute song I feel my body relax into the music. I see my patients doing the same.

References

Bush, Robert A. Baruch, & Folger, Joseph P. 2005. *The Promise of Mediation: The Transformative Approach to Conflict*, Revised Edition. San Francisco, CA: Jossey-Bass.

Davis, William B., Gfeller, Kate E., & Thaut, Michael H. 2008. *An Introduction to Music Therapy Theory and Practice*, 3rd ed. Silver Spring, MD: American Music Therapy Association.

Douglas Stone, Bruce Patton & Sheila Heen. 1999. *Difficult Conversations: How to Discuss What Matters Most*. New York: Penguin Books.

Lederach, John Paul. 2003. *The Little Book of Conflict Transformation.* Intercourse, PA: Good Books.

Lederach, John Paul. 2005. *The Moral Imagination: The Art and Soul of Peacebuilding.* New York: Oxford University Press.

Near, Holly. 2006. "I Am Willing." On *Show Up* [CD]. Calico Tracks Music.

Peters, Jacqueline Schmidt. 2000. *Music Therapy: An Introduction.* Springfield, IL: Charles C. Thomas.

Music Therapy and Strategies for Dialogue

Vanessa Contopulos

Introduction

> In seeking peace, governments negotiate around interests and issues; citizens focus
> on relationships... until relationships are changed, deep-rooted human conflicts are
> not likely to be resolved (Saunders 1999, 30).

How are relationships changed? How can protracted conflicts among people and communities, caused by profound differences of value, identity and worldview, be shifted? Do music and the creative process have a role to play in creating a space in which people can begin to experience one another in new ways? These questions underpin many of the chapter that accompany my own in this volume, and are answered in different ways. In this chapter, I will explore the possibilities for strategies from music therapy to serve as tools in addressing these questions. Here, my specific focus is their potential to supporting the principles of *dialogue*, which itself is acknowledged as a core element of processes of building the understanding which may reduce tensions and transform conflict.

Institutions and practitioners working to create and open up spaces for change often utilize "dialogue," which I will define here as a structured conversation in which a deepened mutual understanding of those participating is sought, and, in this specific context, promoted through: empathetic listening, inclusive engagement of diverse people and ideas, and an emphasis on each person's humanity. Over the past 20 years a wide range of innovative methods and tools have emerged to uphold the principles of dialogue and to support its facilitation (Bojer et al. 2006).

The field of music therapy, as described in the preceding chapter, utilizes music to achieve non-musical goals such as: communication, improved relationships, and expression of feeling (Wigram et al. 2002). Strategies from music therapy are also used to support inclusive and empathetic interactions (Dixon 2002), provide opportunities for personal reflection, and facilitate listening and deep understanding of others.

Through an exploration of the key principles of dialogue, an examination of music therapy and a reflection on the use of music therapy strategies in a facilitated dialogue process which I designed and implemented in Fiji, this chapter explores how music therapy strategies can support the principles of dialogue and thus be of value to dialogue practitioners, the dialogue process, and ultimately, people's relationships and feelings of connection.

Dialogue: A Critical Tool for Building Relationships

There are numerous definitions for dialogue. In Latin, dialogue refers merely to a conversational exchange between two or more people. Given this broad definition, we might say that dialogue exists wherever human beings exist together. However, when it relates to peace building activities, dialogue takes on a more specific definition.

Dialogue is a structured conversation that is acknowledged by international organizations promoting engagement of civil society as a tool for building "mutual understanding and trust across differences" (Pruitt and Thomas 2007, 9). Many community-based organizations identify dialogue as an instrument to create, deepen, and build human relationships and understanding (Public Conversations Project 2006). While there are many different purposes for dialogue and contexts in which it is used, dialogue is defined by its key principles. Dialogue practitioners select and implement various tools that help support the principles and objectives of dialogue.[1]

A primary objective of dialogue is *deepening understanding* around substantive issues (Bojer et al. 2006; Yankelovich 1999). Another objective of dialogue is *building, changing, and strengthening relationships* (Saunders 1999). Upholding the following key principles helps to fulfill these objectives:

- The process is inclusive
- Judgment is suspended
- Each individual's voice is equally heard and valued
- Listening is done with empathy and respect
- There is an emphasis on each person's humanity (Bojer et al. 2006; Yankelovich 1999)

Ultimately, dialogue practitioners aim to create a space in which conversations can take place, while the key issues are explored and emotions engaged with.

The Connection Between Dialogue and the Use of Music Making in Building Relationships

Tools that Build Personal Connections

There are existing dialogue tools and processes that can be connected to the use of music in helping participants build or rebuild relationships. Through a variety of creative ways, these tools build opportunities for participants to share personal stories and interests. Music making has the potential to play a similar role. Stories and histories can be communicated through the sharing of a song or dance. Music also has the capacity to create opportunities for play. In moments of shared musical interaction or moments of musical play, participants might be able to experience one another in a new way.

Circle Processes

Circle processes are often used in dialogue and incorporate wisdom from many traditions in which individuals gather to communicate, celebrate, or make decisions for the community. Christina Baldwin acknowledges the benefits of this tool in her book, *Calling the Circle* (1994). She suggests that a circle process can help create shared leadership among all the participants, which can be used to address power inequalities. This is often done through the use of a prop such as a talking stick that is passed around the circle, providing an opportunity for each participant to speak. The shared nature of communication within a circle is often used to open up conversation or as a tool for building intimacy among the participants (Baldwin 1994).

Communities that traditionally gather in a circle often include music making and dance in their processes. A direct connection can be made to music therapy, as music therapists often gather groups in a circle to promote sharing and relationship building. Frequently an instrument is used to facilitate shared leadership and creative engagement among all the participants. In these music circles, sharing is done through song or rhythm instead of spoken word and an instrument often plays the role of the talking stick.

Traditional Dialogue Practices

Dialogue literature acknowledges the importance of drawing from worldwide knowledge surrounding practices that support the principles of dialogue. This literature reveals an existing richness of practice that, as Bojer suggests, ought to be considered and utilized when developing tools for dialogue practitioners (Bojer et al. 2006). It is interesting to note the use of musical elements in some of these practices. For example, many Native American traditions incorporate art, dancing, drumming, and song in their customs of communication and dialogue. The use of music therapy strategies, such as improvisation or song writing might serve as a way to incorporate these more traditional forms of dialogue in a facilitated process. In addition, the use of creative musical strategies in the dialogue process may offer an immediate relevance within cultural contexts where music and dance are already deeply embedded in community ritual and storytelling.

Music Therapy

From its foundation,[2] music therapy has been shaped by an acknowledgment of the importance of music in cultures throughout the world, and by the acknowledgment and evidence of its healing capacity. While the field of music therapy comprises a collection of varied models and approaches that have emerged from a range of disciplines and countries, The World Federation of Music Therapy defines music therapy as:

> The use of music and/or musical elements (sound, rhythm, melody and harmony) by a qualified music therapist with a client or group, in a process designed to facilitate and promote communication, relationships, learning, mobilization, expression, organization and other relevant therapeutic objectives, in order to meet physical, emotional, mental, social and cognitive needs. Music therapy aims to develop potentials and/or restore functions of the individual so that he or she can achieve better intra- and interpersonal integration and, consequently, a better quality of life through prevention, rehabilitation or treatment (1996).

I have been working with a broader understanding of music therapy, similar to that articulated by Barbara Dunn in her PhD thesis, *Transforming Conflict Through Music*. She suggests that, with its many models, music therapy can be seen as an "active vehicle—a tool to create change" (Dunn 2008, 4). With this understanding of music therapy, and finding myself—a music therapist—in a dialogue setting, I was particularly interested in how its strategies could support existing dialogue tools and also stand as their own tools in promoting the principles and objectives of dialogue.

There is limited research on the use of strategies from music therapy used in the facilitation of peace building activities such as dialogue; however, the field of community music therapy seemed to offer a viable starting point, and throughout my work and research in designing and implementing music therapy strategies in the dialogue process in Fiji, I referenced the work of this nascent area of music therapy.

Community Music Therapy

The emerging field within music therapy identified as Community Music Therapy (CoMT) explores the possibility of music therapy work taking place outside of the traditional clinical setting. Furthermore, Community Music Therapy expresses a rising concern for attention to social, cultural, and political awareness and involvement within music therapy (Pavlicevic and Ansdell 2004). It also makes a case for a broader understanding of the scope of goals that might be appropriately addressed through music therapy, considering social change as a legitimate music therapy goal (Stige 2004). Community music therapists propose that, if music therapy is to continue to develop internationally and have an impact, it must be flexible in moving out of clinical settings and into the community. Furthermore, community music therapists are beginning to expand their work to include music performance and other activities that have traditionally been considered outside the realm of music therapy practice.

Brynjulf Stige (2004) observes that community music therapy may actually be the oldest form of music therapy, as group music making is so deeply embedded in many traditional cultural practices. As described above, many cultures continue to use music in their community life. While the idea of "therapy" is not specifically considered in their mu- sicking, their musical exchanges often achieve non-musical goals. These goals include communication, building relationships, and promoting expression. If music therapists are to bring their work into new cultural contexts, the existing emphasis on musicking in such communities may provide a natural bridge.

From July to September of 2009, I had the privilege of working with the Pacific Centre for Peacebuilding (PCP) in Suva, Fiji. PCP is currently facilitating emerging dialogue processes in Fiji, and in my time there I was able to work alongside the staff to design and implement music therapy strategies in a regional dialogue process.[3] Community Music Therapy literature contributed to my conceptualization of the use of music in dialogue in Fiji in two ways. Firstly, there was practical insight to be gained from music therapists who are working with music therapy strategies outside the traditional music therapy context. Secondly, the work of community music therapists demonstrates that there are growing spaces within the field of music therapy to contribute to peacebuilding activities. Such activities will now be described in my following story of my work in Fiji, starting with an account of its background to set this work in context.

Music Therapy in a Facilitated Dialogue Process

Background

Fiji is a country of diverse peoples that is seeking to find its identity as a nation. It is a former British colony that gained its independence in October 1970, and has experienced four coups[4] since 1987. This has resulted in individual and collective trauma and a currently tense political climate. The Pacific Centre for Peacebuilding (PCP) was set up in 2007 with the mission statement stating that it:

> works to strengthen traditional and western peace building knowledge and strategies with communities, government and non-government organizations and institutions to transform, reduce and prevent conflict in Fiji and the Pacific (Pacific Centre for Peacebuilding 2008, 1).

On May 8-11 2008, Koila Costello-Olsson, director of the PCP, co-facilitated a pan-Pacific, UN sponsored workshop on conflict resolution, which focused on the importance of dialogue. Senior civil servants, civil society leaders, and academics from Fiji were among those who attended the workshop. The Fijian delegates were impressed with the prospect of dialogue contributing to resolving the pressing concerns in Fiji, acknowledging its potential in creating a small and hopefully growing space for people who might not normally talk to one another, to gather and engage in significant conversation and build relationships (Costello Olsson 2009; Baleinakorodawa 2009; Lenisaurua 2009). Some of the delegates formed a group that would meet periodically to take an active role in helping resolve Fiji's political problems (Dialogue Fiji 2009).

This initiative has evolved and is now known as "Dialogue Fiji." The first objective of Dialogue Fiji is to develop a national dialogue process through a number of dialogue platforms. The Dialogue Fiji team believes in the capacity of dialogue to support people-centered development, interactions that build a common and national identity across ethnic lines, and inclusive political processes. Dialogue Fiji wishes to promote dialogue as a mechanism for long-term conflict resolution and peacebuilding (Dialogue Fiji 2009). While this emerging dialogue initiative is continually evolving, there is a current plan to continue organizing dialogue processes at a local level of the country's "Divisions." The hope is that these dialogues will feed into a national process involving senior political leadership.

PCP facilitated the first two divisional dialogues, and was contracted to facilitate the Northern Division Dialogue. It was here, at a three and a half day residential process in a small resort, that I was able to put a number of music therapy tools into practice within the facilitated dialogue process. Many participants traveled a lengthy distance, some coming by boat from other islands, to take part in the process. The intention in inviting participants was to create an inclusive process that would, as much as possible, bring together a group of people who were representative of the northern population. Twenty-eight participants represented major stakeholders in the community, including women's organizations, youth, churches, people with disabilities, the private sector, government, and police. Participants also represented age, ethnic, religious and political diversity.

The following is a reflective description of some of the music therapy strategies that I brought into the dialogue process. It is important to note that all music strategies used in the dialogue were implemented through careful planning, but that opportunities were also embraced for spontaneous adaptation. Through on-going discussion and creative partnership with the staff of PCP, I was able to strategically adapt and apply music therapy strategies to support the evolving dialogue process.

Music Circles

As previously mentioned, music therapy group work is often done in a circle. Frequently, the music making is improvisational, employing percussion activities such as circle drumming, which have great potential to facilitate interactions among the participants and build relationships. Music circles were implemented throughout the three-day process and were often used to gather people at the beginning of the day or after a break. These circles were highly improvisational and evolved into a combination of percussion, singing, and dancing. Many of the percussion exercises were facilitated in a way that provided each person the opportunity to lead a rhythm for the group to follow.

A music circle was used at the start of the second day. The energy in the group was a bit low. The first day had been long and intensive. People had also stayed drinking and talking late into the night. We wanted to energize the group, get people engaged, and set our space for the coming day of dialogue. I began with recognition of the level of the energy in the room, which was quite low. This meant that I started with a slow beat that everyone began to attune with. Once we were all playing together, I sped up the tempo and started to sing a song titled, "I'm So Glad You're Here." The lyrics of the song direct the participants to do different movements, "I can clap my hands, I can stomp my feet, I can dance around." Not only did this get the participants moving, it created a playful mood. People began to sing along and dance. We moved into a call and response activity that moved around the circle, giving each person the opportunity to lead a rhythm that everyone would follow. This created an opportunity for listening and engagement.

Many percussion activities have the potential actively to engage participants without the use of spoken language. This can be exceptionally useful in settings where multiple languages are spoken. It can also be helpful in engaging participants for whom words are not the primary medium of expression. Music circles can give individuals who are less verbal the experience of being engaged in the group and being important to the process (Pavlicevic 2003).

The staff of PCP noted that, while circle processes can be an important tool in dialogue, it is often difficult to allow a space for each person to share while maintaining a timely process; however, the music circles were able to achieve this balance. They also served as a time of play among the participants, something that the staff of PCP noted as an important factor in building cooperative relationships.

Guided Song Writing

Guided Song Writing is a music therapy strategy that can be structured in a variety of ways to achieve a broad range of goals. It is an effective tool for encouraging personal expression. Song writing and discussion in group work also has the potential to deepen mutual understanding of those taking part (Faire and Langan 2004). I was interested in how a guided song writing activity could be used as a tool in the dialogue process, particularly as a creative way to encourage expression and strengthen new ways of listening among the participants. I also imagined that, through this creative manner of sharing, new avenues of thought might emerge.

A space opened in the final day of the dialogue process to use a guided song writing exercise. The dialogue process had come to a place where the participants were beginning to suggest action that could stem from the dialogue, and I was interested in using the guided song writing to encourage creative and collective thinking. I gathered the group in a circle and each person was given a percussion instrument. I used an existing song structure and began singing the chorus of the song "I Choose" by India Arie; "Because you never know where life is gonna take you and you can't change where you've been, but today I have the opportunity to choose." As we continued to play our percussion instruments I asked each participant to imagine building toward the future. The participants were still playing the beat as I sang the chorus again. I then went around the circle to every participant and, as I approached each person I would say, "I choose," and the person would fill in the gap with their word. Some of the words the participants chose were: peace, joy, freedom and friendship.

The facilitators appreciated the song writing exercise as a simple tool to allow each person's perspective to be heard. They also felt that the act of writing a collective song was symbolic of how individuals might work together in their communities and as a nation (Baleinakorodawa 2009; Lenisaurua 2009).

Music and Lyrics

Music therapists often use music with lyrics in *Lyric Analysis* activities to foster insight and promote discussion. This is done by exploring themes or emotions that arise in response to the lyrics presented in a song. While time limitations did not allow for lyric analysis, I imagined that employing songs with certain themes might serve as an effective tool in supporting the dialogue process. Hence, throughout the dialogue in Fiji, music with lyrics was employed to introduce or reflect on certain activities. The lyrics to the songs were written and displayed throughout the dialogue space.[5]

For example, one dialogue tool used by the staff of PCP is the Name Activity. In this activity, each participant shares with the group the history or meaning of their name. This simple tool can help the participants to see one another's humanity. I imagined how reflecting on the lyrics of the song "No One Like You" by singer-songwriter John Denver, a song that speaks of the uniqueness and importance of each individual, could deepen the impact of this dialogue tool.

Throughout the Name Activity, the dialogue participants shared deeply personal stories relating to their name, their family identity and their personal history. Directly after everyone had shared, I and a friend from PCP played the guitar and sang "No One Like You." Some people seemed moved with emotion while others closed their eyes and listened to the music. The music seemed to hold us in the sharing space for a moment longer. As I sang the lyrics to the song, I looked around the room at each face and remembered the unique and personal stories that had just been shared.

The facilitators saw the use of music and lyrics as a tool for bringing people to a pause. Facilitator, Vosita Lenisaurua noted, "This use of music provided a space for people to sit without talking and reflect, perhaps allowing an opportunity for people to dialogue within themselves" (Lenisaurua 2009). Finally, the PCP director observed that the use of music with lyrics served as a mechanism to re-emphasize key messages that emerged within the dialogue (Costello-Ollson 2009).

Conclusion

This brief exploration of facilitated dialogue, music therapy, and the use of music therapy strategies in a facilitated dialogue process suggests that music can be strategically used to support the principles of dialogue. The following is a reflection on these key principles and how the music therapy strategies may help to strengthen them.

The process should be inclusive. The engagement of all the participants in music circles, particularly with the use of percussion instruments, is an effective way of facilitating inclusive interactions. Similar to circle processes in which a talking stick is used, the use of drum circle activities in the Fiji dialogue served as a way of rotating leadership among all the participants. The particular power of the musical exchanges is the interactive nature of many of the exercises. For example, a *Call and Response* percussion activity required the participants to actively listen to each person in the group so that they could be engaged in responding to each musical message.

The use of simple percussion activities is a way of including each participant without the use of language. This is helpful for a number of reasons. First, shifting the communication style has the potential to shift power dynamics that might exist in the group. I observed this in the dialogue process in Fiji. There were times when one person or group of people dominated the conversation, and the change of activity to music circles with percussion instruments brought all the participants back to a place of equal participation and engagement. Second, providing a space for non-verbal communication and leadership is beneficial for those participants who are not highly verbal in their communication style. Finally, in contexts where language is divisive, activities that facilitate non-verbal communication play a crucial role in creating opportunities for inclusive interactions.

It is crucial to acknowledge that the use of music can also exclude people. Before using strategies from music therapy as a tool for dialogue it would be important to recognize certain instruments or songs attached to a particular group or history that might be divisive.

Judgment is suspended. The use of music to bring the participants to a pause for reflection and "inner dialogue" before and after interacting might help people to slow their immediate responses and suspend judgment. Facilitators could also consider using music with messages of non-judgment to encourage this atmosphere in the dialogue.

Each individual's voice is equally heard and valued. Similar to the use of music circles to create an inclusive process, they can also serve as an opportunity for each participant to be heard. *Guided Song Writing* is another tool that could be used to incorporate each participant's voice. The act of creating a collective song also suggests that each person's voice and perspective contributes to, and is important to, the completed work. Finally, for the facilitator, the structure of a song may serve as a useful tool in the challenging work of creating a space for each individual to be heard and valued.

Listening is done with empathy and respect. The process of music making and creative interaction can be an intimate form of engagement between people (Dixon 2002), and can be used to foster empathy. It is also interesting to consider how changing the form of communication (from spoken to musical) might heighten dialogue participants' attention and listening skills.

> *There is an emphasis on each person's humanity.* Throughout the dialogue in Fiji, strategies from music therapy played a role in connecting people to the heart of an issue. John Paul Lederach acknowledges the ability of art and music to do this in his work *The Moral Imagination*. He states,

These are not moments defined by the analytical endeavor. They are deeply intuitive—short, sweet, and synthetic to the core. What they synthesize are the complexities of experience and the challenges of addressing deep human dilemmas (Lederach 2005, 69-70).

Participants also shared that the music strategies helped them to think of each other in more humane ways. In particular, they referenced the use of songs with messages discussing each person's humanity, like the song "No One Like You." I observed that the use of music to facilitate play seemed to allow people to make personal connections and build relationships. It is interesting to consider how the joint experience of music can serve as a medium through which people "experience" each other in a different way, possibly allowing them to see one another first and foremost in their humanity.

There are lessons to be learned from the use of music therapy strategies in the dialogue in Fiji. First, as dialogue practitioners continue to explore new and innovative tools for dialogue, music therapy strategies should be considered, as they have apparent potential to support the principles of dialogue. In certain contexts, the use of music may be particularly helpful to foster new ways of communicating, listening and understanding. They can be structured in a way that complements existing dialogue tools and processes and might also serve as a connection to more traditional forms of dialogue.

A "one size fits all" approach to the use of music in dialogue would not be appropriate and could in fact detract from the effectiveness of the process. If considered appropriate, professionals from other fields such as music therapy could contribute to the dialogue process either through consulting on the design of music strategies or directly implementing music strategies in the dialogue process. Finally, if music therapists are to continue to broaden the scope of their work to reach outside of traditional music therapy settings, it is crucial that they position themselves within the collective knowledge of a collaborative team of professionals. There is great possibility for music therapists and other music practitioners to contribute to peace building activities. If done properly, this could deepen the work of understanding and change and also add a richness to their respective fields.

Notes

1.   For access to a broad selection of dialogue tools and resources see http://pioneer-sofchange.net/library/dialogue.
2.   Music therapy was first established as a professional field in the UK and the US during 1890-1940, which involved an increase in musicians playing in hospitals. The onset of WWII brought additional attention to the role of music in lifting the morale of patients. During this time musicians continued to play for patients, and also began to engage patients in the act of music making.
3.   This was a three-day residential dialogue that took place in the northern region of the Fijian islands. Twenty-eight participants represented major stakeholders in the community including women's organizations, youth, churches, people with disabilities, the private sector, government, and police. Participants also represented age, ethnic, religious, and political diversity.
4.   The first coup was led by Col. Sitiveni Rabuka on May 14, 1987, the second on September 29, 1987. The third coup was led by George Speight and the elite unit known as the Counter Revolutionary Welfare Unit on May 19, 2000. The fourth coup was led by Com. Frank Bainimarama on December 5, 2006.

5.   While participants were encouraged to speak in their first language if that was most comfortable for them, the dialogue was facilitated in English. This was because English was the common language among all the participants. For this reason, we decided to use songs with lyrics in English to introduce or reflect on activities.

References

Ansdell, Gary. 2004. Rethinking Music and Community. In: Pavlicevic, Mercedes. And Ansdell, Gary. (eds.) *Community Music Therapy*. London: Jessica Kingsley Publishers; 65-90.

Baldwin, Christina. 1994. *Calling the Circle*. New York: Bantam Books.

Baleinakorodawa, Paulo. 2009. Interviewed by: Vanessa Contopulos. (10th September 2009).

Bojer, Marianne, Knuth, Marianne and Magner, Colleen. 2006. *Mapping Dialogue a research project profiling dialogue tools and processes for social change*. Johannesburg: Pioneers of Change Associates.

Contopulos, Vanessa. 2009. *Creative Spaces in Dialogue: Exploring the Possibilities for Music Therapy to Contribute to Dialogue*. Unpublished MA dissertation. University of Bradford.

Costello-Olsson, Koila. 2009. Interviewed by: Vanessa Contopulos. (10th September 2009).

Dixon, Matthew. 2002. "Music and Human Rights." In: Sutton, Julie P. (ed.) *Music, Music Therapy and Trauma International Perspectives*. London: Jessica Kingsley Publishers; 119-132.

Dunn, Barbara. 2008. *Transforming Conflict Through Music*. PhD thesis. Union Institute & University.

Faire, Rosemary, and Langan, Dianne. 2004. Expressive Music Therapy: Empowering Engaged Citizens and Communities [Online] *Voices: A World Forum for Music Therapy*. Accessed: November 12, 2009 from http://www.voices.no/mainissues/mi40004000159.html.

Laurence, Felicity. 2008. Music and Empathy. In: Urbain, Olivier. (ed.) *Music and Conflict Transformation: Harmonies and Dissonances in Geopolitics*. London: I.B. Tauris & Co Ltd.; 13-25.

Lederach, John Paul. 2005. *The Moral Imagination the Art and Soul of Building Peace*. New York: Oxford University Press.

Lenisaurua, Vosita. Interviewed by: Vanessa Contopulos. (10th September 2009).

Pacific Centre for Peacebuilding. 2008. *Pacific Centre for Peacebuilding Strategic Plan 2008-2011*.

Pavlicevic, Mercedes. 2003. *Groups in Music: Strategies from Music Therapy*. London: Jessica Kingsley Publishers.

Pavlicevic, Mercedes, and Ansdell, Gary. (eds.). 2004. *Community Music Therapy*. London: Jessica Kingsley Publishers.

Pruitt, Bettye, and Thomas, Philip. 2007. *Democratic Dialogue A Handbook for Practitioners*. Sweden: International IDEA, CIDA, OAS, and UNDP.

Public Conversations Project. 2006. *Constructive Conversations about Challenging Times: A Guide to Community Dialogue*. Watertown: Public Conversations Project.

Saunders, Harold. H. 1999. *A Public Peace Process: Sustained Dialogue to Transform Racial and Ethnic Conflicts*. New York: St. Martin's Press.

Stige, Brynjulf. 2002. *Culture Centred Music Therapy*. Gilsum: Barcelona Publishers.

Wigram, Tony, Pedersen, Inge Nygarrd, and Bonde, Lars Ole. 2002. *A Comprehensive Guide to Music Therapy*. London: Jessica Kingsley Publishers.

Yankelovich, Daniel. 1999. *The Magic of Dialogue: The Art of Turning Transactions into Successful Relationships.* New York: Simon and Schuster.

The Case of the *Ahwâsh* Dance of Morocco:
A Contribution of the Specific
to the Universal

Ahmed Aydoun

Introduction

Although the idea of music as a universal language is accepted by many people, this is not a precise statement: it is not the *language*, but music's *modes of reception* which can be universal. Within each culture, there are unique musical understandings, forms and functions; it is interesting to examine the contribution of each culture, through the uniqueness of its music, to a form of active musical universality.

In the case of the musical and choreographic performances of the *ahwâsh* dance of Morocco, there are contained some mechanisms for intra-tribal conflict management, specific to this musical form; it is the question of seeing how to translate that spirit on a broader plane—from the specific to the universal—that is addressed in the following pages.

It is widely accepted that language, signs, and attitudes are the tools at the base of all communication, while artistic expression can also contribute to the role assigned to language and sometimes overtake it, deepening emotion and the feeling of belonging to the same large family, that of humankind; how many times during a concert have men and women from different cultures and views, carried away by the sound of the music, forgotten their differences and rediscovered themselves in the most secret aspects of their being?

Since the dawn of time, humans have expressed the need to listen to and to feel music, not only as an organization of sound in their space, but also as a condition of their integrity. The *need* is universal even if the music is not itself a universal language, notwithstanding a longstanding discourse which holds this to be the case. According to that need, and across the centuries, people have developed musical and choreographic expressions with characteristics specific to that particular geography, history of cultural mixing, and social or ritual function which each of these expressions can explain.

It is this way of thinking that enables us to understand the musical and choreographic performance of the *ahwâsh* of Morocco, a total performance that, starting with a dance, integrates other artistic expressions as well as mechanisms of conflict-management within the tribal setting.

I suggest that characteristic features of this dance can acquire meaning beyond its localized presence and its primary concern of identity. In describing the practice of this dance, and examining the idea that music, in the form of this dance, can play a significant role in conflict management, I will argue its relevance and contribution to universal humanistic musical purposes.

An "Active" Universality

I would like firstly to propose a basis for an "active" universality before seeking some lessons taken from the Moroccan *ahwâsh*. The debate on universality/specificity in music is a recurring subject, but one that is always topical. Music is not a universal language; if it ever really was, we would not have struggled to understand the different styles of music, each of which requires training and different customs of practice and listening. It is practically impossible to reproduce the accents of some popular songs for those who were not born in the area, and all the efforts to transcribe this music only succeeds in oversimplifying the act of music. As described above, it seems that we should shift the question of "universality" from the scope of the practical to that of perception; this would, moreover, invite people to listen to each other and to look to one another to find ways to regenerate themselves, without one civilization claiming exclusive rights to masterpieces.

What I call "active universality" would be the movement both towards oneself and towards the other, and would be a process that does not impose a supposedly superior model, but which would try to distribute values which are taken from all that is best in the human experience.

In (re)cognition, there is the idea of knowledge but also the idea of memory, and the knowledge of oneself and others allows a climate of confidence in which to move. This was in any case the creed and the wish of UNESCO, in which governments recognized the need to put different cultures in dialogue to avoid or at least to mitigate conflicts and wars. Today it is acknowledged that we must strive to use everything that brings out the best in humankind; it is the responsibility of all of us progressively to build a new universality that integrates the values of humankind in its diversity. I turn now to a musical practice that offers perhaps some of the building blocks for such a process.

The Specific: An Episode and Its Development

In Morocco, in a large area between the center of the country and the Saharan regions, an important village dance dominates the musical and choreographic activity; it is called the *ahwâsh*. It is a musical and choreographic genre that joins dance, rhythmic sections, antiphonal singing, poetic jousting, and a multitude of other features belonging to the ancestral culture and to the ecosystem.

In the map (see Figure 1), the area of the *ahwâsh* is located in the polygon south of Marrakesh, including the regions of *Haha, Souss, Massa, Ayt Baamrane, Draa,* as well as the middle part of the High Atlas.

Figure 1

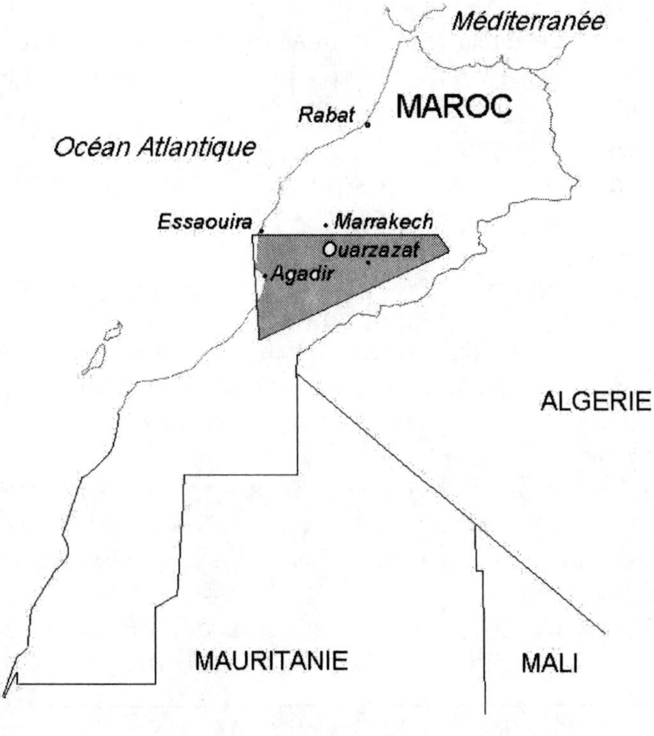

Different, multiple variants of this dance exist: it can be exclusively feminine (as in a variant in the Anti-Atlas), performed entirely by women, exclusively masculine (as in the *Haha* region near *Essaouira*), or mixed, as elsewhere. The *ahwâsh* dance offers entertainment to its participants and watchers, but there are other functions, most notably that of the management of conflicts within the tribe, or between two tribes. The three principal roles that make up the *ahwâsh* are:

- the role of entertainment, pleasure, and relaxation. This is its major function.
- the ritual role, which is linked to agrarian life, especially the life cycle of barley, but also to some beliefs of pagan origin. This can sometimes function as a rite of passage.
- the role of socialization, which is shown by the group's cohesion, and in particular, in conflict management.

When a conflict arises, there is recourse to mediation by family members, or by the wise men of the tribe who have recourse to the customary legal system *(azerf)* at first instance.

But one can also have recourse to the music performed for the *ahwâsh* dance by submitting the problem to the poets, who have power inspired by both the respect and fear of the community. They are respected for their art and their ability for improvisation, but they are also feared, because with a simple poem they can raise or lower the reputation of a person, a family, or an entire tribe.

The two parties in conflict agree to submit the problem to two poets; it also occurs that a third person does this without the knowledge of the two parties in conflict. The two poets simulate a verbal battle (*an'ibâr*) opposing the arguments of one to the other by criticizing in a lively manner and then trivializing the problem; the two parties in conflict acknowledge, by agreeing to dance together, that they are tacitly declaring their conflict ended; generally they cannot do otherwise without spoiling the villagers' joy and upsetting the poets themselves—both unacceptable.

The role of the dance is to drain off tension, to break psychological obstacles, and to prepare for reconciliation; this does not, however, preclude a return to customary law to finalize the agreement of settlement or reparation.

In what follows, I will offer an impression of this generic form with the following description of the *ahwâsh* of *Ouarzazate*.

The *Ahwâsh* of Ouarzazate

A General Overview

Ahwâsh is a collective village dance that is performed differently from one tribe to the next because of the variety of oral traditions. Nevertheless, the general structure is almost the same; in its highest form it joins poetry, song, and dance movements.

This dance is a part of all of the celebrations in the land of the Chleuh (of Berber dialect in the south of the High Atlas). Usually coeducational, it begins with a song in the form of a dialogue.

The call to the *ahwâsh* is announced by the drummers, with a sound that rips the silence of the night; the participants gradually take their places and get organized in the space (*assayes*).

To begin, the flautists strike up an unmeasured melody; this will be followed by the singing of the poet, which may or may not require replies from other poets. When the pitch is well established, the drum beat calls for dancing, first in slow movements, then accelerating to the quick and playful conclusion.

This framework will be repeated tirelessly throughout the entire night, interrupted by poetry contests, while the drummers take turns heating their drums by the campfire.

The positions of the participants can vary according to their number and functions:

- with a medium-sized *ahwâsh*, the male and female dancers are in two separate rows, distinct from the musicians and drummers.
- in a group where there are numerous drummers, the men sit together in the middle, and the dance is performed by the women, who surround the musicians and drummers.

The number of dancers, musicians, and drummers varies accordingly; here is an estimate of a few famous *ahwâsh* (see Figure 2).

There are at least two differences between dances intended for festivals and spontaneous village dances: in the first, both the number of participants and time are limited; in the second everyone participates in pursuit of a mass effect, and time can pass without constraint.

When the dance fills a large part of the night, one of the improvisers sends out a rhyming couplet that will be taken up first by the men's choir, then by the women's choir. Another soloist steps in with another couplet, then the choirs again, and so on, while the drums punctuate

Figure 2

	Poet	Flautist	Drummers	Male Dancers	Female Dancers
Imintanout (Southwest of Marrakech)	2	2	3	8	8
Haha (Essaouira)	-	2	3	12	-
Ouarzazate (Pre-Sahara)	2	3	12	-	16

the slow phrases using a burst of percussion (staggered and successive strikes). After a while, the dance as such begins when the drummers move between the two rows of singers/dancers, where they sit down and play. The song will gradually lose its pre-eminence, becoming a simple accompaniment of drums for the alternating voices.

The Four Pillars of the Ahwâsh

The *ahwâsh* dance would not hold up or make any sense without its four core components, which occupy space and share functions: they are the poets symbolized by the letter P, the musicians symbolized here by the letter M, the male and female dancers with the letter D, and finally the public or the crowd with the letter F (for *foule*).

The configuration and the functions of each of these four components or "pillars" are shown in Figure 3 below.

Figure 3

P	M (m + p)	D	F
Poets	Musicians (m) and Percussionists (p)	Male Dancers and Female Dancers	Public
Improvisation Satire	Pentatonic Rhythmic Division Progressive acceleration	Collective Gesturing and Code of Signs	Participatory

It is the poets who "open the ball" and who structure the *ahwâsh* by periodically restarting the poetic phases, alternating between singing and dancing. On the scale of value, they are placed ahead of the musicians, by the power of spoken language.

The most highly capable have the ability to improvise during the whole night, ranging from pious advice to themes of love, or social satire, for example.

The musicians and the percussionists move in a system based on the simple pentatonic mode, rhythmic division, and progressive acceleration from the slowest to the fastest.

The dancers carry out a set of group gestures and turn toward the leader to see the signals he or she gives and which will be received as a code and a gestured command. For the women's version of the dance, there are two types of complementary and cooperative hierarchies: the poetess of the group is often but not always an older woman, but there is also the one who actually leads the dance: the main drummer.

The public participates by occasionally mixing in with the dance, and encouraging the poets by calling out expressions of surprise and satisfaction, using phrases such as "ifkâk rabbi ssaht" (may God bless you and provide health for you). Women cry out "youyou"s—where the "youyou" is an approximation of the sound of the ululation of the women; in fact it is the combined result of a breath and a lateral beating of the tongue inside the mouth.

These four pillars maintain relationships between each other, either of opposition (in the poetic games), of collaboration (between musicians, percussionists, and dancers) or of sanction (by the public), which is what gives the dance its particular dynamics see (Figure 4).

The poets (P) are in opposition because they lead the poetic jousting; often the quality of a battle (the simulated verbal battle as described above) depends on meter and rhymes chosen by the protagonists.

The relationship of collaboration is established on the one hand, between the percussionists (p) and the musicians (m)—if this were not so, the *ahwâsh* could not get under way musically; and on the other hand, between the musicians and the dancers, who need the melodic phrase and the rhythmic accent. This relationship also plays in the other direction, the dancers having the possibility of suggesting melodic or rhythmic changes.

The public sanctions the agents—those people of the *ahwâsh* who are the active participants in the dance: the poets, dancers, flautists, and drummers. There are the women's "youyous" as mentioned above, and

Figure 4

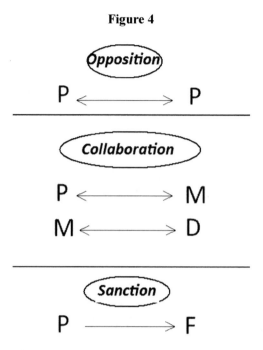

Figure 5

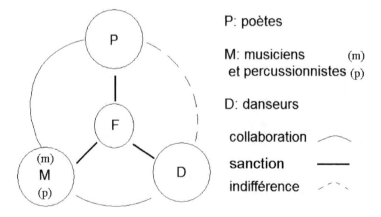

applause or cries of joy, while disapproval may also be expressed of a poet, musician, or dancer; the public may even demand their replacement. Such disapproval for a bad poet is shown in several ways: either by shouting it to his face, or by asking him to leave, or else by discreetly pushing another poet to take his place.

The four pillars support six binary relations, of three different types (two of collaboration, one of indifference, and three of sanction, as shown above). Binary relations can only be understood in a wider framework where we see the articulation of the parts to the whole.

Seen thus, *ahwâsh* is not a spectacle, although cultural tourism has ended up making it one; the public is an integral part of this collective dance. In this vein, the public can be considered as having a central function, not because it is sought after as the target of the dance, but because it participates in, and influences the dance. This is clarified by the management of space.

The Space

Ahwâsh is a performance out-of-doors that can be held on any type of terrain able to function as a village square, and there are various possible configurations of space(s). Poets, musicians, percussionists, male and female dancers, all take their places, respecting a tacit code of progressive positioning. A special place for the campfire can be added here; it is interesting to note this element, because the public can use it to make tea, and to help the percussionists by providing preheated *bendirs* (drums on a frame) from time to time; the fire is used to heat and re-heat the *bendirs*. (However, the space of the fire has in recent times tended to disappear, owing to the use of synthetic skins). (See Figure 6).

Figure 6

1:   musicians' space, closed

2:   poets' space, semi-open
     but rigorously controlled

3:   dancers' space, open

4:   public's space, participative

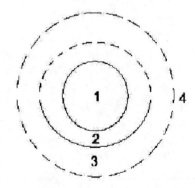

Discussion

Since music is inseparable from the social act, it is usually linked to all the verbal, corporal, and physical expressions produced by humankind, which requires a constant reassessment of the definition of music and avoiding consideration of its acoustic nature alone. One of the definitions which, I would argue, comes closest to the act of music in all its complexity, is offered by the Franco-Greek composer Iannis Xénakis, who wrote that:

> Music is a matrix of ideas, of energy-filled actions, of mental processes, which themselves are a reflection of the physical reality which we have created and which carries us... (Xénakis 2008, 16).[1]

This is an idea that applies as well to popular music as to contemporary music, and especially to those who reintegrate gesture and improvisation. In the present discussion, what is especially interesting about this definition is that it allows music to be connected in the strictly acoustic sense with dance and poetry; and this is exactly what is needed to approach the total performance in a dance like the Moroccan *ahwâsh*.

When one speaks of understanding, harmony, and collective unity, in relation to music, or being produced by music, a paradox arises; for music itself emerges as the source of contradictions, where melodic, rhythmic, and structural states are governed by antagonistic pairs which take turns in the dynamics of musical discourse. The language used and the energy felt refer to concepts such as "contretemps," "syncopation," "dissonance," and also "tension," "diversity" (a biological concept assuming natural selection) and "contrast."

These terms evoke conflict—how, therefore, can they be part of a source of understanding and harmony between peoples? But let us not forget that we are speaking of a multifaceted space of production; so that even admitting the implication of conflict, it is possible to resolve this apparent contradiction by considering musical participation as a form of catharsis draining off negative energy and potentially contributing to a better acceptance of differences.

It can also be taken into account that these moments of tension and asymmetry have been considered, at least in tonal and modal music, as preparations for relaxation and symmetry. Among my contemporaries there will of course be those who deny this need for the resolution of tension, sound having acquired a liberty of discourse which excuses thinking in terms of a restrictive resolution of notes and rhythmic accents.

Within the *ahwâsh*, provided that the poets use metaphors whose meaning is sufficiently accessible, all problems can be dealt with, and real or potential tensions can be trivialized. The dance does this either by using rhythm to drain off bottled-up tensions in the body, or by anticipating a possible conflict, by forestalling it by the beauty of the poem: thus in a contest pitting two Moroccans against one another, one Muslim and the other of the Jewish faith, the faults of each one are laid out before everyone, and what would have been silenced without resolution is shouted aloud; the dance will get the best of the two protagonists, who will take up a famous saying:

Ddîn y gad win rabbi	Religion belongs to God
Ahwâsh y gad i kiwân	*Ahwâsh* belongs to all of us

In their simplicity and at times their poverty, the people of the *ahwâsh* continue to convey values of solidarity and cooperation, values which underpin the dance's role in mediating conflict and alleviating tension. The dance requires the participation of all; moreover, the expression "*tiwiza*" in Berber (or *twiza* in Arabic), refers to collective, unified work, whether it be for the harvest or for creating poetry or music together. There is no notion of a soloist; everything is for the group or for mutual aid, with two or three flutes alternating to maintain the continuity of breath. There is open participation, for the idea of a performance in a discriminatory sense is absent in the spirit of this dance. There is no leader, strictly speaking; it is the *a'allâm* (the one who decides, who gives the signal) who acts as leader, without any other prerogative than to coordinate; but in an *ahwâsh* lasting a large part of the night, this role is passed to several persons.

Thus the specific only acquires its value if it contributes to a better respect for humankind; each country must make an effort itself, and bring its experience to the global society. History teaches us that human abilities, in every field of knowledge and of know-how, have progressed by the accumulation and contribution of successive civilizations. What is this contribution if it is not the uniqueness of each one?

The path to the universal can only be conceived of in the appreciation of the other, and in "appreciation" there is "knowledge": trying to know the other is the first step toward universality, which is first of all a frame of mind.

The message of the *ahwâsh* is a ceremonial one, which celebrates life; it can help give a broader reflection on the management of tensions, by calling on the services of art as arbitrator. But how can this be done if one doesn't speak the same language and if one doesn't have the same cultural references? We have no easy answers, but perhaps my account has opened up a way of considering this question; let's trust human ingenuity and the forces which love peace and solidarity, and make a list of all artistic forms likely to present a positive image of human existence.

Conclusion: From the Specific to the Universal

One of the definitions of universality presents it as "the characteristic of what extends to a set of places, times, beings" (Littré 2000).[2] It is thus that, within Europe and the Western classical music tradition, cultural and artistic productions have been established as universal masterpieces, because they were able significantly to influence countries and groups of people, and they remain since that time in the general global memory. However, by recognizing this quality only in its own thinkers and artists, Europe was locked into its colonial logic, not suspecting other cultures of universality. I would suggest however that elements of universality can be found everywhere, and that while in each musical work claiming universality there is nevertheless some quality that is specific and non-transferable, there is also within each specific genre, a part to share with other peoples.

So rather than looking to erase unique characteristics, which seems to be the legacy of globalization, we must look for values *within the specific* among different groups of people, which can enrich and fuel a collective contribution to what may become universal knowledge and value in musical practice. In the *ahwâsh*, we may see such an example.[3]

Notes

1.   Xénakis, Iannis. 1971. Casterman; "Music is a matrix of ideas, of energy-filled actions, of mental processes, which themselves are a reflection of the physical reality which we have created and which carries us."
2.   The definition of *universalité* is in the 2000 edition of the dictionary: (2000) *le Littré en un volume*, Hachette; 1741.
3.   Photos of *ahwâsh* can be seen on the following site: http://www.toda.org.

References

Aydoun, Ahmed. 1992. *Musiques du Maroc*, Eddif: Casablanca.
Aydoun, Ahmed. 2009. *Essai sur les Musiques Amazighes du Maroc*, Editions du 12o centenaire de Fès, Casablanca.
Chottin, Alexis. 1938. Tableau de la musique marocaine, Paris: Geuthner.

Jouad, Hassan. 1978. *La saison des fêtes dans une vallée du Haut Atlas*, Paris: le Seuil.

Littré, Émile. 1877. *Dictionnaire de la Langue Française*, Paris: Hachette.

Lorat, Jacob Bernard. 1980. *Musique et fête au Haut Atlas*, Paris: Edition Mouton.

Olsen, Miriam Rovsing. 1997. *Chants et danses de l'Atlas*, Paris: Actes Sud.

Schuyler, Phillip D. 1979. The music of the Rwayes, Washington: University of Washington.

Xenakis, Iannis. 2008. *Music and Architecture: Architectural Projects, Texts, and Realizations* Compiled, translated and commented by Sharon Kanach, England: Pendragon.

Musicking and Empathic Connections

Felicity Laurence

Imagine a warm evening at the edge of a huge ocean, the breeze just perceptible. Here there is a stage set up, partly open to the sky, and facing a large grassed area; behind, the sea. On the stage stand hundreds of children, layered in colorful tiers, one row above the next. Bright T-shirts proclaim "African Madonna," bright faces look this way and that, towards the audience who sit before them on the grass, towards the piano tucked away at the side and the small group of musicians clustered around it, and towards two women who stand in front, microphones at the ready, waiting for the music to start. There is such an aura of joyous agitation that you can almost touch it. Expectation, excitement, anticipation—and a sense of "thrillingness" stream forth from the children. But what is utterly extraordinary is that there are black children and white children, and those of other "colors" in this rainbow array, black musicians and white musicians, a black soloist and a white soloist. This is why those tiers are so colorful, but what makes this kaleidoscopic scene so amazing, is that it hasn't happened before. You can scarcely believe the evidence of your eyes. Simply the fact of all of those children standing side by side, even before they begin to sing, disturbs your sense of equilibrium, startles you, and perhaps you can feel the ground shift a little beneath your feet, as it soon will do again when the dancers dance.

For we are in apartheid South Africa, where it is not permitted to mix the colors together, on pain of punishment and much grief.

The music starts—quiet, sweet with the children's singing; the audience is still, and there is a peace here. The children sing, punctuated by the solo voices in front, of many things: pity, compassion, despair and inhumanity, but also of hope, beauty, and of their beautiful Africa as a font of celebration and love. The pace picks up as the music moves through

171

the songs, and now come the dancers, young black people who dance to the drum with mesmerizing skill, and speed, and art; "this is who we are" they are saying, and there is no mistaking this. The audience cheers and applauds and cheers again.

The music continues its journey, and time gradually slows after the dramatic climax of the dance. We come to its theme song, and the children sing:

> African Madonna, your children are our children
> their joys are our joys, their suffering is ours;
> each one who dies leaves each of us diminished,
> and for each one who dances, and shouts, and sings,
> we too rejoice.

The singer who is our African Madonna picks it up:

> "My children are your children" she sings, "and for each one who dances and shouts and sings—we all rejoice."

The music is richly calm now, but her voice soars, and there is passion in it, and the children gaze at her in wonder.

At the very end, they sing a small phrase—"Give us peace"—over and over again, in an intermingling of languages, Zulu, Afrikaans, English, others, all blended together, and coming to rest in unison on the final "Dona nobis pacem."

The audience stands, claps, calls out—there is such affirmation now. "A person says: 'This is where we are— it must change, it will change.'"

Children run everywhere as children do; here is a group with a television reporter who asks them: "Did you feel good about being in African Madonna?" and they answer "Yes!"—they felt fine. Look at the group—again, children of every racial background, standing together, talking together!

And then one girl says: "It was good to be united as one. We were united as one…"

Imagine this scene, in 1988, when the end of an utterly divisive political system was on the horizon, and everywhere in the air, but still elusive, not manifest, not discernible in the everyday lives of people there. This concert, repeated five more times, seemed to "catch" a vision, and enable those musicking in it—in Christopher Small's conception, as performers and as audience—to see how things could be, and to think about what might be needed for such a transformation.

African Madonna

African Madonna is a musical work for children to sing together with adult soloists, one of whom is the symbolic *African Madonna* of the title (Laurence 1990). I wrote this piece in 1986 as a response to the terrible famine in Ethiopia that caught the world's attention then. At that time, my job was teaching singing to hundreds of children in schools all across London, and I found that the children, like everyone else, were desperately concerned to help the other suffering children they could see every evening on their television screens. They told me that they wanted to send a plane to bring the Ethiopian children to London, to send all of their toys, and food, to the starving children; and some of them also said that they felt responsibility and even guilt for the way that our rich country exploited poorer countries. These children were only about 10-11 years old, and I was struck by their concern, their vision and understanding, their sense of right and wrong.

So I wrote the piece *African Madonna* as an attempt to give voice to these children's ideas, and to help the children do something real to help the Ethiopian children, by raising money from performances to send to them. In writing the lyrics, I drew on the words and ideas of the children themselves, and also those of the poet William Blake who two hundred years before had also demanded in his poetry that we look at each other with care and concern, what we might now conceive of as the solidarity with which we are engaged here.[1] He wrote:

Pity would be no more if we did not make children poor

And Mercy no more could be if all were as happy as we (Blake, 1789-94)

words which, if you read them carefully, are deeply challenging.[2]
And he also wrote;

… can I see another's woe and not feel in sorrow too?

Can I see another's grief and not seek for kind relief? (ibid.)

And these words, written more than two hundred years ago, evoke that sense of fellow feeling, that empathic response of sympathy and the deep impulse to respond to another's pain.

We put on three performances across London where hundreds of children sang, and hundreds of people came to hear them. We hoped that through musical means, some solidaric feeling towards those distant other children might be heightened; and as the composer, I tried to make music which would give as much meaning and emotional "charge" to the texts of the songs as possible, but always foregrounding the words themselves and making sure that the musical elements would not intrude in any way which might take attention from those words.

This piece lives still, has been sung in many languages and countries, and continues to be performed because its concerns are perhaps even more pressing than they were twenty five years ago, and the need to think in better and *different* ways about the relationship between poorer and richer countries remains acute. And during all this time, I have been thinking about the ways in which musical pieces like this one are doing their "work."

In this chapter, I will revisit this early production of the piece, "word-painted" in the opening paragraphs above, and, paraphrasing Christopher Small's own deceptively simple question in his investigation of the nature of musical meanings, I will ask what might have been "really going on" (Small 1998, 10) in that performance, which was, in fact, illicit. In that time of apartheid, a hierarchy of the participating children was brutally enforced in terms of their wealth, their access to education, their movement as free people, their very voice and existence. By law, they were not allowed to *be* together, and *certainly* not to sing together. But in this performance, three hundred children from all four hitherto separated ethnic backgrounds challenged this whole basis of existence; and there arose an *unprecedented* situation, when the children sang—together—such words as:

Africa, beautiful Africa, you can give us a new picture of ourselves

You have given us so much, your love, your music, your rhythm, your joy in celebration,

If only we don't let you starve, and exploit you, use you, abuse you...

and

If only you'd listen to me, if only you'd open your eyes...

If only you'd see the person in me

who loves her child with all the passion that any mother would feel.

In such texts, a very specific, and perhaps unusual view of Africa is both *expressed* and also *demanded*; and in singing these texts, the children were able to share feelings, meanings, experience, as they had never been able before to do. The original purpose of the piece therefore took on a new and acute dimension; no longer was it an expression of solidarity towards a distant "Other," as with the London children who first performed it, but between the very children standing right next to each other as they sang and danced together. These children of Africa had been taught *not* to "see" each other as equal in value, and any notion of mutual care was permeated and tainted by the enforced physical separation and emotional distancing in which the black children can be argued to have been allotted a less-than-human status. Here there was no conception of each other as "*an*other," which, as I have argued (see Introduction), might form a basis for an understanding of what it is to be "solidaric." Here instead, was truly the "Other," foreign, strange, unable to be empathized with, and a locus of danger.

So when we hear the child who spoke of her feeling that they had been "united as one" in the musicking, we are hearing nothing less than a revelation. She was indeed using a kind of language we hear often enough now when people try to articulate their responses to powerful massed musical experiences. But this young girl's comment was by no means for her a cliché; these words were an expression of her wonder at being in what was arguably the middle of a paradigm shift, or perhaps, a prophetic glimpse of a paradigm shift. For the first time in her life, she had experienced an equality of voice, and her own voice had been allowed to soar together with all the others, in a way which was normally completely impossible, but which was created now in the moment of the music.

In attempting to "unpick" and analyze processes at work in this performance, I will at this point briefly introduce two pivotal concepts that I have been contemplating for many years, each on its own, and (the nub of this analysis) in relationship to each other. These are the concepts of *musicking* and of *empathy*, and in pursuing the intricacies of their potential conceptual connections, I have kept always in mind the early suggestion of a link between them by the great ethnomusicologist John Blacking who suggested that:

> Through musical interaction, two people create forms that are greater than the sums of their parts, and make for themselves experiences of empathy that would be unlikely to occur in ordinary social intercourse (Blacking 1987, 26).

Musicking

In his opening Prologue, Christopher Small has given us a synopsis of his celebrated philosophy of "musicking," which is profoundly and widely influential within musicological and music educational discourses. As he explains above, his neologism "musicking" gives a concept of the meaning of music that looks to music as a human *activity* rather than as an *object*. Of course it remains undoubtedly very important to examine the music itself—that is, in the context of this piece, the songs and their rhythmical and sonic elements, their texts, and the instrumental elements—and to try to discover what it is *inside* music which might contribute towards its beneficial effects upon human relationships; and this is indeed the focus of interest in many of the chapters in this collection.

But what I want to argue here is that it may be of critical importance to look at the *act*, and indeed the very fact—of these children's co-operative music-making, with *at least as much attention* as we might also give to the music itself.

As he describes above, Small suggests that we should be concerned *not only* with the musical structures and relationships themselves (within the music "object"), *but also* the relationships between the *people* who are *doing* the musicking. This is how he states his thesis in his original book *Musicking* (1998):

> The act of musicking establishes in the place where it is happening a set of relationships, and it is in those relationships that the meaning of the act lies. They are to be found not only between those organized sounds which are conventionally thought of as being the stuff of musical meaning but also between the people who are taking part, in whatever capacity, in the performance; and they model, or stand as metaphor for, ideal relationships as the participants in the performance imagine them to be: relationships between person and person, between individual and society, between humanity and the natural world and even perhaps the supernatural world (Small 1998, 13).

As we have seen above, he further suggests that the meaning of musicking lies in the way we "explore, affirm and celebrate" a whole matrix of relationships which are the "right" ones for those specific participants in a musical performance—the *ideal* relationships as *the participants themselves* conceive these to be. This is no Platonic ideal, and musicking carries no connotation of inherent virtue, so that it is as possible for musicking to serve harmful purposes as it is to be used for good. In this view, the *way in which we music* reflects the kinds of values we hold, or would like to explore; the kinds of musicking in which we choose to participate (as listeners, performers, or composers) reflects our views of what are—for us—"right relationships."[3] With his own words so close by, and so germane at this very point in my argument, I invite the reader to study them again in the following excerpt from his earlier Prologue to this volume:

> A musical performance brings into existence relationships that are thought desirable by those taking part, and in doing so it not only reflects those ideal relationships but also shapes them. It teaches and inculcates those ideal relationships—we might call them values—and empowers those taking part to try them on, to see how they fit, to experience them without necessarily having to commit themselves to them, at least for more than the duration of the performance. It is thus an instrument of exploration.

In articulating those values it empowers those taking part to say, to themselves, to one another, and to anyone else that may be paying attention: these are our values, our concepts of how the relationships of the world ought to be, and, consequently, since how we relate is who we are, to say, this is who we are. It is thus an instrument of affirmation.

And, thirdly, in empowering those taking part to explore and affirm their values, it leaves them with a feeling of being more completely themselves, more in tune with the world and with their fellows. After taking part in a successful performance one is able to feel that this is how the world *really* is, and this is how I *really* relate to it. In short, it leaves the participants feeling good about themselves and about their values. It is thus an instrument of celebration.

In this African performance, and during the five that followed in subsequent days, the children not only sang and danced together, they walked around arm in arm, and spoke openly of their feelings of community and oneness. I remember always one of the adults attending to the children who remarked to me in some anguish: "If they can do this in one week, why can't we?" In the performances, what they were doing was proclaiming the *rightness* of this *new* way of being; at least for the duration of that performance, they were able to live in an equal relationship with each other, and find—if only for a moment—a sense of "right relationship" with each other. They were also demonstrably engaged in Small's exploration of these relationships, "trying them on" to "see how they [might] fit."

It seemed that this relationship was also characterized by a sense of seeing things from each other's points of view and of having more in common than not; by taking part in—indeed creating—a *joint project*; and by actively striving to *reach out* to the "other"—the person who has until now been estranged from you, and being strange, also feared.

These are all aspects of *empathic* relationship, and this takes me to the second core concept underpinning this exploration; namely, the ability and—crucially—*willingness* to empathize, which lie at the heart of solidaric and cooperative existence.

Empathy[4]

The philosopher Edith Stein offered a theory of empathy as a *process* with different stages, in which you must cognitively "grasp" the experience of the other with whom you wish to empathize. The process may involve the arousal of sympathetic feeling in the empathizer, and when it is "complete," it can yield a sense of *community* and a feeling of oneness. This in turn is conceptually different, and in terms of experience, almost "opposite," to the "emotional wave" to which she referred as emotional contagion, which may accompany the act of empathizing but which achieves a yielding up of self rather than the retention of self which must be a condition of real community. Empathizing is thus not a function of raw feeling, but requires an *act of imagination* (Stein 1917; 1922).

Among suggested stages and aspects within the empathic process are: the *perception of similarity*; the *specific situation*; and the *context* in which empathizing is undertaken. Importantly, there has been widespread agreement that without "enough" perception of similarity, the empathic process cannot even begin; this offers immediately a role for musicking, where making music together can provide a shared experience which in turn may allow or enable those crucial feelings of similarity to develop. Certainly, it seemed that it was the experience of the musicking which enabled the children in this performance to bypass the political barriers set up so blatantly to emphasize difference between them.

Empathizing as a process leads to an empathic relationship, which, as mentioned above, is characterized at its core by being *non-hierarchical*. That is of course an ideal state; but it is the state which empathic relationship can be conceived as tending towards. In such a relationship, the "other" is enhanced and not diminished: and there is, as described above, an *active* striving to "grasp" the other's consciousness, and the other person's inner state, in a framework of care and sympathy.

A Concept of a Potential Relationship between Musicking and Empathy

Taking *musicking* as essentially having to do with human actions and relationships, and *empathizing* as a core requirement of interhuman relationships based upon values of solidarity as defined earlier, I suggest that these two forms of human action may, *in certain circumstances*, have some mutual resonance in which they may affect and possibly enhance each other.

The fundamental premise here is the notion that there may be particular points in the empathic process, and some elements of empathic relationship, which may intersect with elements of *certain kinds* of musicking. Furthermore, where this intersection occurs, there may arise a reciprocal effect whereby the musicking may "catalyze" and help build empathic relationship, which in turn affects the quality, content and ongoing effectiveness of the musicking.

Thus, for example, in musicking that incorporates and promotes attention and response to the other, which was an explicit aspect of this performance, empathic relationship—as inherently "other-enhanc-ing"—may be strengthened or indeed created.

Likewise, musicking which focuses upon the other's humanness and which is non-alienating, as the *African Madonna* songs were written to be, may support that aspect of empathic response which humanizes the "other," acknowledges the other's humanness and human rights, sees the other as human and not as object, and accepts difference.

And in musicking where non-hierarchical "ideal" relationships are being "explored, affirmed and celebrated," as I have suggested was occurring during this performance, then empathic relationship—be-ing inherently non-hierarchical—is also being supported, sustained or brought into being.

Many people attending the Durban performance spoke of it as reflect-ing the powerful yet fragile "Zeitgeist" of the moment—a moment when a feeling of change was almost palpable. In this way, the context for the performance gave it a particular and vital validity, and provided a unique potential, and perhaps indeed a critical condition, for this musicking to do "empathic work."

A Different View

The corollary of this analysis of course is that another kind of musick-ing, where, for example, relationships of power or malign or dehuman-izing goals are sought or expressed, will be detrimental and inimical to empathic "work." Quite simply, in this case, the posited "link" between musicking and empathy no longer exists. Furthermore (and this brings us back to Christopher Small's opening story) exactly the same piece of music may be used in different kinds of musicking—so that while the qualities of the music itself may *contribute* to empathic outcomes, they cannot *determine* them. And it is this reality that takes my "story" to the point at which, many years ago, and before I had the benefit of Small's insights, I began to conceive of these things.

In writing the music, I had been imbued with the idea that I had learnt of the composer putting her feelings "into" the music, and the perform-ers and listeners being able to express and understand them and what the composer had intended to convey emotionally. My job, as I saw it, was to write well enough for the music to speak for itself—always—and have the same effects in each performance, arising from the complex partnership between the words and the music that I was making to maximize their expressiveness. Lawrence Kramer has suggested that the music which is bound to words to create a song can be envisaged as the "imaginative space that the text is unable to occupy, a dimension of emotion or meaning that the text may imply but cannot quite embody" (Kramer 2000, 173). For him certainly, the music object, consisting of its timbres, patterns and rhythms, supplies this "dimension" of emotion and adds this and extra layers of meaning too, to the texts. This is what I believed I was doing, and I thought it would be enough for the music to do the work I hoped it would do. And so it seemed; the piece was performed across the world, and everywhere to warm response and reception, with people visibly moved.

But I was wrong of course. I realize now that I was misinterpreting what seemed hard evidence; and the apparent consistency and "matching" of these responses did not in fact come only from the "musical" experience of the songs and the children singing them. This consonance arose also from a parallel match between *context*, *intention*, and in Small's conception, the kinds of *ideal relationships* that were being explored and celebrated. And when the piece came up against another kind of contextual setting, it didn't bring about any of the harmony I had come to believe lay *within* it.

It happened that a few years after this performance, there was another production of *African Madonna*, in the same town, with the same soloists, the same conductor, and again with many children from the different racial groups, though not the same children as before.[5] But this performance was profoundly different in its outcome—this time of alienation rather than unity between the children and also between the participating adults. The children did not link arms, they did not speak of feeling united in any way, and in fact were separated into "black" and "white" as if Nelson Mandela had never walked free from Robben Island. At the end of the performance, the black children returned to their townships confirmed in their separateness, and likewise the white children to their own houses. There were apparently no "magic moments" here, even if the singing itself was powerful and beautiful, and even if the music itself was exactly the same. And I wondered how it was that this could be—that this music had failed so abjectly to move people where before they had risen up in ovation. Using the insights afforded by the musicking-empathy thesis, "in reverse" as it were, we might be able to construct a view which explains what might have been "going on" this time.

There was a different socio-political context; apartheid was gone, but the first rapture had crumbled into a morass of violence and thwarted expectations. The Zeitgeist of hope and promise had evaporated in the realities of the magnitude of change which would be needed to bring to people's daily lives any tangible manifestation of the justice so desperately needed in that country, the justice which must always underpin solidarity and peace. I spoke in my Introduction of the need for enough will and consensus to "get people to the table"—and where our first performance might be seen metaphorically as that table to which so many were prepared and ready to come, in the second performance, that will was fading. True, the children sang together, but it was a hollow singing. The intentionality underlying this performance had perhaps less to do with the demonstration (in the face of the authorities), announcement, and celebration of a new, collective vision seen in the first performance, than with the personal agenda of some of the adults involved in the second one, who now were moving within a far narrower space of both action and ambition. For them, this performance was an opportunity to be seen including black children in ongoing white privilege, and as a forum to display their own musical competence. But the black children were aware of reality of their continuing exclusion from this white privilege, and instead of a singing *with* and a *being with,* there was just a singing—beautiful but empty.

So any initial intention, for example to strengthen a burgeoning sense of empathic connection between former oppressor and formerly oppressed, was undermined by the lack of any real sense of a joint project, or consensus, or shared intentionality. The hierarchical power structures that are, as we have seen, inimical to empathic relationships, were confirmed in the way in which this musicking was carried out. The reaching out to each other, so evident in the first concert, was replaced by a dull acceptance of separation. Elizabeth Bowen has written above of the projects that gave "voice to the voiceless," and this is what African Madonna had seemed to do at the edge of the sea that autumn evening in 1988. Not now; the voices that sang the non-white children "into existence" as they always had, remained silenced once the songs were over.

So it was that music which seemed lovely and effective may have served musicking that in the end was harmful; certainly I wished that that concert had not taken place. The "ideal" relationships prevailing were no longer those of equality, of being "united-as-one," but instead, of power and distrust; and the music simply couldn't do its work as intended and hoped by its composer.

Tao philosophy teaches us to learn from the opposite case; in looking at the second occasion, we may find further ways of understanding the first. It becomes very clear that for musicking to achieve empathic work, there must also be explicit *intention* and also *consensus*. These in turn rest upon further contextual conditions, and where the context is simply too hostile to the kinds of ideal relationships we may be seeking to engender, and "explore, affirm and celebrate," then the musicking cannot succeed, in Christopher Small's words (above), in confirming that "this is who we are," "these are our values," and that we are, through this musicking, "more completely [our]selves, more in tune with the world and with [our] fellows."

But in the first performance, these elements of intentionality and consensus were strong. I reflect of course on the extent of this within each person there; for the musicking happens with each of us as it can, and according to what we bring and how we feel about our own ideal relationships. Most people there came in a spirit of yearning for a better way of living and "being with" themselves and each other. But perhaps some felt the ground giving way when they saw those strong young dancers, so brilliant, so confident in their brilliance, and so powerful. I met a man afterwards who had been there, but he spoke in derisory terms of the black children, and it would seem that the musicking for him did not allow him to be affirmed; his comments made clear enough that for him this was not a vision of the world "as it *really* is," and the relationships being explored by others there were not *his* ideal relationships.

Conclusion

The people who had directed and organized the first performance chose the piece precisely because they wished to declare the new vision it offered. Thus the intention for peace and solidarity lay not only within the innermost musical elements and the very words of every song, but was expressed by those who worked with the children, who in turn expressed their consensus in the kinds of actions and cooperative behavior described above. There was clear and evident consensus too from the audience, the listeners who are also musicking in terms of Small's account of what it means to music.

Thus, in this performance of the piece *African Madonna*, I suggest that the musicking was being "harnessed" at various points within the empathic process, thereby both catalyzing and supporting empathic relationship. This therefore went further than expressing a sympathetic response to an inequitable status quo, as in those original London performances of the piece, but instead, was announcing and even enacting a new, and empathic, vision.

The children sing; three hundred voices with strength and conviction, three hundred young people demanding that we take heed, three hundred individual souls musicking solidarity into existence.

Listen to me
Open your eyes
You need me, I need you
We need each other
Open your eyes and you will see
I need you, you need me,
I am your sister, your brother, your child and your teacher,
as you are mine
as you are mine
as you are mine.

Notes

1. Fragments and excerpt from William Blake's *Songs of Innocence and Experience* were set to music in a number of the songs in this piece.
2. These and other words pointing to the injustice of inequitable relationships were certainly considered to pose too much of a challenge to one children's choral conductor (in a European country) who declined permission for his children to perform the piece on the grounds of what he saw as its political stance.
3. For an extended and authoritative explanation of his concept, written in his own words, the reader at this point can revisit Christopher Small's Prologue in this volume.
4. For a fuller account of the nature of empathy and its relevance to contexts in which peaceful relationships are sought through musical means, see my chapter "Music and Empathy" in *Music and Conflict Transformation: Harmonies and Dissonances in Geopolitics* (Urbain ed. 2008, London: Tauris).
5. While my knowledge of the first concert was gained first hand (I was accompanying it at the piano though not involved in the direction), my information about the second, later performance is gained from detailed written accounts from, and subsequent interviews with, two adult participants.

References

Blacking, John. 1987. *A Commonsense View of All Music*. Cambridge: Cambridge University Press.

Blake, William. 1789-1794/ 1970. *Songs of Innocence and of Experience: Shewing the Two Contrary States of the Human Soul* ed. G. Keynes London: Oxford University Press.

Kramer, Lawrence. 2000. "On deconstructive text—music relationships" in D. B. Scott (ed.) *Music, Culture, and Society: A Reader* Oxford: Oxford University Press.

Laurence, Felicity. 1990. *African Madonna* Cambridge: Cambridge University Press.

Small, Christopher. 1998. *Musicking: The Meanings of Performing and Listening*. Hanover, NH: Wesleyan University Press.

Stein, Edith. 1917/ 1989. *On the Problem of Empathy*. Washington, D.C.: ICS Publications.

Stein, Edith. 1922/ 2000. ed. Sawicki, M. *Philosophy of Psychology and the Humanities* Washington, D.C.: ICS Publications.

Making Musical Space for Peace

June Boyce-Tillman

Introduction

Within Western culture, the twentieth century was characterized by yet another search for a uniformity that might bring peace, based on the methodology of science. But as with previous attempts at the enforcement of a metanarrative on a large part of the globe, it has failed, and we are quite rightly asked again to respect difference in all areas of contemporary life. As noted by Jonathan Sacks, the chief rabbi for the UK:

> The world is not a single machine. It is a complex, interactive ecology in which diversity—biological, personal, cultural and religious—is of the essence... nature and humanly constructed societies, economies and polities, are systems of ordered complexity. That is what makes it creative and unpredictable. Any attempt to impose on them an artificial uniformity in the name of a single culture or faith, represents a tragic misunderstanding of what it takes for a system to flourish... Through exchange, difference becomes a blessing, not a curse. When difference leads to war, both sides lose. When it leads to mutual enrichment, both sides gain (Sacks 2002, 22).

The free market has been seen as an attempt at this idea of exchange as an alternative to war. However, the deliberate secularization of the market by Western cultures has led to conditions in which moral considerations have become marginalized. We now live in an age of bureaucratic and managerial political systems, whose prime aim is to offer maximum choice to individuals with sufficient wealth to access the uncontrolled market. In this current liberal democratic view, religion is seen as archaic and pernicious, and yet in the values of many faiths were, and are still, ideas of "solidarity, justice and compassion and of the non-negotiable dignity of human lives" (Sacks 2002, 11-2).

If the terrorist attacks epitomized by the twin towers disaster have taught that view of liberal democracy anything, it is that religion is an

185

intense driver of human action. Since 9/11 there has been a renewed interest in the urgency of interfaith dialogue for the establishment of world peace. This requires the acceptance of the validity of another's point view in the area of faith, an area particularly problematic for those faiths that lay claim to a monopoly of absolute truth. Religion cannot be left out of debates concerning what Huntington (1996) called the "clash of civilizations." It needs to be included in the analysis of the problem so that it can be included in the strategies for the solution.

In this chapter, I consider the question of whether, and how, we might address these values of solidarity, justice and respect for difference in the context of faith traditions through music making. I will describe the musical project *Space for Peace*, in which spiritual difference is seen as a source of creativity and mutual empowerment, expressed and enacted through music-making. The project involves multiple choirs with a variety of faith identities creating a piece together by chance/choice methods. I will evaluate the outcomes, drawing on many rich participant accounts of the experience, and its potential role in the meeting of multiple religious identities with respect, with a particular focus on the concepts of liminality, complexity theory, and place memory. I will examine how the various domains of musical experience work together to create a liminal space in which difference can co-exist with respect. This will include discussion of the role of place and complexity in constructional practices in the musical experience. It will be preceded by a discussion of identity in the context of religion and civilization.

I begin now with a discussion for the context for this work, of the globalized world and the dilemmas it poses to interhuman connection.

Identity, Religion and Globalization

Globalization has presented us with a variety of problems including an attempt to obliterate difference by means of consumption, with exclusionary results in the area of the poor, and of spiritual traditions. This cultural shift has led to a crisis in identity:

> Throughout history until very recently, most people for most of their lives were surrounded by others with whom they shared a faith, a tradition, a way of life, a set of rituals and narratives of memory and hope... that is not our situation today. We live in the conscious presence of difference. In the street, at work and on the television screen we constantly encounter cultures whose ideas and ideals are unlike ours. That can be experienced as a profound threat to identity. One of the great transformations from the twentieth to the twenty-first centuries is that the former was dominated by the politics of *ideology;* we are now entering an age of the politics of *identity.* ...

Identity divides. The very process of creating an "Us" involves creating a "Them"—the people not like us (Sacks 2002, 10).

The emotional intensity that colors much religious belief, fervor and spirituality makes it potentially a particularly problematic area. Michael Ignatieff has pinpointed the predicament thus:

The more strongly you feel the bonds of belonging to your own group the more hostile, the more violent will be your feelings towards outsiders. You can't have this intensity of belonging without violence, because belonging of this intensity moulds the individual conscience: if a nation gives people a reason to sacrifice themselves, it also gives them a reason to kill (Ignatieff 1993, 188).

In an age of uncertainties, fundamentalisms with all these characteristics are growing. These oppose liberal democracy and the market by attempting to defeat them on their own territory—the imposition of a single way of life.

So how can we set about building religious/spiritual identities based on the dignity of difference? I have become taken up with Derrida's notion of "difference" and the dilemma of how to make relationships across personal and cultural divides without making the "Other" like oneself. How can we relate effectively without abandoning our own identity personally and culturally?

I developed this into a model of the musical experience as one of encounter including four domains of encounter:

* Expression—an Other self
* Values—an Other culture
* Construction—the world of abstract ideas
* Materials—the environment

I have outlined in other places (Boyce-Tillman 2004) how the successful negotiation of a relationship with all these four domains leads to transformative liminality (Boyce-Tillman 2009); to describe this I drew on literature on trance, ecstasy and flow. This notion is drawn from religious ritual, whether it is a Christian Eucharist or a shamanic healing rite (Driver 1998). It draws on Martin Buber's concept of the power of the I/Thou relationship:

But it can also happen, if will and grace are joined, that as I contemplate the tree I am drawn into a relation, and the tree ceases to be an it (Buber 1970, 57).

These ideas are related to those of the philosopher Levinas (1969) who questioned the notion of the "Same" as the basis of ethics, favoring relationship with Otherness as a relationship based on allowing the Other a distinct identity rather than making the Other the Same as the relating "I" (Levinas 1960, 33). As Isaiah Berlin writes:

> to realize the relative validity of one's convictions, and yet stand for them unflinching-ly, is what distinguishes a civilized man [sic] from a barbarian (Berlin 2002, 217).

The challenge to the world faiths is the supreme one which has eluded many of them in the past—that of finding the Divine in a person of another faith tradition.

For Levinas the encounter with difference represented an encounter with infinity, and a way of being in which the spirituality resides in the flow between the two others who retain their differences in the meeting, which I call difference-in-relationship. This links with Derrida's notion of "difference" (Derrida 1972, 19) and also John Dewey's concept of experience:

> [An experience is an] interaction of organism and environment which, when it is carried to the full, is a transformation of interaction into participation and communication (Dewey 1934/80, 22).

This is well described by Rudolf Steiner in a lecture from 1919:

> When I meet another person and through my relationship to that other person express that he or she has something like my I, I engage in the interplay that flows between me and the other person [...] This is the relationship that exists when one person meets another and perceives the other I—that is, devotion to the other—inner resistance; sympathy-antipathy. I am not speaking now of feeling, but just the perception of meeting. The soul vibrates; it vibrates sympathy-antipathy, sympathy-antipathy, sympathy-antipathy (Steiner 1996, 136-40).

Infinity and the Liminal Space

Steiner goes on to describe the process to be like waking and sleeping and by using this analogy he highlights its similarity with the altered time/space dimension of liminality, a concept which I have developed in the area of music, and based on the work of Victor Turner (Boyce-Till-man 2006a, 2006b, 2007a and 2007b). So infinity resides in the spaces between differences and is linked to the concept of mystery which is, as Begara puts it:

> a mixture of certitudes and uncertainties; of probabilities, hypotheses, realities that surpass us, and fundamental questions to which we have no answers... It is one of those words that is indefinable, but that can in the final analysis be part of any defini-tion (Begara 1999, 133).

The idea of a space where paradox is held without resolution is one that has fascinated many theologians and philosophers, particularly those who wish to break away from the Aristotelian right/wrong logic that has dominated Western thought for so long:

> We look at the world through analytical lenses. We see everything as this or that; either...or; on or off, positive or negative; in or out; black or white. We fragment reality in an endless series of "either ... or." In short, we think the world apart. Of course this has given human beings a great power over nature, a lot of success, many gifts of modern science and technology. But we can say that we have also lost the sense of mystery. This dualism of "either ... or" thinking has also given us a fragmented sense of reality that destroys the wholeness and wonder of life. It misleads and betrays us when applied to the perennial problems of being human in this world. Therefore, we need to move away from an "either ... or" attitude to a "both ... and" attitude. In certain circumstances, truth is a paradoxical joining of apparent opposites, and if we want to know that truth we must learn to embrace those opposites as one (Kaggwa 2008).

The challenge to dominant patriarchal cultures is to point to "a diversity of ways of being human" (Johnson 1992, 155). The psychologist Isabel Clarke writes about two ways of knowing. What she calls relational, I call liminal:

> The verbal propositional processing system deals in discrimination; in "either-or". Whereas the relational looks for connection and the whole picture... (Clarke 2005, 98)

So the encounter with differences externally can lead to an encounter with these alterities within the individual self and a greater sense of inner peace based on the acceptance of multiple identities within the self.

In the project described in this chapter, the peaceful co-existence of otherness is a central part of the underpinning philosophy. I suggest that in the area of faith this can best be addressed through music making. Because of (as described above) the richness of the encounter, and by reconstructing the various domains of the experience, we can model value systems that are different from those produced by the market—those values of:

> Reverence, restraint, humility, a sense of limits, the ability to listen and respond to human distress (Sacks 2002, 13).

My thesis is that the creation of a liminal musical space enables the encountering of difference with respect because of its central characteristics:

- respect for difference
- an understanding of the alterities within the self associated with the ability to use these creatively
- the encounter with a wider infinity through encounter with widely differing Others—which can be cultural, spiritual and personal

- •   a sense of shared community-communitas

This chapter describes how musical events can be set up to facilitate the development of these qualities in a culture in which an increasing number of people are marginalized. The capacity of music to create liminal space, and the fact that music seals human cultures less hermetically than language, make it an appropriate tool for such a dialogue between faith traditions and for the respect of multiple identities. Heidi Westerlund is clear about this capacity:

> [...] music could be a genuine way to *create* situations, to *construct* social relations in situations, to *communicate* in a holistic way that combines body and ethics, individual and community (Westerlund 2002, 144).

The Project *Space for Peace*

My thinking about the inclusion of difference in a musical structure has led me to this radically innovative series of events designed for Winchester cathedral, in southern England.[1] Two took place in January 2009 and January 2010 respectively. This magnificent space would become a place for the exploration of difference-in-relationship in the area of religion and spirituality. Jonathan Sacks highlights how there are fewer and fewer spaces where differences meet now:

> Neighborhoods in many Western cities have become ever more economically segregated... Public spaces have grown fewer, their place taken by shopping malls and entertainment complexes, open only to those with the ability to pay. There is less mixing than there was between different economic classes and age groups, and with it a breakdown of that hard-to-define element of social solidarity known as "trust" (Sacks 2002, 30-1).

And yet people long for relationships that are outside the economic sphere, and within congregations, neighborhoods and voluntary organizations. Religious congregations helped to build communities by giving human lives meaning and reminding people that they were not alone. Here I saw a chance to create new community—a new "We" that would give the "I" a renewed identity (Sacks 2002, 202). Interestingly, people who were seeking this came from some considerable distance to take part in the three events following the frame of *Space for Peace*.

It took a great deal of work to set it up. I drew on a web of relationships that had already been formed by a variety of pieces in which local groups had participated. I had written a number of pieces involving local schools and we had co-operated with local music services in a number of projects. I had been involved in interfaith dialogue in London since the

1980s and through these networks had met a rabbi who was an excellent cantor. The contact was made with the local Hindu singer through the network of Arts Asia, which is a Southampton organization that teaches Indian instruments. The Three Faiths forum linked me with the imam in a Southampton mosque. Here I spoke to a number of elders at the mosque. It was not easy to explain what was required of them, as they were used to roles in set liturgies. However, when they grasped the nature of the event they all were in sympathy with the intention behind the musical frame. To make the links I had to draw my considerable experience of interfaith dialogue and my knowledge of their belief systems and rituals, and especially their music. It was often a slow and meticulous process forming these links but very rewarding.

For each of these events, we assembled together local choral groups from a variety of sources—community choirs, schools, the university, the cathedral choristers, and a rabbi who chanted the Hebrew Scriptures, a Muslim imam chanting the call to prayer, and a Hindu singer singing Hindu and Sikh hymns. Some participants used notation, some had no grasp of it and learned everything orally, some were older and singing for fun.[2] Others were skilled classical musicians, pupils from a private school, participants from a variety of religious traditions of whom some were Jewish, some Christians of various traditions, some secularists, and all within an age range of 7-85 years. The participants were contacted in advance and sent copies or sound files of the shared peace chants. I visited each choir or soloist before the event to help with the peace chants and/or explain how the event worked and its philosophy. On the day of the event itself we met for an hour beforehand to go through the peace chants as they fitted together in the first and last movements, and to show the choirs/soloists where they were placed. We used choir companions from the university who knew where each choir was placed and the route for their processional.

We used the cathedral as a resonant meditative space able to contain and merge diversity in a way that accepted it without obliterating it. Each group or individual had chosen in advance what they would sing for peace—some of their favorite pieces. The musical material included popular songs from various cultures, motets, hymns, worship songs, chants and chanting.

The overall plan was that of five movements flowing into one another. It started with all the choirs simultaneously singing peace chants that fitted together, some of which were learned by the congregation/audience. The choirs then processed to their place in the cathedral, to small chapels, parts of the nave, the galleries and so on. Then they chose what and when to sing. Everyone could go and light candles and listen and join in others' pieces. Then they processed back, singing words for peace on a single note and carrying candles, while a saxophonist and solo singer improvised. They returned to the chancel and the opening chants. The third movement of the event was created by the participants on the basis of choice. Each group chose when to sing and could also be invited by the congregation to sing.

The role of the congregation/audience is interesting. They learned some of the peace chants at the beginning and were given a map of where each choir was situated in movement 3. They were in the nave at the beginning and at the end but wandered freely for movements 2 and 3. When the shalom procession started they were able to join the end of the candlelit processions. Some of the audience used the event like a concert and moved round to listen; others joined in with the choirs; others treated it as a time of prayer while others used all these modes in the course of it.

Everyone could move around the building, lighting candles, praying, being quiet, as they chose, but also participating in creating the musical sound. My experience of earlier pieces I had written involving choice of this kind had been that people become very sensitive to their surroundings and to one another. Some of the soundscapes were very complex as pieces were performed simultaneously in various areas of the cathedral, and sometimes it was quite simple. Sacred peace chants that I had written threaded their way through the sound from time to time. A review of the event describes it thus:

> From the Lady Chapel, a children's choir made fascinating duets with Just Sing It, a London-based peace group. In the nave, cleared medieval-style of all chairs, and maybe some of our preconceptions, the effects were especially rewarding. Amid echoes of Sydney Carter, English folksong and the *Missa di angelis* from beyond the chancel, of Taizé chant and South African Alleluias from the west door, and of Tallis from the aisle, the cantor sang from the pulpit. At one point he paused to listen to the rich motet harmonies, before resuming his cantillation from Leviticus—a sweet moment (Williams 2009).

The event was designed therefore to reflect a new model of peacemaking based on the principle that it will only work if we all do what we want to do but also then have the responsibility of working out how far it fits with what other people want to do. Everyone present had a part in the creation of an experience of beauty and togetherness, and they found intuitive ways of relating to and cooperating with others.

The effect of the events was beyond my imaginings. Children singing *I think to myself what a wonderful world* merged with plainchant, Jewish cantillation, Taize chants and motets in a way that saw diversity held in a unity that was not uniformity.

In the following evaluation, I look now at what was going on through a number of theoretical lenses, as outlined in my Introduction above. Liminality seems a fundamental concept here to understand people's experiences.

Liminality

People clearly experienced the liminality of the event. It is very difficult to define fully the characteristics of this experience but some that are found in these accounts include:

- a limen (or threshold) that is crossed from ordinary knowing especially in the space/time dimension
- a feeling of difference in relationship leading to a deep sense of peace
- a paradoxical knowing so that diversity can exist within it easily
- a sense of empowerment, bliss, realization
- a sense of the beyond, infinity
- a feeling of an opening-up in the experiencer as boundaries start to dissolve
- a sense of transformation, change
- an evanescent and fleeting quality that cannot be controlled, which may result in a sense of givenness
- a feeling of unity with the human and the other-than-human world

They wrote:

"thrilled" is perhaps the word to use. I have been pondering on how to best describe my response to *Space for Peace*, the feeling of almost joy and the urge to follow those pure evocative sounds echoing through the spaces of the cathedral.

Have you ever walked the pavements of a residential area of New Delhi or Dhaka or Hanoi in the evening? It's the hot season and the warmth of the evening air cloaks like velvet and every so often, as you pass the little urban gardens the heavy exotic scent of night-flowering shrubs wafts over the walls. The perfume is so wonderful you stop and backtrack, trying to find the source of that heavenly perfume. That was how your choirs and soloists sounded.

Please go on exploring these musical spaces.

I haven't really come down from the rafters yet! Monday evening was an astonishing experience. I think it couldn't have been done without those vast spaces in the vaulting, where all the harmonies could be free-floating and the many melodies meld! And it was only your extraordinary imagination that enabled this to happen. We were all so lucky to be there and to benefit from that most creative experiment; I do hope it happens again in the not too distant future.

My favorite part was at around 8.25 pm sitting in the (then empty) choir whilst the sounds and performances washed in and out. It reminded me of the "offstage" singing of "Praise to the Holiest" in Gerontius - I think that is what Heaven must be like!

I described above how the musical experience is one of encounter and how people can enter the liminal experience through the four domains in the musical experience. Some of the prayer-like experiences were linked with the various atmospheres experienced. In the domain of expression there were (not surprisingly) a number of references to feelings of peace. Some of these were linked with prayer in some way:

Space for peace was one of the high points of my life... The cathedral was cleared of chairs, which was wonderful—one great echoing space. It was all about peace—calls for peace constantly mingling and changing... I was able to sit and meditate on the stone floor in the middle of the North Transept, one of the most beautiful parts. It came to me that "peace is possible."

Children caught the spirit of prayerfulness.

As the whole event drew to a close I noticed a child near me sitting on the floor in the classic eastern meditation position.

Other liminal experiences were linked with freedom of the atmosphere: children were seen skipping round the cathedral enjoying the experience of freedom. In one interview, a child said how at home they felt being placed in a little chapel rather than the singing in the whole building, which can be "traumatic." They liked a "cozy space." The distribution of the choirs had enabled this new experience. As people wandered around in silence, people were seen to embrace one another. Empathy with other performers was felt:

It was inspiring and memorable to hear the other singers and meld our voices with theirs.

Construction and Complexity Theory[3]

The construction of the piece could be seen in the context of complexity theory as applied to the notion of musical construction. This is linked with the feeling of freedom described above, and involved considerable risk:

It was an incredibly brave and innovative venture which worked brilliantly... I loved the fact that you could walk around, sampling different styles and interpretations and, along the way, enjoy the surprise of a lone voice suddenly appearing from a balcony or behind a pillar.

The study of complexity arose in the 1980s when it was related to chaos theory which itself was related to research on creativity. In the context of the argument of this chapter, it effectively brings together the idea of creativity being rooted in the allowing of diversity to flourish. Complexity theory studies how order, structure and pattern can arise from apparently chaotic and very complicated systems, and some theorists see it as part of the challenge to Enlightenment linear theory. It concerns the ability of structures to self-organize and acquire new features not present in the original structure. Some of the features found by complexity theory researchers appeared in the performance.

Firstly, the theory postulates that a complex system is composed of many parts that interconnect in intricate ways. The interconnections in the central section of *Space for Peace* were intense and as the piece moved forward participants became more skilled at creating complex interrelationships. Another characteristic is that emergent behavior is difficult to predict, even though the behavior of each of the parts is predictable. In *Space for Peace,* although each individual choir had set pieces that were predictable and stable, the overall structure was unpredictable and changing. The classic example of this was the moment when the Rabbi crossed over to sing with the imam in the pulpit. This was regarded as a miraculous moment by many people present.

A further characteristic of complexity is that the sum of the whole is greater than the parts. Many of the groups chose short chants which when blended to build up complex soundscapes. Also, a performing artist punctuated the event with a dramatic intervention from a gallery of "Can you hear me? Can you hear me above the sounds of war?" which would have been meaningless on its own. In the concept of dynamic complexity, obvious interventions produce non-obvious consequences.[4] A number of new elements arose that had not been forecast. A Jewish participant asked the rabbi to sing Kaddish for a relative for whom it had not been sung. Some members of the audience formed an impromptu choir in an empty chapel. A liturgical dancer danced for a quarter of an hour in the North transept. The freeing up of the space liberated the creativity of all present.

Cooperation with the Space

We saw above how the musical experience includes an encounter with the materials that make the sound. Here a very important part of this was the huge acoustic space of the cathedral.

Many people noted the ability of the building to contain and embrace diversity effectively and felt that the stones themselves were involved in the process. This notion was common in medieval Europe, because of the theory of the Music of the Spheres with its fundamental principle of a vibrating universe. These ideas, originating in ancient Greece, fitted well with medieval Christianity in the work of theologians like Hildegard of Bingen (Boyce-Tillman 2000) as well as philosophers like Boethius, Johannes Kepler, and Robert Fludd (James 1995, 30). They underpinned the design of many of the great cathedrals of medieval Europe to produce spaces of unparalleled resonances. The elements of the natural world, in this case the building itself, are an intrinsic part of the musical experience. The gradual division of the world into the animate and the inanimate helped the fracturing of the sounds made by humans and the natural world. More traditional societies do not subscribe to this animate/inanimate division of contemporary science, a view that Western colonialism attempted to subjugate wherever it found it (Tinker 2004). In such societies, each place and its associated music will have its own soundscape of the natural world with animals, birds and sounds of wind and sea that are regarded as an essential part of the event. Songs are reworked for each occasion and are associated with particular holy sites and the mineral and animal world. Nowadays these sounds will include louder sounds such as traffic and sirens. These too will become part of holy sound-scapes.

The development of and centrality of notation systems to European music enabled the process of separating music from the context of its performance. The score itself of the classical piece became "the music" and music became separated from the body and the natural world. Classical music became "about" the abstraction of dots on a page, and often lost its connection with anything other than its own internal notated construction systems. The development of recording techniques has enabled this to happen for more improvisatory and non-notated traditions (Boyce-Tillman 2001).

However, contemporary science is assisting the process of re-establishment of the relationship of music and place, by its rediscovery of the notion of a sound coming from the earth itself:

> a relentless hum of countless notes completely imperceptible to the human ear, like a giant, exceptionally quiet symphony, but the origin of this sound remains a mystery… unexpected powerful tunes have been discovered in this hum.[5]

Here is a rediscovery of vibration as the essential stuff of the universe with molecule and atoms circulating in apparently static matter and vibrations of liquid crystal giving the color to digital displays.[6]

The idea of "place memory" is also being rediscovered by theologians, parapsychologists and liturgists. Michael Perry, in his book on *Deliverance* (1987), describes how the memories held in a place can join with later human experience to produce paranormal phenomena. He tells the story of a young father of two children. Three weeks after the death of their third child he was woken by what he thought was burglars. He opened the bedroom door to find groups of people walking along the landing of the house and disappearing through the far wall. They were dressed in seventeenth-century costume and looked very sad. They were carrying bundles. A young police officer saw the phenomenon as well and the police dog would not enter the house. Perry suggests that the man's grief and the memory held by the place itself combined to produce the phenomenon (Perry 1987, 34).

Sacred sites, in particular, like cathedrals, are often regarded as sacred because of the memories of sacred acts that have been carried out across the ages. These memories seem to be stored in the very fabric of the building, and become part of the performance, and the process is in itself reciprocal as the performance itself becomes part of the memories stored in the building. It is an idea explored by T.S. Eliot in his poem *Little Gidding*.[7] Before the event I always go to the cathedral to pray the space, to get in tune with the feelings in the building. I sit and sometimes lie on them and ask for their cooperation in the same way I would ask the human performers for their cooperation within it. It is an idea reflected in one of the audience accounts of *Space for Peace*:

> These huge Quarr stones
> have stood for centuries
> soaking up sounds, divine and secular,
> thinning the human voice to a mere thread,
> de-thundering the organ, damping down the choir.
>
> But when the last trump comes
> and graves give up their dead,
> when kings and bishops, saints and noblemen
> rise from their chests,
> sort out their bones, and are re-fleshed,
> will then the transept walls give up their sounds,
> poems re-echo round the arches
> pillars resound with Benedictine psalms?
> Will youth guitars, visiting choirs,
> sermons of deans and Handel's hallelujahs
> all combine with organ notes

in one triumphant shout of praise
before the world dissolves?

For me the process began last night.
Thank you.

Other comments picked up the relational character of the relationship between the sounds and the space.

> While classic works by Beethoven, Britten and others bear witness to the fact that the pursuit of harmony through music is no mere equivocation, in her *Space for Peace*, June Boyce-Tillman approaches the subject not only as a condition of spiritual grace, to which countless settings of the Mass have aspired, but also as a process. This in turn implies not only musical form, but also dimension and movement... its bold yet simple structure, fruit of many years' preoccupation with exploring the parameters of music and worship, was expertly conceived to turn the venue into a resonant meditative space.

> The result was an extraordinary evening of complex soundscapes which nonetheless yielded an uplifting message: that peace might be obtained not from top-down imposition of values, but through collegial pursuit of diversity within a commitment to beauty and the needs of others... (Williams 2009)

Another account puts it thus:

> I think the fact that the cathedral had been emptied of chairs was an important factor in the experience. First, it created a root to its past back to a time when cathedrals were masses of movement and diverse activities going on at the same time. Second, it literally created the space for sound and movement... I thought this must be what heaven is like, a space where diversity finds its unity and unity blossoms into diversity...

The cathedral in some of its history would have been somewhat like this with masses being celebrated but not synchronized in the chantry chapels. Indeed, the building had an amazing capacity to keep the sounds separate and yet merged simultaneously. It represented a unique co-operation between stone and human agency.

Making a Space for Peace

It is clear that the structures we have developed particularly suit Winchester cathedral, for which it was designed. However, from this project we can draw some pointers to the elements required to make such a space work for peace musically. Some of these concern the organization. The first is the amount of work required to encourage people to participate. The event is unlike either set liturgies or structured musical concerts. It requires persistence and patient work within networks of people who share a concern for ways of valuing diversity. To enable people to feel safe in an unfamiliar structure, written guidance is helpful and we now have a website explaining it philosophically and musically.[8] For those who come as congregation/audience, a map rather than a program is given, showing the location of each musical group in the building.

The space in this case is resonant, and I have argued the power and centrality of this; but it would be worth exploring it less resonant spaces, or example, in a house, which could nevertheless provide the separate corners where people can be separated and yet together, like the chapels in the cathedral. The space itself needs preparing practically (like the removal of the chairs) but also in terms of prayer and meditation and stillness. There needs to be space to move around and carry out a variety of activities like singing, prayer, meditation and silence. There needs to be space where people can all come together.

Musically, it means musicians rethinking the type of pieces they offer. Because the textures are so complex and are made up rather like a fragmentary collage, the component parts are most successful if they are relatively simple—plainsong lines, simple chants work well; and groups need to be able to explore silence. There need to be some shared musical components—in this case the nine shared peace chants and the shalom peace procession. All in all, it needs sufficient structure for people to feel safe but sufficient freedom for people to make choices about how the space is used.

Summary

The project was an experiment in bringing faith groups to value diversity through music. It used a variety of cultures and styles without changing them in any way whatsoever, or requiring any new learning beyond the desire to embark on a voyage of discovery about oneself and others. It had an intention to create a peaceful space expressively. It was not liturgy as we have known and practiced it in the great faiths, but it showed the creativity of a diverse group of people given freedom to exercise their own choices—in *unity without uniformity*. Here is the democratization of liturgy/concert with everyone taking responsibility to create something beautiful; and I offer it as a model for interfaith dialogue and prayer—or perhaps not a model but more of a process, in which paradox can be contained, and celebrated.

Notes

1.   It is planned to repeat it every Holocaust Memorial Day—January 27th—each year. See Space for Peace Website: http://www.spaceforpeace.8k.com.

2.   The developing community choir movement is primarily an orate tradition and represents an attempt to re-empower people musically when they have felt disempowered by the literate Western classical\tradition. The struggle between orality and literacy is well described by Ong, Walter, (1982), *Orality and Literacy: The Technologizing of the Word*, London and New York: Methuen.

3.   The ideas described here applying Complexity theory to musical construction are embryonic and need further development. However, they are helpful to argument of this chapter because of the way in which Western music has traditionally been structured. In the classical traditions, in particular, there has been a great stress on order and, closely associated with it, control, often by a single person.

4.   These characteristics are set out in more detail at: Ferreira, Pedro. 2001. *Tracing Complexity Theory, Accessed: April 18, 2009 from* http://web.mit.edu/esd.83/ www/notebook/ESD83-Complexity.doc.

5.   *Temlan, John. 2008. The Rocks Will Cry Out. Accessed: April 14, 2009 from www. praisecharts.com/live/articles/219/1/The-Rocks-Will-Cry-Out/Page1.*

6.   These ideas are more fully explored in: Boyce-Tillman, June. 2010. *Even the stones cry out: Music Theology* and *the Earth Chapter* in Isherwood, Lisa and Bellchambers, Elaine (eds.), *Through Us, with Us, in Us.* London: SCM; 153-178.

7.   Eliot, T.S., *Four Quartets 4: Little Gidding Analysis.* Accessed: from http://www. eliteskills.com/analysis_poetry/Four_Quartets_4_Little_Gidding_by_T_S_Eliot_analysis.php.

8.   See Space for Peace Website: http://www.spaceforpeace.8k.com.

References

Berlin, Isaiah. 2002. *Liberty,* Oxford: Oxford University Press.

Boyce-Tillman. June. 2000. *The Creative Spirit- Harmonious Living with Hildegard of Bingen* Norwich: Canterbury Press.

Boyce-Tillman, June. 2001. Sounding the Sacred: Music as Sacred Site. Chapter in Ralls-MacLeod, Karen and Harvey, Graham. (ed.) *Indigenous Religious Musics,* Farnborough: Scolar; 136-166.

Boyce-Tillman, June. 2006a. "Music as Spiritual Experience," *Modern Believing: Church and Society*, Vol. 47:3, July 2006: 20-31.

Boyce-Tillman, June. 2006b. *A Rainbow to Heaven,* London: Stainer and Bell.

Boyce-Tillman, June. 2007a. *Unconventional Wisdom,* London: Equinox.

Boyce-Tillman, June. 2007b. Spirituality in the Musical Experience. Chapter in Liora Bresler (ed.) *The International Handbook of Research in Arts Education*; 1405-1421.

Boyce-Tillman, June. 2007c. Peace Making in Educational contexts. Chapter in Urbain, Olivier. 2007. *Music and Conflict Transformation: Harmonies and Dissonances in Geopolitics,* London: I. B. Tauris; 212-228.

Boyce-Tillman, June. 2009. The Transformative Qualities of a liminal Space created by musicking, *Philosophy of Music Education Review* Vol. 17, No. 2 Fall; 184-202.

Boyce-Tillman, June. 2010. Even the stones cry out: Music Theology and the Earth Chapter in Isherwood, Lisa and Bellchambers, Elaine (ed.). 2010. *Through us, with us, in us: Relational Theologies in the Twenty-first Century* London SCM Press; 153-178.

Buber, Martin, trans Walter Kaufmann. 1970. *I and Thou.* New York: Charles Scribner's Sons.

Clarke, Isabel. 2005. There is a crack in everything—that's how the light gets in. Chapter in Clarke, Chris ed. 2005. *Ways of Knowing,* Exeter: Imprint Academic; 90-102.

Derrida, Jacques. 1972. *Margins of Philosophy.* Chicago: University of Chicago Press.

Dewey, John. 1934/ 1980. *Art as Experience,* New York: Capricorn Books; 22.

Ferreira, Pedro. 2001. *Tracing Complexity Theory.* Research Seminar in Engineering Systems Fall.

Gebara, Ivone. 1999. *Longing for Running Water*, Minneapolis: Fortress Press.

Huntington, Samuel. 1996. The Clash of Civilizations and the Remaking of World Order, New York: Simon and Schuster.

Ignatieff, Michael. 1993. *Blood and Belonging,* London: Viking.

James, Jamie. 1993. *The Music of the Spheres: Music, Science and the Natural Order of the Universe.* London: Abacus.

Johnson, Elizabeth. 1992. She Who Is. The Mystery of God in Feminist Theological Discourse, New York: Crossroad; 155.

Kaggwa, Robert. 2008. Unpublished Review of *Between.*

Levinas, Emmanuel, trans Alphonso Lingis 1969. *Totality and Infinity: An Essay on Exteriority*, Pittsburgh: Duquesne University Press; 33.

Ong, Walter. 1982. *Orality and Literacy: The Technologizing of the Word* Methuen: London and New York.

Perry, Michael ed. 1987. *Deliverance: Psychic Disturbances and Occult involvement,* London: SPCK.

Sacks, Jonathan. 2002. *The Dignity of Difference,* London and New York, Continuum.

Space for Peace (April, 2010). Accessed: from http://www.spaceforpeace.8k.com.

Steiner, Rudolf, trans by Nancy Parsons Whittaker. 1996. *The Foundations of Human Experience. Foundations of Waldorf Education Vol. 1*, Allgemeine Menschenkunde als Grundlage der Pedagogik. Pedagogischer Grundkurs, 14 Lectures, Stuttgart, 1919, Hudson, NY: Anthroposophic Press, 136-40.

Temlan, John. 2008. The Rocks Will Cry Out. Accessed: April 14, 2009 from www. praisecharts.com/live/articles/219/1/The-Rocks-Will-Cry-Out/Page1.

Tinker, George E. 2004. -The Stones Shall Cry Out: Consciousness, Rocks, and Indians- *Wicazo Sa Review 19:2* (Fall); 105-125.

Turner, Victor. 1969/ 1974a. *The Ritual Process: Structure and Anti-structure.* Baltimore: Penguin Books.

Turner, Victor. 1974b. *Dramas, Fields and Metaphors: Symbolic action in human society.* Ithaca NY: Cornell University press.

Turner, Victor. 1982. *From Ritual to Theatre: The Human Seriousness of Play.* NY: Performing Arts Journal Publications.

Turner, Victor. 1986. *The Anthropology of Performance.* New York: Performing Arts Journal Publications.

Westerlund, Heidi. 2002. Bridging experience, action, and culture in music education. Studia Musica 16, Helsinki: Sibelius Academy.

Williams, Nicholas. 2009. *Review in the Church Times Feb 27.*

Contributors

Ahmed Aydoun was first a teacher at and then director of the National Conservatory of Rabat in Morocco, and subsequently chief inspector of music education. He is a musicologist, and author of three books and over 300 articles. Also a musical composer and arranger, he was the artistic director of most music festivals created by the Ministry of Culture between 1982 and 1995, and of the National Festival of Popular Arts in Marrakech between 2003 and 2006. He was artistic director of extensive anthologies of Andalusian music (consisting of 73 CDs) and of Moroccan music (30 CDs), and is a musical advisor on national radio.

Fériel Bouhadiba is a musicologist, composer and solo lute player (Eastern lute), and member of the Laboratoire de Recherches en Culture, Nouvelles technologies et Développement in Tunisia. With university degrees in Connaissance du patrimoine et développement culturel (Faculty of Human and Social Sciences of Tunis) and in Sciences et techniques des arts (Fine Arts Institute of Tunis), she is currently a PhD student in Arts and Art Sciences (Sorbonne-Paris). She has written several articles including: *Développement culturel: antinomie de l'uniformisation et néologisme de la singularité* (forthcoming 2010).

Elizabeth Bowen is managing editor and vice general director of Soka Gakkai International Australia. She writes various articles as well as editing a monthly magazine and producing policy documents. Elizabeth has a doctorate in Social Policy and Welfare, having focused her research on young people, changes in employment and risk. Her study of the isolation and disconnection of young people at risk has motivated an interest in their experience of positive social engagement. She has also contributed to a depression initiative and other projects with young people.

June Boyce-Tillman is professor of applied music at The University of Winchester, UK. Her doctoral research into children's musical development has been translated into 6 languages. Active in community music making, she is a composer specializing in music and spirituality. She has composed large-scale works that allow spaces for children's improvisation, including *The Healing of the Earth* and *Step into the Picture*. She is also a hymn writer and a performer, her one-woman shows being widely performed. Her books include *Constructing Musical Healing* (2000), and *Unconventional Wisdom* (2007), among others. Ordained as an Anglican priest, she has long been actively engaged in interfaith dialogue.

Vanessa Contopulos is a qualified music therapist (Music Therapist-Board Certified) and co-founder and co-director of Create4Peace (www. create4peace.com), an organization dedicated to supporting peace building activities through creative initiatives. As a Rotary World Peace Fellow during 2008-2009, she completed her master's degree in Conflict Resolution at the University of Bradford in England. Vanessa has worked in music education and music therapy for the past ten years and has also taught and directed musical theatre. She currently works as a music therapist with a broad range of client populations.

Barbara Dunn is a clinical social worker and music therapist with a private psychotherapy practice in Seattle, Washington (WA), USA and a music therapy program at Whidbey General Hospital in Coupeville, WA. She has more than 25 years of experience using music to help people. Additionally, she is a professional musician and has recorded two CDs: *The Sparrow Takes Flight* (solo recording) and *You Are a Song* (recorded with the Daughters of Harriet). Barbara's doctoral research focused on using music to address conflict with adults engaged in mediation: www. barbaradunn.com.

Soufiane Feki obtained a PhD from Paris IV Sorbonne in October 2006. He is assistant professor in analytical musicology at the Université tunisienne, and a member of the scientific council of the Laboratoire de recherche en Culture, Nouvelles Technologies et Développement, Tunis. He is also research associate at the Centre de recherche Patrimoines et Langages Musicaux (PLM-Sorbonne) and former director of the Department of Music and Musicology at the Institut Supérieur de Musique de Sfax (2006-08). His publications include: *Problèmes de typologie et de terminologie inhérents à l'approche musicologique des pratiques et répertoires musicaux arabes* and *Quelques réflexions sur l'analyse du Maqâm*.

Michael Golden studied music composition in the Pacific Northwest, receiving the doctoral award of DMA from the University of Washington in 1992. He has composed for a wide range of media, with commissions to write solo and chamber ensemble works, large ensemble works, and pieces for jazz ensembles of all sizes. He has also composed for computer-generated tape and live electronics, and for multi-media, website, film, video and theatre productions. His music has been performed throughout much of the United States as well as internationally in many countries. He has also performed as a jazz pianist throughout much of the US and abroad.

Fakher Hakima holds a PhD in musicology from Université Paris IV Sorbonne. He is assistant professor at the Institut Supérieur de Musique de Sousse, Tunis, where he is vice-principal and director of studies. He has addressed conferences in Tunisia, Paris, and Cairo, and is author of numerous publications on the evolution of contemporary Arab music and its instruments, and further scientific articles. He is involved with many creative activities as arranger and advisor, is also a solo saxophone player with several groups in Tunisia and in France, and is founder of the group Saxofans with which he has entered the field of artistic musical creation.

Felicity Laurence, from New Zealand, is a teacher, composer, and children's singing specialist whose decades of international work within the areas of music education and of intercultural understanding is underpinned by the principles of children's innate musicality, and their likewise innate senses of quality and of empathy. Her doctoral study explored conceptual resonances between musicking and empathy, in which she continues ongoing research. She has held lecturing positions at Bergen University College, Norway and at Trossingen Music Conservatory, Germany. She is currently degree programme director for the MA Music and Education at the International Centre for Music Studies, Newcastle University, UK.

María Elisa Pinto García is currently enrolled as a second-year master student in the Peace and Conflict Studies Program at Tokyo University of Foreign Studies with a scholarship granted by the Japanese International Cooperation Agency (JICA). She also holds a B.A. in Government and International Relations from Externado University (Colombia). Her experience and studies have been related to peacebuilding, local development, and the link between music and reconciliation in Colombia which is the main topic of her master thesis. She has also been involved in artistic activities throughout her life.

Christopher Small, a New Zealand native and the forerunner of the study of music as action in a social context, developed and defined the term "to music," with its gerund "musicking," to express this idea. His three books, *Music, Society, Education* (1977), *Music of the Common Tongue* (1987), an utterly original history of African American musicking, and *Musicking* (1998), an analysis of a symphonic performance ("What's really going on here?") have proved highly influential among not only music educators but also among practicing musicians. He lives in Sitges, Spain.

Itır Toksöz is assistant professor at the Department of International Relations, Doğuş University, Istanbul, Turkey. Her areas of research are: security studies, threat perceptions, civil/military relations and human security. She also studies and teaches international relations through art and artworks.

Olivier Urbain is the director of the Toda Institute for Global Peace and Policy Research and the founder and coordinator of the Transcend: Art and Peace Network (T:AP). He was formerly professor of modern languages and peace studies at Soka University, Japan. He is also the founder of the Commission on Art and Peace of the International Peace Research Association (IPRA) and was a member of the IPRA council until 2008. His publications include articles about the power of the arts for peace, a book entitled *Daisaku Ikeda's Philosophy of Peace* (2010), as well as the editing of *Music and Conflict Transformation* (2008).